BIG
SCARY
BROWN
GUY

This story is based on real events, but some names, persons, characters, places, and dates have been changed.

Library of Congress Catalog Card Number 20222933769

ISBN: 978-1-963245-57-8 (print)

Cover design by J. Gonzo
Spot Illustrations by Olivia González

BIG SCARY BROWN GUY

A Memoir

CHRISTOPHER GONZÁLEZ

A FlowerSong Press Imprint

McAllen, Texas

In memory of the places we called home and the people we were when we lived there.

Children begin by loving their parents; as they grow older they judge them; sometimes they forgive them.

—Oscar Wilde, *The Picture of Dorian Gray*

Author's Note

Like most memoirists, I relied heavily on my memories of events that are unverifiable, fact-checking only those items related to time line, history, literature, and popular culture. Whenever I could, I asked family members and friends for their recollections of specific happenings, but ultimately, I privileged my own interpretations. For incidents I did not witness, I deferred to family lore.

I have changed the names of certain individuals—especially those with whom I have lost touch or never had contact—out of respect for their privacy. There are no composite characters in these pages, however; everyone mentioned here is living or was alive when I met them at the various crossroads and cloverleafs of my life. I have also chosen a free-flowing narrative that eschews a chronological imperative. Memory does not work chronologically; it works associatively. And so, my narrative follows suit.

Finally, for those who care about such details, I wrote most of this memoir from May 2021 to January 2022 on my iPhone, composing and revising it with two iOS apps, Pages and Werdsmith. I believe it is critical to demystify the creative process. The most valuable principle of writing, as I see it, is to do it frequently. There is no perfect place or time to compose. You assume the role of author wherever you find yourself. Right now, it is easiest and most convenient for me to write on a smartphone.

Chapter One

No one ever asked if I would like to be a Big Scary Brown Guy. The stereotype was forced upon me, and even now I find myself changed into that person at a moment's notice. I never consented to the typecasting. But after some time, I realized that I had an effect on others that was neither limited to a single instance nor readily explainable. Thanks to my age—stringing together enough years of experience to notice what had become a pattern—I came to understand that I was the incarnation of a particular type of human that certain people were either intimidated by or openly hostile toward in these United States of America.

When this phenomenon first started happening, well-meaning people—undoubtedly believing (naively) that their social circles and workplaces were sensible and free from the strictures of racism and prejudice—would seek to rationalize what I had encountered, what was done *to me*, in one of two ways. They posited that either I had misinterpreted the situation in question, or that the offender didn't mean what they had said or done. In such cases, even as I recognized my own precarity and vulnerability, I was made to feel delusional or unreasonable, sometimes both. Gaslighting 101. So, I was doubly traumatized—first by the experience itself, and later by someone who cared about me and who imagined they had comforted me.

Something about all of this had to do with certain vectors of my intersectionality—that chewy, nougaty spot where my size, my Brownness, my education, and my masculinity converged. For most of my prepubescence, I was cute or adorable, I suppose. Inarguably, I was a manifestation of geeky dorkiness. I wasn't scary then. An administrative assistant (whom we called a secretary) at my elementary school often cooed breathlessly that I had "eyes like Julio Iglesias."

I should state that besides being creepy, the remark about my eyes was made repeatedly by a white woman in flattering, quasi-sexualized ways. Thenceforth, this woman would go on and on about my eyes, to the point that I hated going up to the office. I knew the fawning was coming, and I dreaded it. But I never said anything. Instead of telling her I didn't like what she was doing, I would smile uncomfortably, sheepishly, playing along with her bit and grinning, waiting for it to be over. I was too young to object, and I was afraid of upsetting her or making her angry with me.

See, I knew who Julio Iglesias was. A singer who mostly sang in Spanish, he had recorded a duet with Willie Nelson in 1984 called "To All the Girls I've Loved Before," which likely put him on the American radar more than ever. Though I didn't have the vocabulary for it at the time, Iglesias was a "Latin lover," the persona imposed on most Latino artists, at least initially.

Iglesias, his son Enrique Iglesias, Jon Secada, Ricky Martin, the list goes on. These men were billed as lovers, with a kind of inherent sexual prowess or animal magnetism. They could get women to drop their pedal pushers with a glance, and these women were eager to oblige. I was unnerved whenever this adult white woman spoke sweetly about my eyes, with good reason. As a kid, I was keenly aware of sex and sexuality. Hollywood had already shown me how it was white women, for the most part, who were eager to have sex. As my Latino family saw it, white women were more than likely to be immodest and sexually promiscuous. But perception is reality, as they say, and my family perceived a lot of weird shit.

Someone might argue that this woman was simply being nice, perhaps teasing me good-naturedly. That she was complimenting me in a purely affectionate way. But whatever was going on, I found it weird. At eight years old, I had to quash my feelings and accept that this woman didn't mean any harm. I had to suppress my discomfort while being sexualized by her. When I finally told Rene, my mother, she didn't find the comments endearing at all. It's possible she went up there to tell that woman to knock it off—except Rene probably threatened the secretary, demanding she quit her stupid shit or else. (My mother always solved problems at my school like that. Her hobby was haranguing anyone in power who dared to insult or hurt me. I am grateful she was there for me at such times, even if she was glaringly absent in others.)

As a kid, I was lanky, skinny, undoubtedly awkward, and soon a four-eyes with lenses so thick they seemed like spare parts for some multibillion-dollar telescope. My uncle-brother Tom (that is, Rene's younger brother by lineage; my brother by association because we grew up in the same house) would alternate between calling me Barney Fife—the goofy but lovable character played by Don Knotts in *The Andy Griffith Show*—and Porter Wagoner—the lanky, high-coiffed country singer to whom Dolly Parton dedicated her song "I Will Always Love You." He probably saw me as the Knotts character in *The Incredible Mr. Limpet*, when the introverted book and aquatic life lover becomes an animated fish! Tom, ever the comedian, teased everyone as a matter of course. Back then, my brown skin and dark hair were nothing but ordinary and unremarkable in my environs. Another run-of-the-mill Latino boy in Texas with a too-tall pompadour. We were a dime a dozen in the Lone Star State, and I thought we were all treated the way I was being treated. I'm sure we were.

Many Black men also describe this phenomenon of being cute and lovable before the metamorphosis to "ferocious beast" around their teenage years. Jesmyn Ward, in her novel *Salvage the Bones*, made the all-too-disturbing analogue between young Black men and pit bull terriers in the eyes of white society. I think something similar happens with Brown men as well, though Black and Brown men do not have the same engagements with America, even if there are shared characteristics in their respective experiences. My Brownness comes from my Latinx heritage, rooted in the Indigenous peoples of the Americas and the subsequent *remezclas* of the mestizo, but other Brown men likely have similar experiences—be they Native American, Persian, Turkish, Indian, or a descendant of other heritages where men have a skin color ranging from rusty cinnamon to burnished bronze.

Perhaps you know a Big Scary Brown Guy or are one yourself. Maybe you are married to one of us big lugs or can count yourself among our best friends. Perhaps you are of a similar persuasion but haven't quite realized that you, too, are a Big Scary Brown Guy. ("Knowing is half the battle!" as they used to say on the '80s animated show *G.I. Joe: A Real American Hero*.) My hope is that something in my experience will help give you perspective and perhaps even armor for your own journey. I hope it opens up frank conversations between you and the people you meet along the way.

¡Vamos!

Chapter Two

I admire people who can instantly respond to an aggressor with righteous indignation and outrage. I once saw a colleague—a professor of psychology and a Latina—immediately shut down some bullshit that occurred in a committee meeting, where a white man made a joke that was in poor taste and hurtful to several of us from othered communities. His joke was self-deprecating, to be sure, singling out his straight white male identity during his introduction, but it came off as egregious to those of us who can't easily joke about our marginalized status. Like, he was the only white man on the committee, so, ha, ha, he's the minority now! Get it? As I said, a poor joke in terrible taste.

I sat there at the committee table, stunned and quiet, the morning's caffeine still percolating through my bloodstream but not yet at full redline. I was processing this man's quip the way Lieutenant Commander Data does when he twitches his head slightly as his yellow eyes dart back and forth while he's trying to understand why a human has done some dumb shit or other. "Curious," he would say, and that's what I thought. As we went around the room introducing ourselves, I replayed the joke several times in my mind, trying to evaluate if I had heard incorrectly. Might I be overreacting? (And right there's an example of me trying to excuse disturbing behavior and exonerate the party who is out of line.)

But when it came time for my amazing colleague to introduce herself, she broke the proverbial emergency glass, pulled the fire alarm, and went right back to the joke—because she was about to perform a vivisection before a live studio audience. She expressed her distress and shock to the group. I was in awe. All of us, me included, shrank to the size of the shortest Lilliputian.

She admitted that she did not think she could proceed with the meeting after this outrage. For his part, the man who told the joke took it seriously (now) and offered to leave himself, for he realized he had truly stepped in it. I learned a lot that morning from my colleague who'd had the courage and wherewithal to clap back immediately to the demeaning exchange and the person behind it.

Did I mention that this was a university-wide diversity, equity, and inclusion task force subcommittee meeting?

I have never been able to do what my colleague did, not until quite recently. I find that age and a more authoritative job title (i.e., job security) have helped in that regard—but rising to the occasion in real time is still mighty work for me. One contributing factor to my reticence is my designation as a Big Scary Brown Guy, which influences how I respond to people who make offensive comments to me.

When I go anywhere, I am hyperaware of the way I might come across to others—because I already know how I tend to be regarded by people I meet at restaurants, convenience stores, government offices, and so on. I can sense them stiffening, their blood pressure going up ever so slightly. They seem jerky and unnatural. And I already know that the first words I speak will make a vast difference in the exchange that follows.

But how can you know that? you might be wondering. *How do you know they're going to react to you in that way? Aren't you prejudging them?*

Let's stop with the bullshit, okay? Let's banish the ludicrous and erroneous "reverse racism" mantra that so often accompanies white tears of anguish over the possibility of facing unfair treatment. How can I know? you ask. How many times does someone have to piss on you before you start to figure out something is up? How often do you need to have garbage dumped on you before you come to anticipate it? You just know when it's about to happen. *I* know when it's about to happen.

What I've come to realize, without anyone spelling it out for me, is that I must be ultra-nice. Ultra-harmless. Extra jokey! Excessively silly, to the point that my overtures are almost flirtatious (if it's a white woman) or super bromance-level friendly (if it's a white man). Such performativity goes against my nature because I like to keep to myself and speak seldom, if possible—a vestige of how I was raised and my family's distaste for outsiders.

I don't want to have to defuse my own threat level to others. That should not be my problem, but it is. Think about it. Your discomfort with me suddenly must be my issue to anticipate and resolve to spare you from some imaginary unpleasantness.

I must temper my existence so that my interlocutor is at ease. I must maneuver to put someone else at peace with their own unreasonable bias against me. I have also come to acknowledge that this "responsibility" is harmful to my well-being and takes an emotional toll. See, I don't want to make anyone uncomfortable. I don't want to intimidate people. In our world, such misunderstandings can lead to overreaction and end in bloodshed, if not murder. I see Black and Brown men being killed in chance encounters and I wonder when that will be me. I don't want to die like that (who does?), so I perform this song and dance to convey unambiguously that I'm simply a regular guy with red blood who fires up a grill on the Fourth of July and has attended WrestleMania at least once in his life. (It was WrestleMania XSeven at the Astrodome in 2001, before they closed it and as the Rock's ascendancy in Hollywood was about to begin.)

In truth, these contortions are easy enough in public, where the encounters are naturally brief, though I have a greater situational awareness when I travel. I make plenty of eye contact, smile wide, and in my "good," unaccented English ask a question (my voice pitched a little higher) about something I don't truly need to know. It's a gesture that signals they need not fear me. "So, who has the best burger in town?" I laugh, tell a joke, make a silly comment, grouse about the weather. *See, I'm a nice guy.*

But I can't ever slip. I can't have a bad day. I can't show frustration. Ever.

As you might imagine, reducing my perceived threat level is much harder at a place of employment or in a school than out in the wild, which is weird because my coworkers and colleagues already know me. Or they should, anyway. Imagine being "on" every minute of your day, outwardly upbeat and jovial. The downside is that, because you're constantly smiling and japing, you might not come off as a serious person. (Maybe you're not, in fact, ready for that promotion or award or leadership role. See, you're an unserious person. Only serious people get such rewards.)

These days, when I'm at the first of many meetings that will require some tough conversations, I begin my introduction to the group by confessing that

I will likely seem impatient and frustrated because I view my role, especially within the context of DEI initiatives, as doing whatever I can to move things to action. I despise meetings for the sake of meetings. Meetings to plan for the next meeting. I explain that this habit of mine may make me seem unfriendly or difficult to work with during our forthcoming sessions.

Then I apologize in advance. I haven't even done anything, and already I'm apologizing!

Years ago, I grew a goatee over the winter break. (I tend to grow beards and other facial hair configurations over breaks because I get tired of shaving.) When I returned to work, my supervisor, an older white man, remarked, "Hi, Chris! You look like a terrorist." He said it with such aplomb that he nearly suckered me in.

I always pride myself on having a quick comeback to comments meant to tease me, but this was something altogether different. I don't think I said anything. I probably smiled, then continued on my way.

That comment has never left me, though, and I've turned over the implications of it for years now. My ruminations are a sign that his wisecrack left a wound, one I am constantly picking at, a scab that refuses to heal. I am certain this administrator, let's call him Mr. Monty, associated my brown skin, my shaved head, and my goatee with a radical Islamic terrorist. That I was a big guy was merely icing on the cake. He had known me for several years at that point, and he must have assumed a racist, bigoted joke was okay between us friends. Had he derisively called me a Muslim, it would not have been an insult to me. His statement also showed me that, even though we had known each other well, I could easily be a threat to him. In fact, I *was* a threat, and my goatee had confirmed it in his imagination. (Like when evil Spock sported a goatee in "Mirror, Mirror.")

Worse still, Mr. Monty was my supervisor and the person who evaluated my job performance at the end of the year. How could I take this man seriously now? How could I tell him that his comment had created a genuine problem for me? And how could I do that without a potential backlash when he completed my annual review?

When I went to my closest colleague at the time, a white woman I'll call Suze, she quickly came to Mr. Monty's defense, saying that he didn't mean it that way and that I shouldn't dwell on it. "He jokes like that to everyone."

But I was certain that the *you look like a terrorist* comment was reserved solely for me.

"I think you're overreacting," she said with a smile.

Incidentally, white women, above all other demographic blocs, often explain to me how I'm feeling and what I actually mean to say. (It's like mansplaining, but by white women. Whitewomansplaining? Karensplaining?) Again, anyone is apt to do this, but white women do it more frequently in my experience. They try to help or show solidarity, but they come across as patronizing, condescending, and unattractive at a human level.

Though Suze felt sure I was exaggerating, I knew that I wasn't. I tried to drop it, yet the memory of the interaction was always fresh in my mind. In that instance, I thought, if Mr. Monty was bold enough to say that to my face, what did he think of me when I wasn't around? And how did that belief shape his professional evaluations of me, which were supposed to be objective and unbiased? And how was I expected to do my job when I doubted my supervisor had my best interests in mind?

Now, this is a real example of something that happened to me years ago, an offhand and sorry excuse for humor that should never have happened. One might be wondering why I didn't confront Mr. Monty.

Having it out with Mr. Monty presupposes that I'm not so easily perceived as a Big Scary Brown Guy. But I am, and it complicates confrontations when they arise. I quickly go from scary to menacing. Also, we all know there are hierarchies at any place of employment, and retaliation is a creditable issue. In a separate incident, years later, I learned the hard way that your institution cannot guarantee you will be shielded from retaliation if you file a formal complaint with something like an office of equity, though it will try to protect you (whatever that means). Thus, incidents likely go unreported (mine did), and the work environment looks idyllic on paper because there are no formal complaints or investigations.

The other problem is that, as a Big Scary Brown Guy, I'm expected to take more abuse—because surely I must be tougher and have a thicker skin than the average joe. My superpower, apparently, is to be able to take a ridiculous amount of shit without complaint. If I protest, then I'm "not a man" or I'm somehow oversensitive. It becomes a kind of masochistic exercise, then, to see how much I can endure without even a hint of grievance. I then seek to minimize transgressions against me while absolving my tormentors, turning forever to the promise of their better angels in the hope that they are nice people deep down and it's my own problems that are coming to the fore. I nod sagely while noting how it wasn't that bad and how others have it much worse than I do.

But my traumas wreak damage upon the healthiest version of myself, even if it accumulates over time, like lead in the blood. I work hard to remind myself of that fact, and hopefully my observations might inspire others to take better care of themselves.

I want to recount a story related to me by a young educator, who bravely revealed something that happened to him not long ago. I have removed all identifying features of his specific identity (beyond the fact that he, too, is a Big Scary Brown Guy who works in education), and I have his permission to invoke his experience here. His story hit me hard because I saw myself in it, and he expressed both relief that he was not alone in his experiences but also outrage that this sort of thing happened to others as well.

He (I will arbitrarily call him Moises) is the only POC at a school in Utah, where he works. Those of you in education know the drill of retreats and in-services to launch the new school year. It is a time to get to know your colleagues better, to cover any new policies, and to fire up the old motivation engine, in the hopes it will keep chugging along for the entire academic year—or at least until winter break, when you can grow a goatee and look like a terrorist. (Most educators hate this ritual because they feel their time would be better spent setting up their classrooms and preparing their lessons, but that is another matter.)

As part of this in-service, the school resource officer (SRO—a literal police officer whose "beat" is the school itself) presented to the professionals at the school on what to do in various emergencies—an intruder in a campus building, for one. The SRO then generated a scenario that, according to Moises, went like this:

"If you were to see a Hispanic male with tattoos, about five-eleven and weighing between two hundred thirty and two hundred fifty pounds, wearing shorts, what would you do?"

The SRO had basically described Moises himself in front of all his colleagues, and intimated that a person like this was dangerous, did not belong, and posed a threat. Keep in mind that most mass shootings and school shootings in the United States are committed by white or white-passing young men. Imagine what Moises felt—to be subjected to that kind of humiliation! The SRO's comment will ring in his ears whenever he is reminded that he is the one thing at the school that is not like the others.

It happens all too often: *He's a big guy*, they think. *He can take it.*

Sure, he can take it. He always takes it, which makes him resilient. But why does he have to pay continually for someone else's ignorance? That's the tragedy of Big Scary Brown Guys. We care too much about the feelings of those who have made monsters of us.

But, you see, I was not always a Big Scary Brown Guy.

Chapter Three

MLK was not my first hero. Nor was it César Chávez. It wasn't my mom or anyone I knew. It wasn't an astronaut or cop or firefighter or baseball player. Nope. It was Luke Fucking Skywalker.

There are kids who instantly fixate on certain toy tropes. For girls in the time of my youth, it was going to be toys like jump ropes, jacks, blond-haired dolls with blue eyes that snapped shut when laid horizontally, Easy-Bake Ovens, Cabbage Patch Kids, Strawberry Shortcake dolls, and doll houses. Boys would be shoved toward manly pursuits in toy form: toy soldiers, dart guns, bows and arrows, Hot Wheels, fire trucks, tractors, train sets, racing tracks, footballs, and so on. When I became a father, I saw my friends' kids do this. One kid wanted anything and everything to do with Thomas the Tank Engine. For my daughters, there was a time when all was Hello Kitty! (Now it's *Chainsaw Man*.) For me, it was the totality of science fiction and fantasy, which I'll call "the speculative" henceforth.

The period from the mid-1970s to the mid-'80s, or thereabouts, was such a fertile era for the speculative in mass media: *Star Wars*, *Battlestar Galactica*, *Buck Rogers in the 25th Century*, *Star Trek* in syndication and then *Star Trek: The Next Generation*, and anything else that was outside the realm of my reality (which was a lot, truth be told). I didn't give a damn about Hot Wheels or remote-controlled cars, but I thought KITT was spectacular. ("Turbo Boost" was goddamn necessary in all vehicles, as far as I was concerned. You never knew when you might be confronted with some barrier dead ahead—say, a huge pile of gravel or the missing section of a bridge—and need to jump over that motherfucker! That seemed more than practical to me.)

Transformers action figures were my initiation into the world of the car and the mechanic. These toys were a revelation—and orders of magnitude better than the mediocre GoBots I had obsessed over for all of five minutes.

I can still recall going with my mother—whose name is Irene, but everyone, me included, dropped the *I* so that it was Rene (rhymes with *keen*)—to the Western Auto in Hobbs, New Mexico, on my birthday in 1984. She let me buy myself a gift (it was going to be a toy, of course), and this place was, like, the third location we had hit in search of the lame GoBots. The employee said she didn't know about GoBots, but they sounded a lot like this other toy with a different name.

That Western Auto employee had to be a fleet-footed messenger of Zeus himself, sent to undo the lameness GoBots had wreaked upon the world. Yet I didn't know how lame they truly were until I laid eyes on Mirage, a First Gen Transformer of blue and white that resembled a Formula One race car, #26 of the Gitanes Ligier JS11 variety. Emblazoned with a 26 CITANES to avoid trademark issues, Mirage set my brain on fire and gave me hours of fun for only around ten dollars plus tax. Rene said, first, that the Transformer in robot mode looked a little like a football player and, next, that he looked like a cat, thanks to his face, which was framed by headgear not unlike that of an ancient pharaoh. By the time I got home, I had forgotten all about GoBots.

As it turned out, Mirage rarely appeared in the First Gen animated *Transformers* television series, though he was always there in the end credits, transforming from car to robot within a few frames. I soon recovered from that disappointment (I wanted to see more of my toy in action) and began collecting Transformers whenever I could.

I could not have cared less about fire trucks or firefighters, unless we were talking about the kind Ray Bradbury had imagined in *Fahrenheit 451*. Cops were boring unless we were talking about Paul Verhoeven's *RoboCop*, a movie I watched so many times as an after-school ritual that I began to wear out the magnetic tape from the VHS cassette, memorizing every nuance and line of the film. Forget Delta City; Old Detroit was where the action was!

My imagination was ablaze with possibilities. Even some horror films, such as *Alien*, didn't so much frighten me as motivate me to think about why some things were and some things were not. Like, for instance, why was it that I already knew the Black guy on the ship, Parker (played brilliantly by Yaphet Kotto), would die at some point? When he dies because Lambert, a white woman, freezes and obstructs his shot at the xenomorph, it felt natural in all the worst ways. Of course he would die because he didn't want, or was not allowed, to hurt the white woman. Yes, the alien appears ready to use his barbed tail as a speculum on Lambert as the threat of rape creates the tension in the scene. Still, even I was ready to throw her out of the air lock, and I was only, like, seven when I watched the movie for the first time! I'd never seen a character cry so much that they made themselves unsympathetic to the audience. "Nobody likes a crybaby" was a maxim for a reason.

I'm talking about the game within the game of representation here, and even during the green shoots of my youth, I felt I could not fully embrace this genre of storytelling that brought me so much delight. I'm talking about the lack of Latinx people in the speculative wing of popular culture. Except for Edward James Olmos in his brief scene with Harrison Ford in *Blade Runner*, I hardly saw any people who looked like me in that most fascinating and visionary of genres—the speculative!

Of course, it's not as though I had much to choose from if I wanted to see quality, accurate representations of my community on-screen. *Gunsmoke* reruns were on after the nightly news, and I was not much interested in what I saw there. Same with *Bonanza, The Big Valley*, and all the other Westerns my grandfather demanded to watch. The only place I assuredly saw people who resembled me on TV was on Spanish-language networks. And since there were no great speculative movies or shows in Spanish that came across my television transom because Mom and Dad weren't as interested in them as I might have been (*El Chapulín Colorado* didn't count), I quickly concluded that speculative stories were mostly white stories, with occasional Blacks and maybe Asians to keep things a little interesting.[1] They supplied fodder when some character needed to get exploded or the plot called for a higher body count. The cultural invisibility left me feeling like an interloper in my favorite storytelling arenas. As if I were watching stories made for other people. Imagine watching your fellow kids play while you had to sit on the sidelines, a mere witness to the fun.

Still, there were transcendent moments. When I was eleven, one film became a kind of touchstone for me and my family. In 1987, a month before

---

1 Clearly there is a rich and beautiful history of Latin American cinema and speculative genres. Luchadores like El Santo and Blue Demon battled such classic creatures as Dracula, the Wolf Man, and Frankenstein's monster, and these movies fueled imaginative play when my cousins were around. But Spanish-language speculative stories were not foregrounded in my home.

my twelfth birthday, *Predator* was unleashed upon the world. When we got our hands on our own copy of it on VHS, it became a household treasure the way some people might view their own piece of the True Cross. It, along with *RoboCop*, went into heavy rotation in our home, becoming a nightly ritual before bedtime. We'd say, "Looks like it's going to be a *Predator* night," and we already knew what that meant: get your snacks, take care of your unimportant shit, and let's watch this amazing movie for the three hundredth time.

What made the film especially awesome for me was the inclusion of a Latino character *and* a Latina character . . . and the Latina survives! Watching Poncho (Richard Chaves) get blasted by the *Predator* (Kevin Peter Hall) hurt me, but he had made it almost to the end. Anna (Elpidia Carrillo), following Dutch's (Arnold Schwarzenegger's) meme-worthy exhortation to "*Get to the choppa!*" barreled her way to the bitter end. Our shared ritual of watching her make it all the way through the movie reached a kind of beatific significance. *Hail, Anna, full of grace, the choppa is with thee.* It was wonderful.

"Hail Anna, full of grace, the choppa is with thee."

Chapter Four

I was born into a family of talented Latinx people who were as intellectually curious as they were superstitious. We believed in *el ojo* (the evil eye), discussed horoscopes like they were scientific proofs, and never left dirty dishes out overnight lest hungry spirits felt invited to munch on our scraps. We took it as normal that someone would knock on the door at night with no one on the other side. If these things weren't happening, we willed them into existence through sheer determination.

Throughout my childhood, Rene was, in truth, the only person I saw at home who took a genuine interest in books and anything approaching literary writing. Rene and I lived in her parents' home on the east side of Lubbock, Texas, and there her parents all but legally adopted me. For years I thought Rene's parents were my parents and that Rene was my big sister. When I did find out that Rene was my mother, my life was never quite the same.

Elva was Mom, and what we all called Rene's mother. Mom had always been devoted to the daily local newspaper, the *Lubbock Avalanche-Journal*, and even until the end of her life—from where she lived out her final years, right off I-20 in Louisiana—she loyally read her paper from Lubbock, Texas. I placed a copy of the day's paper into her casket as a final send-off at her funeral. If I hadn't, she would have been annoyed with me even into the afterlife. The paper would arrive a day or two late when she lived in Louisiana, worn from travel, but she didn't seem to mind. She did not read literature or books for most of her life; print journalism—and usually the more salacious and fictitious, the better—was the nourishment of her literacy. When I grew older and began to drive, I was always charged with picking up the day's newspaper, along with an assortment of tabloids—the *National Enquirer, Globe,* and other such dreck. If I didn't bring Mom her papers, and perhaps a Big Red soda, there would be hell to pay. I suppose a newspaper subscription, such as the one she had in her last few years, wasn't viable at the time. Spending two quarters a day and a dollar on Sundays was better than whatever a year up front would have cost.

Sometimes the *Lubbock Avalanche-Journal* would be sold out at the Town & Country Food Store or Allsup's, and there I would go, stopping by any vendor that sold a paper, in desperate search of a single copy. If I came home empty-handed, with the bad news that all copies had sold out, Mom would not believe me. Instead, she would become frustrated and say something like, "Oh, sure. I see you remembered to get yourself something but didn't remember me. *Cabrón*," even if I hadn't gotten anything for myself. She was always suspicious of deep conspiratorial plotting and saw an ulterior motive in every breath you took.

Mom was hard on all of us; her acerbic wit and penchant for cussing made us fear her wrath. She was tough on me as well, though in her mind I was her baby boy, one of her lost sheep that she delightedly took in. She did this with Rose, who was her niece but ultimately adopted daughter, a few years younger than Rene. Mom kept me in line with threats of a spanking or some choice words that could cut deeply. But she also was tender and most like a mother to me. Caring for me when I was sick. Rocking me when I was restless. Doting on me when I charmed her. She was an avid crocheter, and when I interrupted her work as a little boy, rather than shoo me away, she handed me a hook and some yarn and taught me how to do it. Rather than tell me it was "woman's work," she took the time to teach me a craft that I still enjoy today.

Rene, on the other hand, was seemingly born with an affinity for artistic and literary culture in a family that didn't give two shits about it. She was always reading—not newspapers but actual books—and it most assuredly left an impression on me. It was she who sparked my interest in speculative fiction, and she encouraged me to read and write for fun. You must understand how significant that was in a family that saw reading and writing as mere laziness, an attempt to shirk one's work in whatever sundry projects were going on.

Imagine my delight when I once saw, tucked in Rene's bulky purse, a thick paperback novel. On its cover, an immense mastodon hauled helmeted riders bearing the trappings of the far future—like so far that shit had gone prehistoric again. It impressed me that she was reading that kind of a book. It seemed a book of pure escapism, and when I think of it now, I can see that Rene was always slipping away from our family. Not actually, but only through the vicarious escape route of imagination. And so, naturally, I did the same.

Most nights, after the local evening news was over, she and I would watch *M*A*S*H* and then *Star Trek: The Original Series* in syndication on a tiny black-and-white TV screen in her bedroom. Later, it was *Star Trek: The Next Generation*. I came to adore *TNG* and its storyworld. Picard was an excellent father figure, a concept that took him forever to realize though I recognized and longed for it instantly. Riker was everybody's favorite uncle— stormy, charming, rule bending, goofy. Data was the new Spock, but with the childhood developmental psychology angle that I could connect with. I saw some of myself in Worf, but watching him getting his ass kicked all the time made me gloomy. Counselor Troi made clear to me that I was indeed heterosexual because her formfitting unitards put her shapely ass where it was hard for me to miss—her derrière loved the camera and vice versa, and I was a big fan. I learned about "the male gaze" from Laura Mulvey many years later, but I experienced it as a reality thanks to Troi.

As a Gen Xer, I was fascinated by *Star Wars* as well, my first real passion, and Rene indulged me with multiple trips to the theater to see it and spent money to buy me twelve-inch Kenner action figures of C3PO, R2D2, Chewbacca, and Darth Vader. The smaller versions of these figures would help George Lucas become a billionaire, and I helped build his empire a few bucks at a time by complaining to Rene that I needed them. You're welcome, George.

Rene also made possible my first forays into such science fiction books as Madeleine L'Engle's *Wrinkle in Time*. I can still see the cover of the 1979 edition in my mind's eye—Mrs. Whatsit as the winged, slightly intimidating centaur flying across the sky, and the Man with the Red Eyes, somewhat reminiscent of the giant floating head from *The Wizard of Oz*, scared me a little. I paused in my reading as I neared the descriptions that would take me ever closer to the red-eyed character. More than once, I left the book long enough to forget it; then I would start again from the beginning.

I also thought these volumes were somehow forbidden in the house because Rene kept this and a few other paperbacks under her mattress, like the mastodon-in-the-future novel in her purse, as if they were dangerous, never where they belonged, like in a bookcase. After every one of my reading sessions, I would return these novels to their place beneath the mattress, away from prying eyes. In this way, thanks to Rene, I discovered Tolkien's Middle-earth, Herbert's interstellar economies of the spice trade and white-boy messiah tale, Asimov's Foundation and Robot novels, Adams's Hitchhiker series, and more. Later, she introduced me to Erich von Däniken's ancient astronaut theories, which coincided with her abrupt turn to agnosticism.

Rene often filled in the gaps of my knowledge concerning world history, making me aware of the injustices done upon Indigenous peoples and why we should have pride in the Aztec, Incan, and Mayan civilizations. She was an early practitioner of critical race theory without realizing it. Her enthusiasm for ancient civilizations gradually inspired me to read more about the Egyptian, Greek, and Roman empires, and the relatively less antiquated Moorish civilization in Spain and other parts of Europe. Because of her, I learned of the Moorish characters El Cid and Othello.

When I happened upon a copy of Edith Hamilton's *Mythology* in my elementary school library at the age of eight, I was enthralled; it was likely the first chapter book I read more than once. By the time I got to the mythology unit in the ninth grade, I was the resident expert in many mythologies. Apollo and Athena have always been my favorite Olympians, and my love for them was sparked in the third grade, when I checked Hamilton's book out of the Yarbro Elementary library in Lovington, New Mexico. I can still see its bright orange library binding.

In short, basically every volume that I could find in our house—whether in Lubbock, Texas, or later in Lovington, New Mexico, was likely traceable to Rene. I read my first Ray Bradbury novel, *Something Wicked This Way Comes*, because she had brought it home, and I tried but was bored with Ken Follett's *Eye of the Needle*. I suppose I wasn't so keen on spy thrillers then as now. She loved books and would often take me to the public library and, when I was in junior high, to the local community college library in Hobbs, New Mexico, where she was enrolled in occasional classes, never having completed a degree.

Chapter Five

Above all worthy things, *Star Wars* dominated my imagination during the earliest part of my childhood. Even as a small child, I experienced that "galaxy far, far away" as a real place, a world beyond me but always tantalizingly within reach.

One day Rene told me of a promotional event at Anthony's—a clothing store that was the forerunner of Bealls and Palais Royal—where some of the *Star Wars* characters would be and you could have professional photographs taken with them. Today, I know it was a marketing ploy to sell expensive photograph packages, but I thought the *Star Wars* characters were actually there. I was desperate to go, and Rene took me to Anthony's, during the day, when she should have been sleeping because she worked nights. We waited for what seemed like hours, wearing ruts into the industrial carpet as we walked around the store to kill time, waiting for our name and number to be called. I could see some of the characters in the photo area—Jawas (creatures that were made creepy by similarly styled, brown-robed, diminutive characters in the cult horror classic *Phantasm*), an R2D2 that was most likely a prop (I'm confident Kenny Baker wasn't in the droid in a clothing store in Lubbock, Texas)—and I was astounded that here was *Star Wars* in real life. I had complete and total suspension of disbelief, which would be a big problem in short order.

Rene had me in one arm over her hip, and before I knew what was happening, Darth Vader was standing next to me. I had not noticed him before, but he was plainly there now. Though it was surely a second-rate costume, likely less sophisticated than your average cosplayer today, it looked like the real thing to my child's eyes. He was huge, and I remembered that he could Force-choke a person from across the room. Vader made some banter with Rene; then he turned his attention to me. I peered into his mask and searched his impenetrable lenses. He patted me on the head with one black-gloved hand.

"What a nice little boy," he rasped in a deep voice through the mask, and tousled my dark brown locks. "And such wonderful hair. It would make an excellent pair of socks."

If someone had set my hair on fire, I would have howled less fiercely than I did at that moment. Terror coursed through my little brown body, and I wanted nothing more to do with this photo shoot. *Get me out of here!* This was the real Darth Vader, and I was in equally real danger! Couldn't everyone see that? I was done.

Rene tried everything to get me to calm down. "Chrissy, it's just pretend. That's not the real Darth Vader, *perrito.*" She said something to the guy in the Vader suit, careful not to get too close, but I couldn't hear, thanks to my own bloodcurdling screams of terror. She probably told him he needed to get me to understand that I shouldn't be scared. Maybe if he had removed his helmet, but the poor guy was probably contractually bound under pain of death not to remove it. Nothing he or anyone *else* did worked to calm me down. That's the way irrational fears work, but my fear was perfectly rational to me at the time because that's also how irrational fears work.

Imagine your typical kid who screams bloody murder when they finally get to meet Santa Claus at the mall, and then multiply that by a googolplex. Santa gives children toys, and the worst he does is give a naughty child a lump of coal or a box of cordial cherries (one of my all-time most hated candies). Darth Vader killed motherfuckers before his afternoon tea! I was inconsolable, unreachable, adrift in a sea of panic, and Rene finally had no choice but to leave Anthony's without the picture, with only a marginally entertaining story for posterity as her recompense. I'm sure she was beyond irritated.

Despite this setback, my passion for *Star Wars* was incurable. I was fated to be born a couple of years before the phenomenon of the original *Star Wars* trilogy, and it naturally dominated so much of my imagination, screen time, and whatever entertainment dollars I could guilt my mother into spending on *Star Wars* toys. It was *Star Wars* 25/8. I dressed up as Darth Vader for, like, five consecutive Halloweens in the early 1980s, and I'd wear that shit for weeks on end, until I wore it out. It was the kind of costume that was mostly vinyl and plastic, the fumes from the mask somewhat intoxicating even if the smell wasn't quite pleasant.

It was the films, however, that fueled my imagination and playtime. *Star Wars* (later retitled *Star Wars: Episode IV—A New Hope*) is the first movie I remember seeing in a theater, and all I can recall from that first viewing was being utterly captivated by the X-wing attack runs in the Death Star trench. Rene had always worshipped at the altar of the speculative, God bless her, and she bequeathed that passion to me. She called herself a Trekkie before I even knew what that was. She would take me to any speculative movie she could.

Ralph Bakshi's *Wizards*, released only three months before *Star Wars*, was another film that left a mark, but when we rewatched it on VHS when I was in high school, we realized we had profoundly misunderstood it. *Star Wars* didn't aspire to such lofty artistic expression in depicting fascism and war. Bakshi had included footage of Hitler giving speeches and a murdering assassin-robot named Necron99 that was essentially reprogrammed and renamed Peace! Of note, Mark Hamill was a voice actor in *Wizards* in his film debut.

Before long, everything I wanted revolved around *Star Wars*. I watched derivative films like *Battle Beyond the Stars* (laughable) and Disney's *Black Hole* (execrable), only to come back to *Star Wars* feeling even more convinced that it was better by orders of magnitude. Nothing since then has consumed me so intensely. Rene knew it, and she would buy anything related to the films, even if it was the cheaper knockoff versions of plastic lightsabers— basically a flashlight attached to a long polyurethane tube that was utterly silent; I had to supply the proper hum of the lightsaber myself.

The Kenner action figures (a.k.a. dolls for boys) were ubiquitous and cherished. I didn't collect baseball cards, but I would get my hands on similar kinds of cards made by Topps that were essentially screen caps of the movies. Sometimes they were stickers. I had coloring books and comics that all siphoned money we couldn't afford to spend and shuffled it off to Mr. George Lucas, who didn't cast a Latinx person in his films until 2002, when he tapped Jimmy Smits to play Bail Organa (Leia's adoptive father) in *Star Wars: Episode II—Attack of the Clones*, the lowest rated of the nine Force-driven films in the Skywalker family saga on IMDb.

Rene was so mindful of my obsession with *Star Wars* that, even into my midtwenties, after I was already married, she would send me books that hit the market either as reissues or new material (thanks to a resurgence of interest connected to the prequel trilogy and Kevin Smith's even greater obsession with these properties). For instance, my mother sent me a book of Ralph McQuarrie's concept art for *Star Wars* and another one with the art of Dave Dorman—out of the blue. *Thought you might like these*, she wrote on a note in the package. She was right.

Chapter Six

That cinematic setting—a long time ago in a galaxy far, far away—was a siren song to me. The problem, my blessing but also my curse, was that Luke Skywalker was the hero. He was my hero, but I knew I could never be Luke Skywalker. Because Luke Skywalker could never look like me.

Perhaps other Brown kids didn't give a shit that Luke was basically a white boy from Kansas. (Kansas, Tatooine—similar in that they are supposed to be where the rubes and country folk live, far from the nerve centers of culture and pools of talent.) Like Clark Kent and Dorothy Gale, Luke Skywalker had to come from humble origins, where he gained his sense of Midwestern values and ethics that would serve him, as it serves Superman and Dorothy, when he must confront evil incarnate and, most important, the temptation to use immense power irresponsibly. Han Solo tries to insult Luke in the original film by pointing out how he doesn't know a damn thing about space dogfights, because Luke's basically an ignorant farm boy who can barely wipe his own ass properly: "Traveling through hyperspace ain't like dusting crops, boy!"

These three protagonists (four, if we include Han Solo—but let's not, because he's only a crucial helper character) are white, even though in the case of two of them, the men, there is no reason they cannot be any other race, ethnicity, gender, or species. Kal-El and Luke Skywalker are goddamn aliens, as far as we earthlings are concerned, but they are played by the most Caucasian, Anglo men you can find. Dorothy is a little white farmer girl because, well, there are a lot of little white girls from farming communities in Kansas. So at least there is logic to that. (Were she from Utah, she'd likely be a white Mormon girl with an eyebrow-raising spelling of her name.)

Demographics are destiny. If you think I'm exaggerating or this discussion is overblown, imagine these characters as non-white, with non-majority identities, and contemplate how that would go over today. I mean, we have seen this and the equal outrage from many white people. Legions in the *Star Wars* fandom figuratively riot and howl in agony when non-majority actors—especially women actors—take up prominent roles in the films. Kelly Marie Tran was so pestered and harassed for playing Rose Tico in the sequel trilogy that she deleted her Instagram account. Rey Skywalker was dismissed as a Mary Sue—a woman character derided for seemingly unearned or undeserved powers or perfection—as if Luke weren't exactly the same thing. On the other hand, we are informed that issues of representation are not such a vital matter. When marginalized identities want more representation, we're told to wait. But when we do get meaningful representation, it's white genocide. So, does it matter, or does it not matter? I get confused sometimes. (Last two sentences dripping with venomous sarcasm.)

Hollywood acts like there isn't a history of Latinos in the United States, and certainly that there aren't many Latinos who go to movies and buy merchandise that is based on Hollywood and TV productions. That would be news to Rene and the rest of my family. We watched all kinds of movies and television shows, and we didn't have the luxury of boycotting this entertainment or that until we saw more Latinos on the screen, because we'd have been shit out of luck. Nothing like that would be coming, not for decades.

In any case, we were spending a lot of time watching networks like Galavisión, Univision, and Telemundo when we wanted to see some storytelling that seemed to reflect some aspect of our culture. I lost count of how many Vicente Fernández flicks I saw as a kid. For people like my grandparents, that's where you tuned in to see Latinos as the stars of their stories. They didn't care that people like us never appeared as the stars of American films, or else it never riled them the way it did and does me.

When they saw a stereotype of the Latino in an American film, they laughed at the stereotype because it seemed to them that we Latinos had infiltrated an American movie to muck things up. We were trickster figures. This happened in movies that incorporated Mexicans into the story, like *The Three Amigos*, a movie I dislike with a passion, or the Mexican *bandido* who appears fleetingly in *Blazing Saddles*, a movie I adore, when Harvey Korman's villainous character is enlisting other unsavory figures to help in his cause.

As the *bandido* signs up and is given a badge, his response harks back to the character Gold Hat from *The Treasure of the Sierra Madre* when he repeats the line "Badges? We don't need no estinking badges!!" My family laughed at that moment, and I did, too, even if it did make me feel uncomfortable for reasons I could not yet articulate. I laughed harder at the movie's infamous fart scene because we ate a lot of beans—such comic and room-clearing flatulence happened often in my home whenever my uncle-brothers Tom, David, Robert, and I put away a pot of Mom's *frijoles*.

Even so, I hardly saw any characters who looked like my family, and that made me think we Latinos were much smaller in number in society than we actually were. And by smaller, I mean of less importance. Insignificant. It also gave me the sense that we weren't worthy enough for an interesting film. That we were invisible. That's how early such thinking can take hold, accepting cultural inferiority as simply the way things are. Well, things are that way because of deliberate policies and attitudes, both codified and unspoken, enforced by people in power. White supremacy isn't a natural phenomenon.

The irony here is that kids play pretend all the time. They pretend to be shit that is so different from them: dragons, elves, trolls, *Minecraft* Steve, Link, Sailor Moon, Rainbow Dash, Eren Yeager, Harry Potter, and other fantastical characters. No kid says, "Well, I can't technically be an elf in real life, but I can sure as hell pretend to be one on my own time and for my own entertainment." A child runs with it, no ruminations on the technicalities and no rationalizations. Similarly, I could as easily have said, "I'm Luke Skywalker! I'm here to rescue you. *I'm here with Ben Kenobi!*" and simply had fun.

But beware the literalists walking among us as children, classroom lawyers who are ever at the ready to explain, annoyingly, how you can or can't do something. These would-be junior counsel most often seized on certain kinds of play they deemed out of bounds, either because of racial or gendered rationales. See, a little girl can't be Luke Skywalker because, well, Luke is a boy. And a Brown boy like me couldn't be Luke, either, for obvious reasons. In other words, little girls and non-white little boys could never pretend to be the most important character in the most popular of films. They couldn't even pretend to be the savior of the universe. We had to be a sidekick (not Han Solo, though, he's too cool and he's white—so maybe Chewbacca!).

Of course, what I should have said was, *This is pretend, motherfucker, and I can pretend to be whatever I want.* But somewhere deep down, it felt wrong to make believe I was a white character. It felt like a betrayal of my identity, and no wonder: In my community, when I was growing up, striving to be white was something you should never want to do. The keepers of authenticity in my culture were always quick to judge you and flag you as not Mexican or Latino enough—too *pocho*—and if you weren't Mexican or Latino, well, then you must be a gringo or a *gabacho*. Didn't matter that you were as Brown as the day is long, had a Hispanic surname, watched *El Chavo del Ocho* whenever you could, and ate homemade tortillas with every meal. I was always fending off accusations and appraisals from my Brown kinfolk, who took to calling me white. As I got older, their judgment bothered me less and less.

Because Luke (played by Mark Hamill) was white and I wasn't, part of me always felt like I was trespassing in a place that wanted to—that was designed to—keep me out. I mean, Luke was, like, the whitest guy I knew, with his bleached-blond hair and brilliant blue eyes, plus the way he was constantly whining in the first film. If I tried to whine my way out of whatever work I was supposed to be doing at home, I'd sure as hell get it.

I understood the whining to be a feature of Luke's whiteness and privilege. And no way could I easily have left the old homestead to belatedly train as a Jedi after Stormtroopers murdered my whole family. The souls of my family would have haunted me like Force Ghosts if I didn't keep the moisture farm going! Luke's hair got darker with each sequel, which confused me a little—he was getting darker in hair and clothing the closer he got to the Dark side—but that didn't bring him any closer to *me*. The darkening hair only confirmed my suspicions that the darker you were, the more dangerous you appeared to the universe around you.

Weird kid that I was, I soon began to pretend that it was not Luke Skywalker that I wanted to be . . . but Darth Vader. While I still recognized Luke as the savior of the galaxy, his father, and the films, I was bound by some rule that said I *couldn't* be Luke Skywalker—even in my own flights of fancy. Today, I'd tell my single-digit-aged self that I could playact and role-play whatever character I wanted. Hell, wanna be a rancor and bite off people's heads? Fucking knock yourself out, kid! Wanna be the sarlacc pit and slowly digest your victims over a thousand years? Why not! Or be ahead of your time and channel Boba Fett!

But back then, I resolved to be the villain. Milton had cast Satan in a heroic light when he gave him the words about reigning in hell as preferable to serving in heaven. So, too, would I reign as Lord Vader. If I couldn't rule the galaxy as a handsome young white guy, I would overlord it as a cyborg in all black as I wielded the greatest of all lightsabers, the Sithian red one. Red has always been my favorite color.

But what kind of bullshit was that, anyway? I was willing to be Darth Vader, the villain, instead of the hero? Vader was a loser! Old, fading fast, clinging to his sorcerer's ways as a part of his sad devotion to an ancient religion. All true, of course, but he was still damned formidable. He struck fear into everyone, especially white people, which was predictable when all the major characters except for Lando, who came later, were white.

How easily I took on the persona of Darth Vader around the house! In my young mind, I thought Vader was like C3PO, R2D2, and IG88, a blasted robot! And even I knew robots weren't white, Brown, or Black. If C3PO sounded like Jeeves on helium, that was because he was programmed with that voice! Vader's voice was all-powerful, and when I learned that a Black man named James Earl Jones was the voice of Vader, I was amazed and overjoyed. Later still, I learned that an imposing British man named David Prowse was the one physically on set and in the suit. But, like many fans, I was sold on Vader as a character in large part because of Jones's voice.

That voice loomed in my periphery for years. I thought about it often and could hear it clearly in my mind's ear after I had memorized Vader's every line. It was a voice of power, and even as a small Brown boy, I felt that if I could speak like that, I would enjoy a similar kind of respect without having to resort to Force-choking a person to make a point. Respect, but without murderous intent. Win–win. Before they created those toy synthesizers that could change your voice (or at least they purported to do so; it never worked for me), I discovered that you could alter your sound if you put your face very close to a box fan while it was on.

In West Texas, you had a box fan for almost every room. When I was bored and left to my own devices, I'd creep up to a box fan and start to growl in as low a register as I could, until I could speak in a kind of guttural vocalization—a proto voice. I would recite Vader's lines. "You are a part of the Rebel Alliance and a traitor! *Take her away!*" and "I find your lack of faith disturbing." What's more, I tried to imitate Vader's (Jones's) quasi-British accent. Like, he wouldn't say *force*; he'd say *fohse*. He wouldn't say *falcon*; he'd say *folkun*. And so, I would too.

One afternoon, I was doing something like climbing on the furniture, jumping from sofa to love seat and back, lording over my domain as Vader had. Annoying behavior typical of kids who don't yet recognize boundaries or why you shouldn't abuse furniture that costs money. Rene and Mom admonished me to cut it out, which would ordinarily have stopped me dead in my tracks. But I was in Vader mode, and Vader didn't stop for anyone, Sith Lord that he was.

I carefully raised my toy, a third-rate lightsaber with a puny flashlight base, and menaced Mom and Rene with it. "Don't you know I can kill you with this?"

"*¿Ah, sí?*" Mom shot back without missing a beat. "*Cabrón,* don't you know I can kill you with this?" She raised the most formidable weapon in the Chicana armory, a single *chancla*. That shut me up quick. Vader role-play on indefinite hiatus for retooling.

But I never thought, *I can't do this. I'm not allowed to do this, because Vader's voice is a Black man's voice and I'm not Black.* I attribute my blitheness to my early belief that Vader was a robot—or more exact to the *Star Wars* universe, a droid. So far as I was concerned, he came from a race of mechanical beings, and was therefore unshackled from whiteness or Brownness or Blackness. It wasn't until the second and third films that it became clear that Vader had been a human being at one point, that he was once a white guy. But by then, it didn't matter. To me he was a robot in black, "more machine now than man," as Obi-Wan told Luke, and I could more readily align myself with his identity than I could Luke's. How was this possible? Hadn't Vader terrified the shit out of me at Anthony's?

He had indeed. But part of my ease in playing Vader was that no one had a problem with pretending to be a Black guy. In fact, I knew white kids who were always claiming to be some Black man from a given part of popular culture or professional sports league. Little white boys called themselves Walter Payton or Magic Johnson (pre-HIV) during recess, and not once did someone say, *Well, now, wait a minute there, Jimmy. Those guys you're talking about are Black men, and well, ah, you ain't Black, son. Why don't you pretend to be Larry Bird or Kurt Rambis or Danny Ainge?* (Well, nobody wanted to be Ainge, that's for damned sure.)

And a few years later, Gatorade would bust out a genius ad campaign in which little kids wanted desperately to Be Like Mike. Michael Jordan's apotheosis made it permissible to want to be him. No matter who or where you were, Air Jordan was universal. But remember that simile—you can be like Mike; you can't be Mike. And let's not talk about all the white kids who loved Michael Jackson (I'm not being facetious or intentionally ironical) and emulated him by trying to reproduce his dance moves in the school hallway. Moonwalking belonged to everyone!

Just as society had created these invisible but insuperable barriers to whiteness, it had also made Blackness a buffet where you could indulge in all that you wanted, and still go back to your non-Black privilege at the end of the day. Though I couldn't put it into words at the time, I could feel that it was okay to be a man in black who spoke like a Black man, but I couldn't be a blond, blue-eyed white guy. And since I wanted entrée into the *Star Wars* universe, it would have to be Darth Vader for me. And so, even today, I have an abiding fondness for Darth Vader. Not Anakin Skywalker but big-ass, black Darth Vader. It ought to make no sense, but when you look at mass media storytelling, both then and now, it makes perfect sense.

Chapter Seven

Whenever people talk about representation in storytelling, usually around the time of awards season, we get to read and hear grievances about the lack of diversity in, say, feature films. In reaction, we also get wind of complaints that representation is fine the way it is, that diversifying storytelling contributes to white genocide, that it makes for sorrier films and characters, that Hollywood—which conservatives despise so much yet long desperately to be a part of—is somehow made even more irrelevant by being so politically correct, or PC.

It's a simple fact that those communities historically in the minority in the United States are growing larger and at a greater rate than whites. That whites will one day not compose the majority group in America is inevitable. This demographic shift is so scary to many whites—the reality that they will someday be a minority. Perhaps select whites believe their indifference and hatred toward minority groups will ultimately be turned back on them. Since that's what they have done to others, they believe it will be done to them. The Golden Rule also has a karmic, unspoken inverse to it: Do harm unto others, and harm will be done unto you.

My recognition that Luke Skywalker did not look like me, did not come from my culture or community, was not an anomalous or accidental observation. In other words, Luke Skywalker was not a one-off, the only white savior of the universe. On the contrary, white saviors are practically a given in storytelling in the USA. As I write this, it's everyone's favorite white boy, Timothée Chalamet, playing the messiah Paul Atreides in *Dune* this time around (despite the fact that the actor they cast as his father is a Guatemalan-born Latino, Oscar Isaacs!). Even many Christians, at least in this country, have made representations and paintings of Jesus look like, at various times, Viggo Mortensen's Aragorn, '80s-era Kenny Loggins, and Ewan McGregor's

Obi-Wan Kenobi. These ornately framed versions of Jesus are everywhere in Utah. Sometimes it seems that whiteness is often next to godliness.

I remember another space-themed movie of the early 1980s that came out in the wake of the *Star Wars* phenomenon and was titled *The Last Starfighter*. The hero, Alex Rogan, wasn't from another part of the galaxy—he was a trailer park kid, colossally average, who was going nowhere fast. But thanks to his mad video game skills (his loserdom is an asset here, you see), he finds himself on the path to saving the galaxy. And, of course, after every other starfighter in the universe is killed in a surprise attack by the Ko-Dan Armada, Alex Rogan literally becomes the last starfighter, who happens to be a trailer park white boy. He's the poor man's Luke Skywalker.

Fast-forward some thirty years to *Ready Player One*, and it's still a white boy saving the universe! If one didn't know any better, it was almost as if only young, white, straight men were up to the challenge of being saviors. I recognized this for the horseshit it was even then, and yet it kept getting replicated ad nauseam. I wondered when we would see a Brown person saving the galaxy. I'd be damned if I was going to pretend to be a white guy hero, even if it was Luke Skywalker. It was like being the cowboy when you played cowboys and Indians. The white hat to me was the hero for killing brown people like me.

I wasn't usually allowed to be a cowboy anyway, because—well, the young literalists argued that I most closely resembled the Indians, and so my similarity to what an Indian looks like would make it more entertaining. Forget that the Indians always lost the game (someone would invoke history but never the Battle of Little Bighorn) and that they couldn't speak English, so I was supposed to make stereotypical Indian whooping sounds. And I did it a few times because even then white privilege allows and empowers white kids to gaslight Brown kids. I was also, invariably, Tonto (sounds like the word for "dummy" in Spanish) in all iterations of the Lone Ranger LARPing I did as a child. But who the hell wanted to be the Lone Ranger when you could be a Jedi knight?

If we think of this in a different way, these mutually reinforcing narratives suggested that you couldn't be a hero unless you were white. The message was both annoying and dispiriting, and it damned sure wasn't accidental. Movie studios and executives wanted white boy heroes like James Dean, Burt

Reynolds, Paul Newman, and Robert Redford. Richard Dreyfuss somehow rigged the Matrix and was an improbable nerd hero in *Jaws* and *Close Encounters of the Third Kind*. While that nerd hero appealed to me and my own nerdiness, I wasn't that interested in building a scale model of Devils Tower out of mashed potatoes or talking about *Carcharodon carcharias* to a dumbass mayor like some damned walking encyclopedia. If I was gonna be a fact-spewing robot, I was gonna be goddamned Darth Vader.

Worse were the films that tried to be more diverse but ended up making a white savior anyway, not for an entire galaxy but instead a small group of people on society's fringe. This narrative is the prototypical white savior story that doggedly continues to be made—movies like *The Blind Side* and *Green Book* give white audiences that feeling of having done something for non-white non-majority people. Instead, I want to see them make a Brown person that is the savior of the universe, or a Brown person who saves a bunch of hapless white people. *Blazing Saddles* kind of manages to do this, but it is deliberately satirical and self-aware. I'm thinking of one that is sober and serious.

You might be thinking of many such films. *Night of the Living Dead* has the Black hero killed by a white cop who "mistakenly" thinks he's the undead. *The Brother from Another Planet* features an extraterrestrial played by Joe Morton, which I appreciated. But he wasn't a Black man saving white people. Michael Jordan saved the Looney Tunes cast in *Space Jam*, which I enjoyed. Sidney Poitier set a bunch of unruly white Brit high schoolers straight in *To Sir, with Love*, and thank goodness he did. *Black Panther* was released in 2018 to acclaim, and many fans from marginalized groups felt that, at long last, a larger-than-life superhero who looked like them had appeared on the screen. Or maybe you thought of *Coco*, but *Coco* isn't so much a superhero film as it is a film about family (which makes it well within the tradition of Latinx family drama and magical realism).

All of these are gorgeous, necessary films. But I want to see more films that feature a protagonist of color who is saving white people. Did you watch *The Book of Eli* with Denzel Washington? He saved *literacy* and the Holy Bible, to say nothing of the postapocalyptic future. And he doesn't survive to the end, just like *Night of the Living Dead*. Such films are still too few and far between, even if you may not be hip to the problem because you are white.

Chapter Eight

When I was a kid, it was white heroes all the time. I wondered if only white people were heroic and worthy of glory on the big screen. (Savior figures were chosen by destiny; by their whiteness ye shall know them!) If the best of us were white, that must mean being white was best. So, then . . . were the people who looked like you or your family in fact the clowns and villains movie and television stereotypes made you out to be? Were your stories less compelling—less important—than those of the white community? A Brown boy idolizing the heroes of white narratives might easily slip into a disdain for non-white groups and their (apparently trivial) stories.

Doubtless, this phenomenon explains why white supremacists see nothing wrong with, say, representations of the kind I am discussing here. They sure enough squeak like rusty wheels when a film or production dares showcase a non-white, non-male, non-straight hero portrayed by an equally diverse actor. In 2022, so-called fans rained hell upon Moses Ingram, a Black actor cast as Reva Sevander in the Disney+ series *Obi-Wan Kenobi*. Ingram received hundreds of racist messages regarding her portrayal of the powerful character, prompting Ewan McGregor to condemn the backlash in a strong statement and video under the official *Star Wars* Twitter handle (@starwars). Ingram had the temerity to play a role—to play pretend—as a meaningful woman of color, who at one point faces Darth Vader in a lightsaber duel—in the *Star Wars* cast of characters, so of course she became the target of a hate campaign. (And this was *forty years* after my own problems with Luke Skywalker!)

To my knowledge, the nine films anchoring the *Star Wars* franchise have never featured a Latina/o/x/e actor in the role of Jedi Knight. Rosario Dawson played Ahsoka Tano (in orange makeup and prosthetics) in *The Mandalorian* series on Disney+, and Pedro Pascal plays the title role, revealing his face usually once a season. Oscar Isaac is a kind of Han Solo figure in the sequel trilogy, as is Diego Luna in *Rogue One: A Star Wars Story* and its magnificent spinoff, *Andor*. I would have loved to encounter these characters when I was a kid.

So, yes, my community and culture *are* slowly making their way into the *Star Wars* universe. And little Brown girls and boys today are able to see something of themselves in the Latinx actors who have begun to inhabit that fictional world—in a way I never could. But some people act like a small uptick in Latinx visibility in speculative storytelling is akin to exponential representation and that it's therefore unfair. Hardly. We've taken maybe a hundred steps in a two-thousand-mile journey! Yes, that's "progress." It's exceedingly slow progress.

I often think of my namesake, a Christopher who in his all-too-short life went on to be a great rapper and hip-hop artist—if not the greatest. Christopher Wallace had several personas: the Notorious B.I.G., Biggie Smalls, and most important for me here and now, a character he called the Black Frank White.

Now, Frank White is the name of a character played by yet another Christopher, this one with the surname Walken. In *King of New York*, Walken plays a notorious and powerful drug lord named Frank White who is consolidating power in NYC while acting as a kind of Robin Hood or Iceberg Slim to the downtrodden community. Clearly, Wallace found an affinity between his own burgeoning image and that of the character Frank White, a white man literally named White.

But rather than fall back because his film hero was a white guy and not Black like him, Wallace simply anointed himself "the Black Frank White." He took the essence of the original character and ran him through the machinery of imagination whereby Frank White could be reimagined as Black. Blackness for Wallace was often painful but hard fought, and for him at least, it had an inherent transformative power, which he cherished. The Black Frank White could surely exist, and it would be the Notorious B.I.G. who willed him into existence, out of necessity and by sheer determination.

This was a sophisticated move that my single-digit-year-old self didn't know I could make, because Wallace himself hadn't done it yet. And why aren't there more Blackified and Browned roles or personas—like the revamped Namor a.k.a. K'uk'ulkan in *Black Panther: Wakanda Forever?* Sure, I get the exhortation to make our own characters, and we should. And we are. But that's a lengthy undertaking, and in the moment, why not do what Biggie did and go with it? Making a white character Black or Brown transforms it into something new. With a mere turn of phrase, *the Black Frank White*, Biggie changed how a lot of people would go on to interpret Walken's original portrayal.

I wish I could go back in time to tell little Christopher González that he can go ahead and like Luke Skywalker and that the weird dissonance he feels is not his fault, and in truth, it's not Luke's fault either. I'd say the following:

Don't worry that you don't have blond hair and blue eyes. Your dark hair and brown eyes are fine the way they are. The thing is that moviemakers in America like more than anything to make white people into heroes, whether they deserve it or not.

But that's not your concern, Crisito. See, you can't be Luke Skywalker, and he can't look like you, because this nation won't let it happen—lest it make a whole lot of insecure but powerful people angry. But you know what? Think of yourself as the Brown Luke Skywalker. That way, you can take the best parts of him while keeping the best parts of you. It's the best of both worlds.

But hurry up, mijito. This country won't be getting any easier for guys like you, and there is real hero shit that needs doing out there. Big Scary Brown Guy work won't do itself.

Chapter Nine

In the summer of 1967, Tomás González and his wife, Elva, bought a house in Lubbock, Texas, over a mile from where they had been living on Spruce Avenue. They would pay fifty dollars a month until they owned the place free and clear. Tomás and Elva were my mother's parents, but we all called them Dad and Mom. (Dad was also the very first Big Scary Brown Guy in my life, and it took me some time not to be intimidated by him.) He had grown up on farms around San Antonio and turned to masonry and carpentry for his livelihood. Mom kept the home and was both law and order for as long as she lived.

Irene, their spirited, know-it-all firstborn daughter, with a cuteness to match her attitude, had been set to attend Alderson Junior High—at the time, a predominately Black school owing to the segregation that bifurcated Lubbock, same as in many cities and towns across the South. However, Dad and Mom did not want their daughter, whom everyone including me would call Rene, to attend Alderson, so they moved a bit southward so Rene could attend O. L. Slaton Junior High and, later, Lubbock High School, where most of the Latino kids went to school.

But later that same year, in a stroke of beautiful irony, Lubbock redrew its school districts, reset the redlines, and Rene eventually found herself at Dunbar High School, where the vast majority of Lubbock's Black students attended, a school named after that titan of American poetry, Paul Laurence Dunbar. Its mascot was, naturally, a Panther. (Incidentally, Dunbar High School no longer exists, effectively erased, its history gone.)

During the 1960s, Lubbock had many similarities to other comparably sized cities in the South: clearly defined boundaries that kept identity communities separated.[2] Unmistakable economic advantages and

---

2 At the time, Lubbock was similar in size to such cities as Greensboro, North Carolina; Knoxville,

disadvantages depending on where one lived, with schools to match in a perverse semblance of "separate but equal." One clear difference, however, was Lubbock's significant Latinx population, which made this demographic the majority minority in the area—a demographic more prominent in the American Southwest than in the American South.

While Latinos were tolerated in cities like Lubbock (which is still considered comically conservative even among other regions in the red state of Texas), they were never treated as first-class citizens—and Blacks were essentially shunned by all other ethnic groups. Couple this racial hierarchy with my family's general misanthropy toward people outside the household irrespective of skin color, and one can see the distorted, racist logic that impelled Dad and Mom to cross school district borders and move into a small house down the road. Fears of miscegenation apply not only to whites, ladies and gentlemen.

And so, this little house where my mother would spend the rest of her childhood would also serve as my childhood home; her parents became my parents in all ways except those that made it a legal adoption. The house—a modest, unremarkable abode with cream-colored ceramic tiles on its exterior—presided over a corner lot in the isolated neighborhood. But that house had stood there a long time, through several previous owners. It was once an old-timey schoolhouse and even a church, according to Rene, and it had seen two suicides before Dad bought it—a history likely undisclosed to him when transferring the title. (Because why tell a Latino who didn't speak English very well about something that might keep a superstitious lot like this from signing on "the line which is dotted"?)

Inside, there were two bedrooms and one bathroom. The living room, what I grew up calling *la sala* (a "great room" per reality TV home shows), was set off from the dining area by a homemade pony wall that rose to about five feet and was covered in dark wood paneling. From the cap of the partition, store-bought wooden balusters, lathe-turned and unvarnished, reached to the high ceiling at regular intervals. This bit of carpentry was known in my family as "the divider," and it did its job admirably, separating *la sala* from the dining room.

Tennessee; Montgomery, Alabama; Little Rock, Arkansas; and Jackson, Mississippi. All averaged around 125,000 in population in 1960, according to the U.S. Census of Population Report of 1960.

Where the balusters met the solid wall of the divider, capped at about eye level for most people, various knickknacks found a suitable landing spot. Loose change, nasal sprays (ubiquitous in the house and called 4-Ways no matter the brand), small tins of Carmex and tubes of ChapStick, deodorant, Wrigley's chewing gum (Big Red or Doublemint, sometimes Juicy Fruit), and other personal items with no permanent home appeared logically arranged there too. The divider was likewise a catchall for essential things like wallets and car keys.

Though the divider abutted the western interior wall, it ended abruptly several feet from the opposite wall, leaving an egress from *la sala* to the dining area. A four-by-four-foot mirror hung on that wall, straddling the two spaces. Below and to the left of the mirror, an old gas wall heater, the kind with a light brown steel cover and ceramic bricks within to radiate the heat, would inefficiently supply warmth to the drafty house. The house had neither central air-conditioning nor central heating, and on cold mornings before school, I would stand in front of this wall unit as I got dressed for the day.

I would clothe myself there not only because it was warm but also because I had no room of my own. In all my childhood, I never did have my own bedroom or even a room to share. I had no fixed place in the house as a kid, always settling my stuff and myself wherever there happened to be a little space left over.

I grew up sleeping on Mom and Dad's large bed or, often, on the couch or in a sleeping bag. I always found it strange to watch television shows and movies that depicted a child having a domain of their own, with the audacity to hang a sign on the bedroom door telling everyone else to KEEP OUT! Conditions in my home would never have allowed for such territoriality. Not a fucking chance, kid!

And it was never lost on me that these children I saw on television were often situated within a family meant to stand in for white America. I was made aware that white people lived differently than the way we did at home. Indeed, as I compared what I saw on the screen to my own experience, these shows defined a very palpable separation between the two cultures. White people lived differently from my family, but why? Television and film were a window on how my family's circumstances were far removed from what was considered normal and mainstream in other American families.

Such representations helped confirm for me that television was powerful and had the capacity to shape a viewer's understanding of the world. It could make a person feel as if their own identity, their own lifestyle and standard of living, was somehow lesser than or different from everyone else's. In my young mind, the reason I didn't have my own room was because I wasn't white. I'm sure there were plenty of white children who were growing up without a room of their own, but at the time, I didn't believe that. Little David, my second-grade classmate who told me it was no problem if I stopped at his house on my way home from school, had his own room, but maybe he was the exception?

The ceilings in our house were high for such a small structure (it was supposedly a schoolhouse or church, after all), perhaps nine or ten feet, and they made the place feel much more substantial than it truly was. As a teenager, I would get a running start and then jump as if I were trying to dunk a basketball, so that I could touch the ceiling tiles.

In the kitchen, cupboards and drawers held items that would have been more at home in a garage or toolbox, like pliers and superglue. It was the kitchen that made the house feel old. Far from aesthetically pleasing, it was downright ugly. But it worked, and good food was always coming out of it. Beyond the kitchen were the utility room and the back door, with its medieval-looking metal bar that we could slide into place to lock up.

The front face of the house featured what we called the porch, a thick platform of concrete that rose several feet aboveground. During those rare times it was free of clutter, I enjoyed getting a running start and jumping from the porch because it seemed to take minutes to land, which gave me the feeling of flying. Standing on the porch and looking through the open windows into the house was strangely entertaining, with only a metal windscreen between me and Mom, who often lay on her bed and looked out onto the world, the same bed I would lie on when watching Bugs Bunny.

She would tell me to get away from the windows. That neighbors must think there's a naked woman inside giving a peep show, she'd say. I didn't think the neighbors cared one bit about what was happening at my house, but being suspicious of anyone who didn't live there with us would become a defining, stubborn, and persistent trait in my family.

The front door was not original to the house; it was an oddity. Whereas the back door was flimsy despite its medieval lock, the front door was ponderous and heavy, and later I learned that it had originally belonged inside a bank. I often wondered how a door that was once inside a bank had ended up on the front of my house. (Most likely, it was salvaged or bought at an auction.) Whenever I closed it, I could tell it didn't belong. Too much potential energy. Too much investment of inertia. Frankly, it was too well made, too dense for its bulk to ever feel comfortable on its solid brass hinges.

That front door was sure to hold up even when the rest of the structure around it collapsed. It would abide after Gabriel blew his horn, I thought. The last thing standing at the end of it all. I felt secure behind that banker's door, but it was only a sense of security I had, not security itself. The tenuous nature of that security would be exposed again and again as our house was broken into at will over the years, our things picked over and often stolen. Burglars would break in through the windows—but never through that big-ass front door.

The house also had a bad temper, and here is the requisite magical realist part of my Latino story: For years, members of my family would remain convinced that a malignant presence lived in our home. Things knocked about of their own accord. Lights turned themselves on for no plain reason. Voices would call out to you from the back bedroom, pretending to be someone you knew when that someone wasn't in the house.

Rene claimed it was the house that made Dad sick, and Mom would explain away her daughter's speculations regarding the supernatural. Mom had a strong belief in God, as seen through the lens of Latinx Catholicism. There were always lighted Saint Jude candles with little slips of folded paper under them. Prayers from Mom that, like secrets or birthday wishes, I knew would be invalidated if shared. So, I never read what Mom wrote on those pieces of paper. Her prayers were more than a match for whatever it was that bumped about in the house.

Rene, born into that same Catholicism, was a self-proclaimed agnostic who turned away from religion when I was in high school. When one of her best friends died in the hospital after pulmonary aspiration, Rene turned her back on the notion of a God who could save or heal or right wrongs. But she believed in ghosts and otherworldly shit. So, agnosticism worked well enough for her. And she fully rejected the idea of a personal savior.

If you were to visit that address today, you would find that the house no longer exists. It was bulldozed in 1999 for my family's failure to pay the property taxes. A house that my family had owned free and clear. Restless spirits were banished, and that enduring bulwark of a door didn't stand a chance. No one bothered to tell me about it till after the fact. One night, I went over and saw the bare yard of my childhood, but the house itself was gone. It may have been an ill-tempered house, but it was my childhood home. The darkness of the night had swallowed it whole.

As for me, I never viewed the house in terms of spookiness or the supernatural. Despite my mother's zeal for agnosticism and her insistence on turning away from religion, she and my family were very superstitious folk, the kind of people who placed great stock in things like horoscopes and fortune-telling. Walter Mercado, the Puerto Rican tele-astrologer, QEPD, was revered in my home. They had a strong belief in destiny and fate, and they often placed too much stock in games of chance and luck.

I believe this superstitious bent contributed to a gambler's sense of reality within the household. My family was always willing to take a chance, even when logic and reason screamed not to do it. Rather than setting money aside for the future or investing it, they imagined a huge payday or "win" was around the corner. If only we had the faith to place our bets. It was a game of chance that, perhaps unsurprisingly, led to clear misfortunes and hardships in our family. Rene, in particular, was someone who always took the chance and would always gamble to improve her position or station in life. She won, yes, but she lost as well.

I remember when the State of Texas finally instituted its lottery system in late 1992, first with scratch-offs and later in the year with lottery tickets. Even though we were living in New Mexico by that time, and I was in my senior year of high school, my family would drive to the state line to the first convenience store they could find to buy at times hundreds of dollars' worth of lotto tickets.

Rene looked forward to playing the lotto. She would excitedly drive to the convenience store to make her purchase, playing her favorite numbers or sometimes relying solely on "quick picks." When Rene returned home, she would be grinning merrily. Already in her mind, she was assured some bit of money but most likely the jackpot. As the time drew closer to the announcement of the winning numbers, she mused extravagantly about how she would spend her winnings.

But it wasn't Rene alone who did this! Sharing fantasies about the prize money was infectious in my family, and even I would do it as a young person. We would sit around and talk about how we were going to spend multimillion-dollar winnings, how we were going to buy a new house or new cars.

My own fantasies related to being "bill free." Bill collectors always threatened to spoil any moment of jollity our family may have latched on to. Rarely did I know exactly what the collectors wanted, and I would have done most anything to wave them away with the flick of a wand. I imagined being some big shot with an assistant whose only job was to carry a large briefcase wherever I went. I'd go to these collectors, snap a finger, and like a Secret Service agent, my assistant would open the case with a loud click and pay these bastards in cold, hard cash. For as long as I could remember, I yearned for a future that liberated me and my family from financial anxiety.

And then, when inevitably our lotto numbers did not turn up, everyone was surprised and crushed. My dreams of throwing fat stacks of money at relentless bill collectors disappeared. There we were again, depressed and discouraged, left with the cruel fact that we were stuck in our reality without enough money, without enough time. Losing the lottery placed even more pressure on the next drawing, and our silly drama would repeat itself more often than it should have.

"It would abide after Gabriel blew his horn, I thought."

Chapter Ten

In Lubbock, our neighbors across the street and to the south were the Shues, Kennith and Joyce. An older white couple, they had lived in that neighborhood on the east side of Lubbock at least as long as my family had. Most likely, they were there even before Dad and Mom moved in. The Shues' tiny sand-colored home was well kept and well maintained. My memories of Kennith Shue are as flimsy as gauze. I remember him as a tall man who had male-pattern baldness and reddish-brown hair. To me, he looked like Winchester, a character played by David Ogden Stiers in the TV series *M*A*S*H*. (In my mind's eye, Kennith is decked out in the same olive drab fatigues they wore on the show—but in fact he was partial to denim overalls.)

Someone in our family had dubbed Kennith *el pelón*, which is like calling him Baldy. It was an unimaginative nickname, but descriptive and relatively good-natured. Mom, always quick to invent nicknames that stuck, likely gave it to him. What I'm entirely sure of is that I did not come up with the name, though I had no problem using it.

El pelón scared me in the way large, deep-voiced men sometimes scare little kids. He was a big man, and he hated animals. He had killed some stray dogs and cats in the neighborhood simply because they messed with his plants and his lovingly cared for yard. He was always setting out poison bait and animal traps, which made me want to stay well away from his property.

El pelón owned, or at least had access to, several tractors and some heavy machinery, and because we lived on an unpaved, unmaintained road, he would take it upon himself to grade the dirt and clear the bar ditches so water could flow along the roadside when it rained. He watched over his quaint section of the neighborhood, which was also our own. His wife, Joyce, looked like a stereotypical librarian or schoolmarm. She wore horn-rimmed glasses, pinned her brown hair up in a bun, and generally seemed very friendly and pleasant to be around.

When Kennith was diagnosed with cancer (perhaps it was a brain tumor), he insisted on clearing his life's ledger of the debts incurred by his actions or words, and so Joyce brought him to our house so he could ask Dad and Mom's forgiveness for anything he might have done against them. All was forgiven, of course, because he was a nice man and a terrific neighbor—even to us, who were without question borderline shut-ins and misanthropes. Joyce held her husband's hand as he stood in our living room, frail now, no longer an imposing, strapping figure. Kennith died not long after that, and our patch of the neighborhood would never be the same.

I don't recall attending Kennith's funeral; if any of us went, it would have been Mom and Dad. Our family felt sorry for Joyce now that she was alone. Though her adult children lived not far away, my family disliked that she was by herself in her home. Afterward, she would often come over to visit, but we tended not to go to her house. That behavior is typical of us, even now. Maybe a select few are welcome to visit or call (to a point), but we will not go out of our way to reciprocate. We claim we don't want to bother people, but that's projection; in reality, we don't want people to bother us. And so, we left Joyce alone and gave her privacy, but whenever she chose to pay us a call, we gave her a warm welcome. She was always so nice. They both were. The Shues were the nice neighbors—the neighbors we were happy to get along with, the ones we trusted, the ones we wanted to know slightly better. I would surely have trusted them with important matters concerning our family had circumstances ever called for it.

Perhaps we should have been suspicious of them. They were, after all, a white couple. What did they know of being Latinx? What did we know of being white? Perhaps the Shues had moved into the neighborhood back when it was free of minorities and lived there long enough to see their environs slowly change in demography and color, as when the change of season turns things brown in West Texas. Perhaps they should have been suspicious of us because our cultures were so distinct. Perhaps they should have been wary of us.

The Shues were the only white household for several blocks, and they were our neighbors from the mid-1960s until 1999, when we left the neighborhood on E. Thirty-seventh for good. It would not have been surprising if they were mistrustful of or prejudiced against us. But for as long as we knew them, that simply wasn't the case. The Shues were kind and generous to us, even if Kennith was a brute when it came to stray dogs and cats. That aside, it was a privilege to have them as neighbors. They treated us as if we were almost normal.

Chapter Eleven

The Shues may have been damned fine neighbors, but the same cannot be said of the Rivases, our neighbors to the east. Their extensive family—Latinos, like us—was downright strange, even by my household's freaky standards. Mom always called them a family of hoodlums, but looking back, I tend to disagree. Our neighbors were probably a typical Latinx family in Lubbock, Texas, not a band of criminals.

Sure, the Rivas kids were involved in petty delinquency (the same went for a lot of the neighborhood youth then), and they forever seemed to be trying to hustle someone, to screw someone over. Suffice it to say these were not children and teens who went out of their way to help a person out. Our family may have been reclusive, but we weren't trying to take advantage of anyone. Or, at least that's what I believed at the time.

Yes, even I had been complicit in petty theft as a child: For the thrill of it, I once took a crayon—a single crayon—from a box of them at Furr's Supermarket because I was obsessed with its color, a kind of electric pink. In 1972, Crayola had created a pack of exceptionally colored crayons they called fluorescent, and this one hue struck my fancy. It may have been Hot Magenta, and it seemed to give off its own light, so intoxicatingly bright. I'd never seen a crayon that color before. I may also have pilfered a small piece of candy for good measure.

In fact, I did. Sometimes sweets were made to look like toys or fast food. One particular candy was designed to look like an itty-bitty hamburger. My teacher had introduced it as a reward for student achievement—a prize I did not earn. So, I lifted the candyburger along with the single crayon and came out of Furr's walking on air. I knew I might be in trouble if I were to get caught, but I was, like, six and doubted I'd go to jail over it.

When I hopped in the car, I showed Rene what I had swiped.

She shook her head. "Don't ever do anything so goddamned stupid again."

And for a while, I didn't. I felt some shame and embarrassment after my little heist, a sign that I wasn't so far gone, and had some hope of turning from a life of petty larceny.

Around the same time, I went on a trip with Mom to visit some people I didn't know. They were Latinos, so either they were good friends with Mom or perhaps related to us somehow. This home had a certain smell: a mixture of fried meat, corn or flour tortillas, beans, and probably onions. I'm sure that's how my own house smelled, but I had gone nose blind to it; I was super aware of it at this place. Their home was comfortable and reminiscent of our own; even so, I wanted to leave almost as soon as we had arrived. But the adults were conversing, and I had no choice but to wait it out somehow. I knew better than to complain to Mom that I wanted to go home.

One of my cousins was also there, and we were playing with the child whose cozy house we were in. Juan Carlos, a year younger than me, was cunning even as a kid, and the kind of punk you loved to hate. I spent a good deal of my childhood with him—he was a friend, but he also infuriated me endlessly. I had not expected Juan Carlos to be at this house, yet there he was. Because I had a hard time pronouncing words as a kid (for example, Kool-Aid was *Toonaise*, while the Incredible Hulk was *Treble Holt*), I couldn't say Carlos. I had yet to develop the skill of rolling my *r*'s and I ignored his name Juan altogether. Instead, I said *Colo*, and that's what I called him until we grew into adults. (I still think of him as Colo, though.)

It was soon nighttime, with the smell of West Texas rain in the air—the aroma of dirt and precipitation and ozone from distant lightning—and I was bored, ready to head out. But the kid who lived there was younger and nice enough to play with, so I took consolation in that.

The boy had some plastic army men, except these figures were cowboys and Indians. Army men, toy soldiers, whatever you call them, were fun but dull. They didn't move the way *Star Wars* figures could, and they damned sure didn't have the joint articulation of a *G.I. Joe* action figure. But the toy soldiers this kid had fascinated me, and one in particular had me transfixed (as when I was under the spell of that neon crayon): an Indian with an arrow nocked and ready to loose from his bow. When no one was looking, my sticky fingers made damn sure that plastic warrior made it home with me.

I thought I had gotten away with it, too, but the next morning, Colo was over at my house in Lubbock, the slippery bastard. I was too stupid to realize Colo would notice the toy I'd snatched, and of course my cousin recognized it at once.

"You stole that from the kid last night!" he accused.

I denied it. Anyway, who was he to talk? I was certain Colo had taken stuff from me, many times over—so often that I was urged to hide my things whenever he was coming over for a visit. The time I got a die-cast *Millennium Falcon* for my birthday, you best believe I hid that motherfucker where no one would find it.

So, if the Rivases were hoodlums who committed petty theft, could they be any worse than me? Yes, without question. The Rivases had a bunch of kids around the same age as the kids in my house. They were like our weird counterparts, Bizarro versions of me and my uncle-brothers. David had a Rivas double. Robert had one. And I had one. You might imagine that we all spent time together, getting into scrapes and scuffles the way friends do. The way neighbors do.

In fact, none of us were friends. Paul was a boy about a year older than me, and I recall wanting to be friends with him. He was the only kid I saw near my house who was about my age and who might potentially be interested in playing and doing the kinds of things I was doing at that age. But he always seemed to want to trick me, to make fun of me, to accuse me, to cuss at me. He refused to be my friend for reasons I cannot fathom. Maybe he matured into a stand-up guy, but as a kid, Paul Rivas was a little shit.

Paul had some toys on his side of the backyard fence, while I had some toys on my side. (For families with children, two backyards in their natural state.) He didn't have many toys, to be honest, but he did have things I didn't have, and the unfamiliarity gave his sorry stuff an attractive patina. I wanted to play with some of his toys and thought a trade might be in order. But not a permanent trade. More like a kind of borrowing. He had a croquet set that he never played with, and it was a strange game to me. The colored balls, most of all, fascinated me like that fluorescent crayon, as did the mallets. The set was something I had never seen, never played, and I wanted to get my hands on them. But only for a while.

The opportunity came one day after school, and I asked Paul if I could play with his croquet set. He said, "Sure, if you give me that toy you got there." He pointed to a large Tonka dump truck of mine, and I agreed. He pointed to several other toys in my yard I didn't even play with anyway, stuff I can't remember now, so I gave over whatever toy I had. A Nerf football. An aluminum softball bat. A Frisbee. Now, when he said, *give me*, I took that to mean "pass it over our fence." I didn't understand it as a transfer of ownership. That's why I didn't have a problem handing over the goods.

But that wasn't enough for this cur; he wanted other toys I had. More toys. He wanted them all. And he kept going until at last he had maybe half a dozen or more large toys of mine that he had no intention of giving back. But I didn't know that. I wasn't giving my toys to him. I thought we were simply doing like a temporary trade, where he would have these toys awhile, I would have the croquet set awhile, with no change in ownership. But when he gave me only one measly croquet ball to play with, the yellow one, without the mallet, I should have known. Not fair, I thought, but whatever. At least I had custody of the strange croquet ball for a while. It was somewhat heavy, and I wasn't sure whether to throw it like a baseball or bowl it—as in bocce, another game I didn't know about at the time.

Paul had duped me, and his father, Gus Sr., came over at dusk, knocked on our mighty banker's door, and angrily explained what his youngest son had done. He whirred in Spanish, and Mom stood there in seething silence, listening to him rant. Gus Sr. and Paul had their arms full of my toys, and I stared at them, horrified and thunderstruck. I didn't accurately realize how many things I had passed over to him. Had I given him all of that?

Mom told me to give up the little yellow croquet ball, and Paul returned all the toys I had exchanged with him. Right there, at the threshold of our house, I could finally see the trade disparity: Tonka trucks, fire trucks, secondhand Fisher-Price playsets, a blue aluminum Louisville Slugger that wasn't even mine (it was Mom's), and so much more, while in my right hand I had one croquet ball. The yellow one.

Once everything was made right and the neighbors had returned to their house, Mom proceeded to dress me down and clarify for my dumb ass how stupid I had been. I tried to explain why I had done what I had done, but to no avail. It didn't matter that I had only lent my stuff to Paul. I was truly under the impression that we had merely traded for a while. I couldn't make Mom understand anyway, and so she called me every degrading name she could think of and then admonished that I had better never do anything so goddamn stupid again.

Chapter Twelve

In time, these neighbors would come to represent the generic "kooky family." Need some shorthand for an eccentric clan? The Rivases. Need to describe a group of hoodlums? Oh, you mean like the Rivases! And so on. And whenever we wanted to suggest strange or weird occurrences in a family, we wouldn't name-check TV characters like the Clampetts or the Addamses. We would simply point to our neighbors, the Rivases.

Not only were they odd, but they would also engage in behavior seemingly intended to set people's teeth on edge. At one point, Gus Jr. came into possession of a drum kit, and he must have had visions of being the next Bonzo from Led Zeppelin. He practiced loudly, but his playing was shit and never ever seemed to get better. This went on for years, at all hours of the day and night. But at least he got the opportunity to play music, so he ultimately had one up on me.

Shortly after the toy fiasco—the trade that made me the world's biggest sucker—changes were afoot. We returned after visiting Lovington one day and noticed an enormous fence going up between our homes, extending the barrier from the backyard up through the front of the property. There were no zoning issues, apparently, and the Rivases wouldn't have cared anyway. Part of me felt responsible for the ridiculously huge fence. Exaggerated and overdone, it sent a clear message.

Whereas most people who erect a fence around their house would build it with reasonably sized posts, Gus Sr. had somehow come into possession of several telephone poles—whole goddamn telephone poles—over eighteen inches in diameter, stained with tar. He decided to use them as fence posts, with industrial-grade chain-link fencing between each post. But Gus did not erect a similar fence on the other side of his house. No, that monstrosity was reserved for us. And the moment we saw it, David joked, "Gus is making a

King Kong fence!" It was grossly oversized, as if Gus were trying to keep King Kong out, or in. It was on a par with the entrance gates to Jurassic Park! The fence was an instant eyesore, and I despised it.

Brown-on-Brown hate is a real thing, make no mistake. For instance, you'll find thousands of Mexican Americans all along the Rio Grande Valley in South Texas who will indulge in vitriol against undocumented border crossers, conveniently forgetting that their parents or grandparents had made the same crossing years before. Doesn't matter. There is less solidarity among Latinos than the national media seems to imagine, which is why so many journalists and data crunchers speak wide-eyed about all the Latinos in Texas and Florida who voted for Trump. For anyone who is a part of that community, it was no shock.

A third of Floridian Latinxs are of Cuban descent, and their adverse experiences in their country of origin have allowed them to embrace staunchly conservative politics in the United States. Some Cuban Americans did want to spend astronomical sums of money on a border wall between the United States and Mexico. And no wonder—"the Wall" didn't affect them, and never would.

My family had plenty of antipathy for other Brown people. When I was a kid, even though I saw something of ourselves in the Rivases, we still pegged them as undesirables, regardless of our shared culture. Everyone in our family seemed to dislike everyone in the Rivas family except for the two heads of the households. Dad genuinely seemed to enjoy his friendship with Gus Sr., and vice versa. (Or, if they didn't, they sure put up a good act around me!) Gus Sr. would come over to sit and talk with Dad for what seemed like hours, and Dad would go visit him sometimes too. They were good friends. They got along. They seem to share a connection.

I was grateful for that. I appreciated how Dad was able to build a friendship with these neighbors, or at least with Gus Sr. Whereas the rest of us seemingly could not connect to any of the Rivases in any meaningful way, I was envious that Dad could so easily have a friend next door. Despite vain attempts on my part, my own Rivas double wanted nothing to do with me. But the friendship between Gus Sr. and Dad lasted for as long as Dad lived near Gus.

The last time I saw these two men together must be the greatest spectacle between the two families that I can remember. I was sixteen, full of vim and vigor, and it was a glorious June. Mom and Dad were seasonal farm contractors, employed by an area co-op business to hire field hands to work agricultural crops, and at different turns, all of us pitched in. Mom had taken over this assignment years before, when her brother Juan became sick and later passed away.

The weather was summery in West Texas already, hot and dry, getting hotter and drier every day. It was nearing the onion harvest, which we designated as "the clipping" because you had to take oversized scissors that looked like sheep shears and clip the roots and stem from the onion to harvest it. In the spring we called it "the planting" for obvious reasons. (In Spanglish, *el clipeo* and *el planteo*, respectively.) The clipping was upon us, and we were preparing for toilsome seasonal work.

One of my jobs for the past few summers had been to procure and distribute sacks for the harvested onions; I maintained a supply of these sacks for the workers who did the actual clipping. They were much like potato sacks—burlap, itchy, and very durable bags that would hold sixty pounds of onions easily. One sackful of onions earned a worker between fifty and sixty cents at the time.

Robert and I made sure there were always plenty of sacks because if the workers had no sacks to fill, they couldn't do their work. They could fill only so many buckets with onions before they had to empty the buckets into the sacks, so it was our job to see that they never ran out. (If that ever happened, it was our asses!) We would take a fifth-wheel trailer to various locations and load it with fresh sacks to deliver to the workers. And so, this trailer was indispensable.

We had to prepare the trailer to make sure that it was roadworthy, empty, and in working order. During the rest of the year, when we weren't using the trailer, it was typically a repository for miscellaneous junk from around the yard, or else we put it into service for assorted tasks. Dad had once sold watermelons out of it on the highway near our trailers in Lovington, where we moved after my second-grade year. The watermelons were given to him, and they were not high-quality produce, but he made some pocket change at any rate, and that made him happy.

Dad had decreed that on this beautiful June day, we were going to empty the trailer and do maintenance on it because we needed it the next day. There we were—Dad, Robert, and I—slowly unloading the trailer on a warm June afternoon, and we made leisurely work of it. We were having a fine time too. It was like those movie montages when a family is having such a pleasant, untroubled day, you know shit is about to go to hell with all speed.

It was such a splendid afternoon that you wished you could bottle it like liqueur and drink from it whenever you felt blue, the kind of moment you prayed heaven was built of, like granite blocks cut from a paradisiacal quarry. This afternoon, before Gus Sr. showed up, would surely be one of my heavenly cornerstones. It would have a short dedication on it, the way people can buy inscribed bricks at a memorial fundraiser. The block would say, GLORIOUS JUNE DAY WITH DAD AND ROBERT BEFORE GUS SR. FUCKED IT UP.

Chapter Thirteen

Dad was always very serious, especially when it came to work, so getting him to laugh was extra special. That day, as on others, we had Dad laughing about something or other, and we told jokes and stories to make the time go by quickly. Robert and I were likely teasing each other, playing the dozens. (Of course, around Dad, we'd leave out the cussing and refrain from such terms of endearment as *bastard*, *bitch*, *fuck*, *faggot*, *pussy*, and so on.) Robert always had a good sense of humor and could quickly find funny ways of mocking a brother or cousin. That was his shtick.

One of my techniques for making Dad laugh was to exaggerate my emerging masculinity and capacity for hard work. I was the youngest boy around and the smallest, as the Big Scary Brown Guy gene had yet to kick in. (You could see it in proto-form, but I still had a long way to go.) So, I would pretend to be bigger, stronger, faster, and smarter than I doubtless was. That was my shtick.

See, Dad had always staked his reputation on an ability to shoulder a near superhuman workload and perform remarkable feats of brute force. For instance, when he was a young man in the Hill Country of Texas (basically the Greater Austin and San Antonio areas), Dad would work the region's many cotton fields with his family.

Cotton picking did not go away with the abolition of slavery; it simply became slightly less brutal by virtue of the meager wages tied to it. But, like the workers who harvested onions and basically every other crop that required handpicking, people who worked the cotton fields were paid in proportion to the cotton they collected, by weight. The workers would file along the furrows created between two rows of cotton plants, a long canvas bag tied to trail behind them, and they would literally twist the cotton fibers out of the bolls. This was grueling work. The worker moved forward while bent fully at the waist, dexterously picking dirty white cotton lint and filling the bag one handful at a time.

Dad was legendary for the amount of cotton he could pick in his youth, and that rep was part of what made him so attractive to women looking for a husband who could support a family. My relations, on both sides, had been farmers and laborers, and received a negligible education. Dad had only a few years of school in Texas as a young child before he was expected to do the backbreaking work of a farmer—full-time.

There is a Polaroid that I have in my possession, taken many years before my birth. In the picture, Dad sits on a bed, and Rene and Rose, my aunt, are sitting on either side of him in their pajamas. They are probably the age my girls are as I write this, between fourteen and seventeen years of age. He holds a book in his hands and appears to be reading them a bedtime story.

This picture pains me today, and I feel sorrow whenever I look at it. The tableau is staged. The girls are clearly too old to have a story read to them by their father before bedtime. I know now that Dad was illiterate, and Rene was a voracious reader then as she is now. She must have been aware that the photo was wholly a fiction. It portrayed a make-believe world—an alternative reality where her father could actually read her a bedtime story. I never asked Dad why he didn't try to learn to read in a more formal way. I didn't want to embarrass him, and Mom had given him a few lessons along the way, like writing and signing his name. I think he had managed to live his life without learning to read, and likely saw such learning as not as important as the "real" work he needed to do elsewhere.

When I was a teenager, I saw Dad reduced to tears because he could not read. I was in the shower, and he and I were the only ones in the house that day when Dad answered the phone. The call was important, and the caller had given him precise details that needed to be related to Mom when she returned home. When I got out of the shower, Dad called me over to the dining room table in a panic and asked me to read what he had tried to scribble after his own fashion. He pointed to the writings, which to me were little more than squiggles on the page.

"What does it say?" he demanded.

I paused for a moment before I gave my answer, which was surely going to disappoint this man I admired so much: "I don't know."

He then tried to explain what he thought he had scribbled, growing annoyed that I couldn't read it.

"I don't know," I repeated like an idiot. "Can you remember more about what they told you?"

In an instant, his green eyes flooded with tears of anguish and shame. "I can't read!" he whimpered, his voice cracking as he said the last word.

I was stunned, for I had never seen Dad shed a tear in all my life to that point. This was a stout, tallish man who always seemed to be tamping a storm in his soul. He was fierce and unapologetic, never mincing words with anyone. I loved him, but when I was a child, I was intimidated by him and his booming voice. And now he was weeping because he couldn't do something I could do without a second thought. I loved him even more in that moment. I wanted to tell him that his illiteracy didn't affect who he was as a man by one iota. He possessed the most naturally gifted mind I would ever know, made all the more impressive because he had to memorize and calculate instantly without the advantage of reading and writing. I wanted to say all of this and all the things that my heart felt for him. But being the kid I was, I failed him in that moment.

"It's okay," I reassured him. "They'll call back. Or Mom will know who it was." I gave him a smile. "It's okay." I leaned and put my arm around him as he sat at the table.

He nodded as he wiped his eyes, still staring at the little scrap of paper and the mysterious glyphs he had transcribed but could not decipher.

The memory of that day is fresh in my mind, and when I see the staged Polaroid where everyone is pretending to listen to Dad reading aloud, it breaks my heart. He died years before I even considered a life as a teacher or a writer, and I have mixed feelings. I am certain he would have been proud that I have been published. I also think it would have frustrated him that he could not read any of the books I have written.

Despite his missed opportunities at a formal education, Dad's orienting philosophy was to work hard and not be lazy, because that was how he had come up. For him, working hard—or simply working—was what others might call working like a mule. He knew hard work intimately, and he would find it funny when I exaggerated my own strength and ability because he knew I was full of it.

Like the time we were driving to Petersburg on some *clipeo* errand. This time it was me, Dad, and Mom in the red and white Ford F-150 Lariat truck. In the distance, to one side of the road, I saw these huge hay bales shaped like giant cinnamon rolls. They lay on their sides, and it seemed you could push one over or even get it to roll. Because of my inexperience, I could not get a sense for how much these rolls of hay weighed. Hay itself was light, yet I knew the compacted roll was dense beyond my imagination.

"Dad? How much do those things weigh?" I asked. "Those hay bales. The round ones."

Dad took a moment before answering. His eyes left the road briefly to gaze at the field of rolled hay as he continued his calculation. "I'm not sure," he said at last. "They're pretty goddamned heavy."

"I bet I could push one over," I said with mock confidence.

Dad laughed, a deep, baritone guffaw that came from his belly. "Shit!" He composed himself. "One of those bales might be a ton. You couldn't move it."

I didn't miss a beat. "A ton? I don't care. I'm pretty sure I could push it over. Pull over and let me try."

"Ha!"

That's the kind of thing I did to get Dad to laugh. I loved to hear him laugh because he always seemed so serious or even annoyed or angry about things. He had a short temper, and if temper is inheritable, I get my temper from Dad. So, as I made my way through puberty, I cultivated a persona that indulged in braggadocio and quixotic exploits that never materialized. I also liked to ask Dad all sorts of questions because, even though he could not read, he had an impressive and logical way of looking at the world.

Chapter Fourteen

Already on this June day, Robert and I understood that we had to do most of the strenuous work, as Dad's health was by now clearly precarious. Though we didn't know it at the time, he had around ten years of life left.

We worked hard but easy, if that makes sense, cracking jokes, playing the dozens like we did, keeping Dad smiling and laughing at our dumb remarks. We suggested that he sit in the shade on the porch and tell us what we needed to do, which went counter to his work ethic, but we had his best interest in mind. He would sit occasionally if we seemed to be doing things to his approval and get up to correct us when necessary.

We had completed the major phase of the day, and Dad said: "Okay, boyzes, let's take a break," like that because though Spanish was his first language, Dad often liked to speak in broken English with a heavy southern accent. Looking back, I gather that Dad must have learned English from South Carolina or Georgia natives because his English was peppered with the same sort of southern drawl. For instance, he'd say the word *here* as *heah*.

Dad called the shots when it came to anything concerning the workday, so if he announced a break, it was time to take one. We all proceeded single file into the house, where the swamp cooler was going nice. This class of air conditioner works via evaporative cooling and is common to areas of high heat and low humidity, like the American Southwest. Robert had given the cooler's wood-wool pads a good soaking with the water hose because the pump was broken, and soon the pads would cool the air entering our house. I was looking forward to a cold drink and something to eat. Dad was listing what we still needed to do that day, and I noticed that at the very same moment Dad entered the house, so did Gus Sr. He came out of nowhere. He actually beat Robert and me into the house, literally pushed past us and nearly barreled over Dad to get inside—strange behavior, even for Gus Sr. He typically would give us a moment to open the door and invite him in, but undoubtedly, something had agitated this man to the point where he could not wait even a second more.

I was confused. I couldn't understand why our neighbor would barge in like that. It was disrespectful to enter our house that way, even if you were Dad's good friend! None may cross the threshold without approval. I was offended, but probably more annoyed that he had accessed the cool interior before I did. I'm the one who had been working outside for the last few hours, motherfucker! I prepared for Dad—but probably Mom—to smash Gus Sr. to smithereens for being so rude.

Finally, when all of us were in the living room, two steps inside the screen door, I noticed how nervous Gus Sr. was. Tears were brimming in his eyes, and he talked as if in shock. He was in full meltdown, disheveled, his pants unbuttoned and his belt unbuckled. I don't make it a habit to stare at anyone's pants, especially some crusty old Brown guy, but he was holding them up by the waistband, as if he had run out of his house in great haste with no time to dress himself properly. Shirt untucked, he had a generally unkempt look about him. I knew something wasn't right. It was, like, three in the afternoon already.

I looked at Robert.

Robert looked at me.

And we exchanged a lot in that glance. We knew something was happening, and Robert took a guarded position, alert for danger. Fight or flight, and Gus Sr. was flying high with fear. Was the man going to do something to Dad or Mom or one of us? We were baffled and more than a bit scared.

Dad laughed at Gus Sr. because it was all so comical. He couldn't understand why Gus Sr. had rushed in without even bothering to knock. Now we all stood in a sports huddle, as if someone were about to call in a dandy of a play. And we had been putting Dad in a good mood all day, so he was relaxed and easygoing.

Dad said, in deliberately broken English, "Gus, what's the matter? Whatchu got going on?"

And Gus Sr. kept saying in a loop, "He's trying to kill me He's trying to kill me He's trying to kill me," a robot programmed with only one line of speech. But he said it in Spanish, *mequierematar*, as one word over and over.

Dad was still trying to laugh this off. He said, "Whatchu talking about, Gus? Who trying to kill you?"

Right at that moment, we heard a voice outside our door, beyond the porch. Someone screaming. We didn't know who it was. We looked out. A noise, a pop, a report, something like a gunshot, but it couldn't be a gunshot. Who would be firing a gun at this time of day? It's afternoon. At night, maybe. But not now.

Gus Sr., in a panic, tried to close our boss of a front door. See, even Gus knew that door was the real deal and not to be fucked with. He wanted to be behind it.

When I looked out the front window, I could see his son Gus Jr. with a rifle in his clenched hands, screaming, tears of anguish flowing down his cheeks. The expression on his face made me uneasy. He was awful to look at, his face a contorted mask as he kept repeating, "Come on!" yelling at his father to step outside.

I think we were all still confused about what was going on, what was happening right in front of us. This deranged Rivas family drama had boiled over now and involved our family, landing squarely in our living room.

When Dad at last realized that this young kid, this punk, was outside our house with a gun, threatening his friend Gus Sr. to come out, Dad lunged toward the door as if he were going to talk sense into this armed maniac. Mom suggested he not go out, but it was Robert who stepped in and *commanded* Dad to stay inside.

I had never heard Robert cuss at Dad before. As surreal as the circumstances were, his son cussing at him was what snapped Dad out of his woolgathering, out of his confidence that he could do something about this and talk some sense into the outraged kid. Robert cussed at Dad, saying, "Don't go out there, Dad! This fucking kid will fucking kill you!"

Oh shit!

What was worse than one Latino son with a gun trying to kill his father? How about another Latino son cussing at his father! I well-nigh laughed aloud, and at that moment, I had a near out-of-body experience—as if I were watching this unfold on television, some low-rate telenovela that might not make it to a full season.

When Robert dropped F-bombs on Dad, both Dad and Mom looked Robert right in the eye. *What did you say?* I had seen that reaction on Mom's face before—an expression that said she was going to crush you in about two seconds flat.

It was the drama within the drama. The guy outside with a gun could never have had this effect on them short of cussing them out. But Robert had used the cussword in Dad's general direction. He didn't exactly cuss *at* Dad. He hadn't said, *Fuck you, Dad!* or *Fuck off!* He had actually said "fucking kid," an insult to the punk who had deserved it, and "fucking kill you."

That last phrase must have been too close, too familiar, too much in the way of erasing the patrilineal line between them, as if Robert had spoken to a peer. But ultimately, this word is what stopped Mom and Dad in their tracks. It broke the strange spell they were under and snapped them to the reality of the situation. The danger of it. I can still see Mom's reaction in my mind's eye thirty years later. There is anger in her face. Anger at Robert, her youngest biological son.

Now, a quick side note: Dad and Mom used the word *fuck* like they owned and trademarked it, and cussing in my household was second nature. But one of our inviolable family laws was that, while Dad and Mom could cuss and even cuss at you, you could not return cusswords in kind! So, lest the reader think Dad and Mom were shocked to hear the word *fuck* because they'd never heard it or used it before, don't be confused. When their youngest son used the word forcefully with his father, it made all the difference, in more ways than one.

Chapter Fifteen

I mentioned earlier how superstitious my family is, despite my attempted countermeasures. Though deeply religious, Mom believed in an extended realm of supernatural things and, specifically, evil supernatural things. These entities functioned in our world as something like karma—a force stirred up to teach your stupid ass a much-needed lesson.

Mom, and sometimes, Dad, would occasionally recall stories of their own childhoods in Texas—different parts of Texas than where I had grown up—and these stories would often thrill me like a damned Edgar Allan Poe story. They always invoked some paranormal element, like the story Dad told of a headless horseman figure who could be found on a certain bridge not far from Seguin, Texas, at a certain time of night when he was a youth.

The horse had red eyes, and some of Dad's elder brothers had seen this demonic figure for themselves. When I heard that story the first time, as Dad related it to other elder family members, it freaked my ass out because Dad didn't lie or make up shit willy-nilly. If he was telling this story, it was gospel truth, as far as he was concerned.

Mom's supernatural story par excellence involved a black dog and fits into the general trope of the hellhound tale common to Mexico and Ireland. These dogs are like harbingers, or a sign of an imminent death. Mom would say she saw this as a young girl in Kenedy, Texas, how this black dog appeared shortly after her cousin (her father's brother's son) had punched his father.

Why had he done that? Too much alcohol and the thrill of carousing and womanizing were a growing habit. Mom's cousin, let's call him Jaime, was staying out so late he was becoming a liability at work. One night Mom's uncle tried to rebuke Jaime—to get him to stop his reckless behavior, and in response, Jaime had struck his own father.

There is some internal family debate about the particulars of this story. This is how I remember it: Immediately after Jaime hit his father, this fucking black dog showed up and remained in his orbit. It seemed to follow the guy wherever he went but often kept its distance. It terrified Jamie. Despite the family's best efforts of closing doors and locking windows, the dog would often be found inside the house.

Incredibly, Mom said if you got close enough to the dog and it allowed you to pet it, it would give off goddamn sparks. I half expected to hear that it emitted a sulfurous smell to boot, but Mom's story stopped short of that. The dog lingered until Mom's cousin died of illness, not long after striking his father. As of the day they buried Jamie, that black dog was never seen again.

Robert remembers the story slightly differently, and his version might be more correct because his wife, Linda, was there one of the last times Mom related it: In this version, Jaime, on horseback after a night of drinking and rabble-rousing, felt someone or something watching him in the dark on his way home. He was scared sober, sensing a malevolent presence and the feeling that he was being watched. It frightened him so much that his cowboy hat would not stay on his head because his hair stood on end. (This was a key detail in both versions of the story.) The dog was always near him, and—here is where the versions diverge—no one else ever saw the dog.

As he was dying in his bed, Jaime famously roused enough energy to say, "*Hay 'ta ese pinche perro.*" He could still see the black dog, seemingly waiting for him to die, whereas it was invisible to everyone else. In anguish, Jaime stared at the dog as he lay on his deathbed, knowing he had summoned its presence when he had assaulted his father.

Whatever the truth, the crucial bit was that the son had struck his father and paid dearly for it. It sounded like something out of the Bible. As Exodus 21:15 states, "And he that smiteth his father, or his mother, shall be surely put to death." Well, this dude smitethed his father and got a goddamn devil dog to drag his ass to hell for sure.

Mom would recite this tale as a lesson to us never to do such a thing to Dad. Disrespecting a father could have colossally bad consequences, as she well knew. So, when Robert raised his voice to Dad, waking him up to a clear and present danger, I knew Mom's thoughts had turned to that karmic hellhound.

"As of the day they buried Jamie, that black dog was never seen again."

Chapter Sixteen

Robert wielded the term *fucking* like a mythical word of power, and in so doing, broke the spell of indecision and confusion. As soon as Robert said it, twice, in Dad's general direction, Dad knew the peril we all were in. The temperature in our living room changed instantly. Immediately we slammed the door, and that Rivas bastard outside with the gun was still screaming at his father to come out so he could, what, shoot him? I had never felt the power and security of our front door more than at that moment. No way a little .22 rifle was going to penetrate the thick hardwood banker's door.

But Gus Jr. didn't know our front door had neutralized his threat, which gave us an advantage. He still raged outside, threatening to kill his father, to kill us. He was so furious his voice went into the stratosphere, shrill and breaking. Dogs must have howled in pain for blocks. I knew he must be serious because the more he went on, the less masculine he seemed to me. He was no tough guy with a gun. Rather, he was shaking and pathetic with what looked like a BB gun in his hands. (Good thing Tom wasn't there. He would have returned fire with his sawed-off 12-gauge or his super-short, super-illegal 20-gauge. And he would have been glad to do it! Sometimes Tom had more guns than sense.)

I thought we were surely about to be in an episode of *Cops* as I ran to the telephone and, for the first time in my life, called 911. Robert yelled at me to call even as I was already headed toward the phone. Naturally, I was the one to make the call because, like Rene, I was a designated talker.

When the operator picked up, I told her what was happening. I tried to sound calm, but I was still clearly a young guy on the phone. I'm not sure she believed me.

After she asked for our address and other basic info that I provided, I said: "Our neighbor is outside with a rifle. I think he shot at our house." I don't think he did, because we never found a bullet hole. It's likely that he shot it into the air. I had erred on the side of caution and told the operator that he shot at the house. I may have embellished even more. "He said he'd kill any motherfucker who didn't come out. Those were his exact words."

When the operator wanted more context, I blurted, "The guy's dad is in our house. His name is Gustavo, but we call him Gus. They're both Gus— Senior and Junior. For some reason, his son, Gus Junior, the guy who has the gun outside, wants to kill his dad, Gus Senior. I have no idea why. I've never seen them like this."

That was true. I've said the Rivases were kooky, but they didn't blaze guns and threaten to kill one another. This was unprecedented even for them.

"Do not go outside," the operator intoned with a poise that didn't set well with me. "Don't let the father go outside the house, either. We're sending an officer to your house. Stay inside."

"You're sending a cop?"

"An officer. Yes."

Huh! Bad boys! / Whatcha want, whatcha want, / Whatcha gonna do / When Sheriff John Brown come for you?!

I just knew we were in an episode of *Cops*, and I was morbidly eager to see it unfold. I had already envisioned several scenarios, the worst of which were bloody shoot-outs with multiple casualties. I wasn't so eager to experience that, but I thought there was the slightest chance Junior might be pissed off enough to shoot at a cop. And if he did that, all bets were off. More likely, the cops would put Junior in cuffs, take him away, then there would be an attempted murder trial. We'd be witnesses, and already I was imagining my time on the witness stand.

I knew I could handle it, but what about Robert, who couldn't talk his way out of a wet sack? I wanted to make sure we had nothing to do with this guy. *We are some law-abiding citizens, Sheriff John Brown! See? We speak nice English and believe in (an albeit vengeful) God. No, don't shoot us . . . we're not the problem. Brown? Yes. Scary? No!*

When the cop finally showed up, he spoke to Gus Jr., and Gus Sr. was allowed to go back to his house. I suppose the cop didn't want to have to go through the hassle of paperwork to write up one Latinx guy threatening his father and involving yet another Latinx family. But Gus Sr. was out of our house, so good riddance! The day was shot, so to speak, and we would not be able to finish all that Dad had set out to do. We sat around as evening stepped in and wondered at what we had witnessed earlier, what we had been a part of without our say so, trying to understand why and how it was that a son would take up a firearm against his father.

Mom was angry, likely at Robert and Gus Jr. in equal measure. She was still brooding at the disrespect Robert had shown Dad. "You shouldn't speak to your dad that way," she admonished.

"There wasn't time. That crazy bastard wasn't going to listen to Dad." Robert was showing guts here. Maybe it was the day he grew up a little bit. "I had to get your attention, and I did."

Dad appeared a little shell-shocked. It undoubtedly rattled the normally stoic man I had come to know. That a son would want to harm, perhaps kill, his father, was too much for him to contemplate. It was a bad omen. *La mala cosa.* Bad juju, as the West Africans say. And hadn't his own son raised his voice to him only an hour before? Perhaps it was that Robert's own frankness was the greater transgression and, thus, the greater curse.

We quickly concluded, completely unsupported, mind you, that Gus Sr. must have tried to fuck his daughter-in-law (and maybe it was mutual), or perhaps had tried to rape her, or had been caught in the act, and that Gus Jr. had happened upon the scene. Had he come home early? Did we not notice that he drove up in front of his house when he should have been working at Peter Piper Pizza or wherever? Had he known something unnatural was up, and that's what made him check on his wife and his own father?

In the heat of passion, perhaps seeing his father and his own wife in the throes of a different type of passion, Gus Jr. picked up his gun and chased his father into our house. That would explain Gus Sr.'s disheveled look in the early afternoon on a June day. It explained why he didn't even have time to button his pants and buckle his belt during the fifteen to twenty steps it took to go from his front door to ours. We realized we had many problems in our family. But we never had the issue of a son trying to murder his father because his father was trying to fuck his son's wife. So, we had that going for us.

The contrast of those events makes me think of our two Latinx families. Here we were, working with Dad, having a beautiful, honest time, while next door a son was potentially about to spill the blood of his own father. That should have cursed them. Instead, they annexed the space where I had come to learn so much of myself and my family.

That little place on the east side of Lubbock, Texas—with its cream-colored ceramic tile and large concrete porch and formidable banker's door—went from being my primary residence, which I thought of as home, to a place we would visit occasionally throughout the year, typically in spring and summer. Later, the house would be used by someone else, like David and Rose, on a temporary basis. When my family stopped paying the property taxes, we lost it outright, though the house and the land had been paid for. I found this out well after the fact.

During a night of drinking with Rose and David on a quick trip to Lubbock in 2002, Rose told me the house was no longer ours. At one in the morning, my system saturated with tequila, I demanded she take me to the address of my youth. David lay passed out in the back seat. Rose didn't even have a chance to bring her car to a full stop before I was out, standing under the large sodium arc light that bathed our little corner of the neighborhood in a tangerine glow. I stared at the place where our house, that house with the bad temper, had always been, only to see it was gone forever. Now the Rivases' junk flowed onto our property. I convulsed and wept bitter tears. I had arrived to see that my house was not only no longer ours but had also vanished altogether.

But the memory of that place, like the beautiful day I shared with Dad and Robert, persists in my mind like a lovely dream of gossamer that leaves you if you push it too hard. So, I don't insist. I let that memory, like the memory of my house, come to me as it sees fit. When it does, it feels like a blessing from on high, and I am made whole again, even if temporarily.

And I remember the good and the bad.

And this is what I remember.

Book II

Chapter Seventeen

These days, I often recall my childhood in Lubbock, where I lived, and those first life lessons with a sense of wonderment and discomfiture.

It's 1981, and my home is nestled within a perimeter of warehouses and cotton gins that are scary yet reassuring, like Easter Island sentinels facing outward to keep the cruel world at bay. Ever suspicious of outsiders and allergic to new friends and uninvited guests, we like it this way. There are several neighbors to the north, east, and south—persons we see as annoyances, as oddballs, as pains in the ass (not the Shues, obviously). But west of us, a great plot of empty scrub creates the illusion of isolation and solitude.

As a child, I often catch myself outdoors, looking west, the openness of the field overwhelming me. It offers comfort and protection, a buffer between my family and the world, a shield no one can take from us. I'm not sure anyone knows what to do with this tract of land, so it has remained undeveloped for at least half a century. I live alongside it until our move to Lovington, New Mexico, which will never feel like home to me, not the way this strange outpost in Lubbock, Texas, does.

To the west of my house, a ribbon of pale dirt road runs north–south for about a quarter mile, a demarcation line between our yard and that immense field of emptiness. The undeveloped lot is a remarkable anomaly within a city of nearly a quarter of a million people. (Perhaps not much of a city if you're from DFW or LA or NYC, but Lubbock is a metropolis of the South Plains. It's called Hub City because of all the tiny towns that orbit and rely on it.)

This open space looks wild and bright as the sun climbs above my shoulders any given autumn morning. There are no trees in the unforgiving terrain, only clumps of knee-high prairie grass. At the margins of the dirt road, colossal bar ditches remind me to keep to my own side. When it rains, they fill with water and swell into small rivers in an otherwise parched land, and when the rainwater has been absorbed by the thirsty earth or evaporated by the prickling sun, the surfaces of the ditches crack like shards of pottery. The sun makes its way beyond the horizon at the close of the day, sinking behind my personal nature reserve. If I can overlook the enormous warehouses that stand at the head and foot of the field, this land is pleasing to me. Visitors to this geographic area in West Texas openly point to the ugliness, the dearth of beauty. The meagerness of features. The flatness. I happily ignore these detractors.

Along the west side of the barren runs a railroad track that gently curves eastward as it reaches the foot of the field and then crosses the dirt road (named Hickory Avenue despite a scarcity of trees) before its surface becomes paved in asphalt. Sometimes I hear the rumble of passing trains, and they sound best to me on Saturday mornings, when I can watch Bugs Bunny cartoons in the front bedroom on a little color television. On those mornings, the windows are open, and a cool breeze carries the steel-on-steel ringing of train wheels and railway track. The short freight trains are regular guests that lumber gently with assorted cargo. The lingering blast of an air horn sounds like home.

Observing the field from afar is one thing. Going into the wasteland is quite another. From my side of Hickory, I soon discover that if I shout forcefully enough, my voice will echo across the field and reverberate against the metal warehouses at the other end. I raise my voice and send it across the untamed field, wait for the span of a few heartbeats, and—there!—my own voice answers me, somewhat altered. I like the idea of launching my voice into the world, and honestly, I experience the sound as a living thing, an entity in motion, and not some tinny recording on a cassette tape. Its power captivates me. I experience my voice as a material reality, something created and let loose upon the world, and yet I realize I am the only one who pays it any mind. Except for Mom, who complains about the volume.

Chapter Eighteen

I am told that even as a baby, I was clearly destined for great things. Rene alleges I began reading at the age of two. First it was the words on traffic signs. (Easy enough: I likely memorized them.) Then it was the local newspaper I was reading. Soon, I was making my way through some of Rene's computer manuals from work, books written about the programming languages COBOL and Turbo Pascal, a forerunner of Java.

One of Rene's coworkers, a lovely Black woman named Geraldine, rushed over excitedly to tell her that I was in the other office, *reading*. Rene had taken me with her to work that night shift at a financial data processing center called ShareData. Rene turned as if annoyed, telling Geraldine, "Yes, I know." Rene always treated any achievement of mine as unremarkable, and took them for granted. I don't believe I was as young as she insisted—for sure I wasn't reading about Turbo Pascal at two years old. Let's say I was too young to be reading computer programming books in general principle.

Other miracles soon followed. Rene contends that I was potty-trained in a single day. Even I find that unbelievable, having helped potty-train two daughters of my own. It is not lost on me that Rene generally exaggerated mundane childhood development milestones while downplaying any significant accomplishments I earned through skill, talent, or discipline.

When I was born, I had a voracious appetite, feeding twice as much as the average newborn, and my voice had a gravelly, almost hoarse quality to it. Dad announced right there in the hospital to any nurse who would listen that I would be either a singer or someone whose career depended on speaking, like maybe an attorney. I was going to be a talker! With a voice like that, how could I not? He was half right: I generally can't shut up once I get going, but I can sing only well enough to make a spectacle of myself at karaoke.

Voices have long fascinated me. I thrilled to hear my own voice resound in that artificial canyon of warehouses. But for all my interest in loud, echoing notes, I went into the field only a handful of times as a child. Painful lessons accompanied each occasion. My uncle-brothers used the land for recreation—throwing a football around, riding their motorcycles, things like that.

Tom was seventeen when I was born, and of the three boys, he always felt the most like an uncle, because of the age gap. David, nearly eleven years older than me, was always in a hurry to grow up and get out from under his mother's skirts. I remember him often away with some girl or off to get married, removed from the family but never for too long. Admittedly, David was never far from the family's friendly confines. He was always nearby.

Robert, nearly seven years my senior, truly filled out the role of big brother in all the best and worst ways possible. That is, he was the brother who would stick up for me one minute and then torment me the next. Ours would always be the closest and also the most volatile of my relationships with my uncle-brothers.

Chapter Nineteen

I am a passenger on David's dirt bike. The motorcycle has a blue fuel tank.

Even then, I am sure he is plotting his escape from home. He comes off as older than his years, and is a wisecracking genius. David is handsome, athletic, and tends to have a girlfriend nearby at all times. I admire and love him the way little brothers idolize much older brothers. I always want to be by his side, and would rather hang with David than with the younger Robert, who rides an Indian motorcycle and has no interest in accommodating a little boy who wants so badly to ride too.

Robert is often a bastard that way (but not a literal one like me). He is kind of like the older brother and narrator in "The Scarlet Ibis," a story by James Hurst, indifferent to the needs of his younger brother, Doodle. That makes me either Doodle or the scarlet ibis, I guess: fragile and out of place.

The youngest boy in the house, equally doted on and teased by all, I whine and complain that I want to ride a motorcycle. At other times, I have even been to motorcycle shops with Rose (Rene's younger adopted sister who also rides and has an interest) and David, and noticed small motorbikes that are exactly my size. I want one desperately. They look like toys, but they are real motorcycles. As I watch the bikes wheel and circle in the field and listen to the squeal of their engines from my side of Hickory, I want nothing more at that moment than to be astride one of them, in control of such speed and movement. David and Robert ignore my pleas, my presence.

Mom finally intercedes, taking pity on me, yet also annoyed that I can't seem to handle being left out of the fun. She has terrific command within the family, and no one disrespects her without significant collateral damage. Mom's words are powerful, and the way she says them can be more devastating than the words themselves. She will call the shots, no matter where she is or how frail her body might be, until her dying day in September of 2020.

Mom calls David over and orders him to take me on a ride for a few minutes so I'll shut up. He laughs at me good-naturedly, tousles my hair, and tells me to hold on tight. He lifts me and places me in front of him, nearly on top of the blue fuel tank. And we are off!

I have never felt speed like this, so different from riding in a car. It is as if I am flying, only the rough ground below reminding me that I am very much on terra firma. I hold the handlebars as tightly as my tiny arms can manage, and soon we are going so fast that I am no longer enjoying it. I am scared I will fall! I am losing my grip. My arms are too puny to handle gravity, inertia, momentum. I want off, but David cannot hear me. It's quite possible he's deliberately ignoring me, to scare me out of wanting to ride again. The plan is working. I'm dangerously close to becoming a scarlet ibis.

We are following a track my uncle-brothers have already carved out with the dirt bikes. It's always a left turn. There is a sudden dip, and despite the efforts of my arms, I can't avoid head-butting the handlebar as we barrel over a hillock. Like a cartoon character might, I see stars swirl in my field of vision. Perhaps I am experiencing my first concussion and don't know it yet. When David sees me flail, he brings the bike to a halt. I feel as if a horn has sprouted from my forehead at the impact, like when Sylvester the Cat gets hit with a huge mallet. It's my own poor judgment that has caused this explosion of pain, I know—I am to blame.

I cry and wail. David laughs, chastises me for not holding on more tightly. "It's your own fault, *cabrón!*" Soon I am sitting on the kitchen counter with something cold against my head. Mom is upset with David for not being more cautious, and she is angry with me for being such a pest earlier. In not so many words, she, too, tells me it's my own fault for wanting to play with older boys: that's what I get.

And though my first real foray into the neighboring field ends in pain, it won't be long till I doggedly head right back in.

Chapter Twenty

A few years later, I am in the second grade on a day I will be walking home from school. Why my family let me walk home is anybody's guess. Typical Gen X latchkey kid stuff. It is over a mile from my house to Harwell Elementary School. I had walked home once before because no one could pick me up from school, but on this occasion, I specifically asked permission to walk home, for fun. For fun? No doubt I was a different kid. It made me feel older, I guess. I asked Mom if I could, and after some hesitation, she relented. She gave me a few bucks and said I could stop at the convenience store situated at the midpoint of my journey home.

The majority of the route requires that I walk west to east on E. Fortieth Street until I get to Hickory Avenue, where I turn left past Armstrong's Heating & Air Conditioning. The only major worry is that I must cross Avenue A, a very wide and busy thoroughfare, with no crosswalks at the time. But I have done it once, and I am not worried much. Yet today, something is different. I have a classmate and friend, coincidentally named David (I'll call him Little David to avoid confusion with my uncle-brother David), who is also walking home and going in my general direction. For about three-quarters of the way, we will be following the same route. Little David invites me to stop awhile at his home before continuing on to my own. When I try to decline his offer, he says, memorably, "It's no problem." Famous last words.

At the bustling intersection of Avenue A and E. Fortieth Street, there is the convenience store, my planned stop, called Town & Country Food Store. Today it's an empty building that takes turns being restaurants and fly-by-night businesses. Little David suggests we go in and get something to drink. For such a small kid, much smaller than me, he is quite pushy. Like me, he is a little Latino boy; unlike me, he is of the fair-skinned variety.

We go in and he immediately introduces me to "suicide soda," where you combine a little bit of every soda fountain flavor available. What kind of alchemy is this? You mean you don't have to get only one kind of Coke? (Yes, I'm from Texas, and we call all sodas Cokes. Conversations go as follows: Want a Coke? Sure. What kind? A Dr Pepper.)

The suicide concoction is a syrupy revelation to my seven-year-old brain. What now? We linger at the convenience store, thanks to an arcade game—probably *Tempest*, with a slightly lesser chance it's *Defender*—and after dropping a few quarters, we are off. I am already feeling a little uneasy at taking longer than I should; my internal chronometer is buzzing uncomfortably, but Little David and I are now on the move again, crossing Avenue A. Little David is a damned persuasive guy, and I'm happy to follow his lead.

To get to Little David's house, I must detour slightly from my regular route. He lives west of Globe Avenue, which forms the western border of the empty field I see every day. It turns out he lives on the other side of my field.

His house is comparable to mine but more organized. I am surprised that Little David has his own bedroom, and he shows me many of his toys, which I covet. I refrain from letting my sticky fingers stuff my pockets and instead allow Little David assume the role of docent. We play for several minutes, or maybe it's the better part of an hour. Mostly he's busy showing off all the shit he has. We have lost all track of time, our grasp of which was tenuous at best. I am having a great afternoon with Little David! This is the first time in my life that I have been invited over by a friend who is not related to me. Further, it's the first time I've gotten to play at a friend's house without being accompanied by a family member. I am exhilarated. That elation will be short-lived, as you might expect.

After who knows how much time has passed (an hour? two?), Little David officially introduces me to his mother. She is kind and instantly offers me refreshment and something to eat, like every other Latina mother I know. I still have my fountain drink in hand, all the ice long since melted. And now something begins to creep inside me, like an itch where itches don't usually occur, like when you have hives and your palms prickle with discomfort. My mind processes the scene: Home. Mother. I should be home by now. Right?

But it is Little David's mother who finally trips my internal alarm system. NORAD has hit DEFCON 1. Shit is being launched with reckless abandon. She asks where I live, and shouldn't I call my mother to let her know I'm here, *mijito*? She walks over to the phone, unhooks the receiver, and gestures her willingness to dial the number for me.

Yes, I think. I should call home now. The problem, however, is twofold. First, my house, I now realize, is right across my beloved empty field. I can cross it in a minute at the most. That's basically as quick as a call, I think. (It's not.) But the thing that kills this plan is that, if I call home, I'm up shit creek because I'm somewhere I didn't have permission to be. I am trying to process the equation and am not sure how to continue.

And Little David's mother, she's so nice and sweet. She seemed pleased to see me, and she'd met me only minutes before. In point of fact, I'd like to know her better. Does she need another little boy? Plus, I'd make a good brother to Little David. What gets to me is how welcoming she is. It's almost as if—and I know this is a real stretch—but it's almost as if she *likes* having a guest in the house. This prospect drives my confusion as well.

Chapter Twenty-One

Let's pause a moment—leaving me in tilt mode, like a pinball machine, in Little David's home—to ruminate on this a bit.

I come from a family of misanthropes, truly. We are reflexively mistrustful of people not living in our house. That goes for relatives—cousins, uncles, in-laws—as well as neighbors. Yes, even the damned fine Shues. For you to be any of these and nevertheless get the welcome mat unfurled in your honor means you have done some impressive shit for someone in the house. And your racial-ethnic identity, sexual identity, gender expression, religious affiliation, or whom you voted for doesn't matter. If you don't live in our house, we begin our introductions already choking down an intense antipathy and suspicion, looking for a reason to confirm why we hate your guts beforehand.

This is not hyperbole for the sake of a memoir. When I was growing up, our front door—that huge banker's door—was rarely opened for others. I was taught to be ever vigilant for the slightest knock on that door and to freeze should someone rap on it. At first, I didn't understand why, but a knock at the door would terrify me. We would play the quiet game, and that family from *A Quiet Place* doesn't have shit on us. We would win that fucking game, and it would make for a boring-ass movie because we knew how to shelter in place decades before our national schoolchildren became experts at it.

Two examples will illustrate:

Once, in kindergarten, I was sick and thus stayed home from school, which happened a lot in my youth. I had been absent several days in a row, actually. I distinctly remember being crushed that I would miss out on the Valentine's Day party, at which we were to exchange cards and candy.

Rene admonished me when I whined about it. "Who cares? It's some stupid cards and candy. We have candy here. Besides, you're sick."

She didn't value this expression of kiddie sentimentality and commercialism. But you know who did? Ms. Sylvia Owen, my ur-teacher, and she was going to make sure I didn't feel left out. This teacher, who must surely be retired by now, belongs in the canon of teaching saints because, unbeknownst to her, after her long day with those tiny brutes, she had decided to deliver valentines to *a bunch of freak people-haters*! I wish I could have warned her, prepared her for what she would find, but I never thought she would visit me at my home. I would have told her not to come to the house, but thanks for the thought.

But she did it, man. And she knocked on our door. Our big-ass banker's door. And everyone froze the way we always did when someone came unannounced.

"Who is it? Who is it?" Mom and Rene whispered to each other. And we did what we always did: we stayed quiet, preparing to wait it out. This might be a minute, or it could be longer. Bill collector? Jehovah's Witness? Tío Pancho?

Incidentally, we didn't bear the anxiety of the undocumented, worried that *la migra* was coming to deport us. We were simply outsider averse.

But Ms. Owen was tenacious, God bless her, and kept knocking. She must have known we were inside. Must have known I was in there. And thinking about it now, I suspect she was aware that it may have been a cultural thing that was keeping the door closed. Knowing that her whiteness made her a stranger and thus suspect, she began talking through the door in her always-pleasant kindergarten-teacher voice.

"Hello? Is anybody home? I'm Sylvia Owen, Chris's kindergarten teacher at Chris Harwell Elementary." *Knock, knock, knock.* "Hello?"

That's all she needed to say. I was a star at the school, and apparently Ms. Owen was worthy of opening the door, as far as Mom was concerned. I loved that teacher the way little boys latch on to women of a certain age who aren't their mothers. I could already read before I hit kindergarten (this I can confirm), and I knew she recognized that I was different. When other kids got to take a nap, I was doing sentence-writing exercises with Ms. Owen. She's also the first white woman I got to know as a person and not as some television personality, and she left an enormous impression on all of us. But especially on me.

Ms. Owen left the big bag of valentines with Mom, who spoke to her briefly, and then my teacher went home, to her family and supper, having never been allowed to set one foot inside our house. She was neither invited in to have a seat nor offered some coffee or a *panecito*—the typical hospitality one might find in other Latinx homes. You had to be a part of the inner circle to cross our threshold. And though she was a good woman doing saint's work, Ms. Owen was not admitted to our temple of doom.

That should have been my first warning that we were different.

My second example concerns one of Rene's uncles on her father's side. Though he bore several names—Francisco, Frank, Pancho—it was Rene who christened him "the Amazing One," or simply, the Amazing. Rene had always loved to write, and one Saturday she wrote a story about Tío Pancho that was satirical and a gross caricature of the man. But in a lot of ways, the man was a gross caricature of a person. He had grown old without wife or children, and he tended to make the rounds visiting relatives, which was nice in theory. But his visits could last weeks, even months. He smoked cigars (the King Edward variety), had terrible body odor from infrequent showering, refused to do anything around the house to help, and it all contributed to no one wanting him around long, not even his younger brother, Dad. Rene's story was clever and funny, and she had the guts to read it aloud to her mother and father. Ordinarily they would have frowned on the disrespect, but they had to admit she made a good point about Pancho. So thenceforth, he was dubbed "the Amazing."

One time (we were in Lovington by this point), the Amazing showed up on a random morning. And we knew this was going to be a long visit because his visits were never short. Mom and Dad were back in Lubbock for some reason, taking with them our only working vehicle at the time, the red and white Ford F-150 XLT Lariat, and we were going to have to wait it out. Tom, Rene, Robert, and I were quiet, but the Amazing probably had nowhere else to go. And I remember we waited for hours, hoping he would go away. And he simply sat there in his truck with the driver's-side door open and smoked his King Edward cigars like he had all the time in the world. A regent in exile regarding a potential fiefdom. At dusk, finally, mercifully, he left.

When we thought it safe, we relaxed and turned on some lights and the swamp cooler air conditioner. But an hour later, the Amazing returned—like

Michael Myers, seemingly indestructible—catching us unawares, and we had no choice but to let him in and concoct some story about having been gone all day. I'm sure he knew better. We may have thought ourselves crafty, but Tío Pancho wasn't stupid. No vehicles had come or gone! That's why he was the Amazing. He could hack into our misanthropic systems and gain access like few others could. We shared genetic material, after all.

In short, we didn't want anyone entering our home, and we insisted on returning the favor. (We weren't coming to your house, get it?) And so, standing there in Little David's house, with his lovely mom sweetly asking if I should call home—as if there wouldn't be serious fucking consequences if I did—I was paralyzed with dread. If I had dialed home, I would have avoided the bigger shitnado to come.

But we all must take our lumps. As Herman Melville said through his iconic Ishmael, "And so the universal thump is passed round, and all hands should rub each other's shoulder-blades, and be content." My universal thump, one of many, was at hand.

Chapter Twenty-Two

I am startled and scared, but I want to remain calm. Perhaps this is the first time I have experienced pure panic. I have tarried too long walking home from school; I know that now. How long has it been? I am west of Globe Avenue, perhaps a quarter of a mile from my house, but I feel as if I am on the other side of Texas. I bolt out of there in sheer terror, my feet hardly touching the ground. I do not stop to thank Little David's sweet mother for her hospitality, or Little David for inviting me over.

He'll probably never ask me to come over again. (My fears prove true, though he does return the favor and visit me at my house sometime later. We don't go inside to play, naturally.) I run for home, seeing the empty field from its western side. It appears to me as a bothersome obstacle. If I don't get home right now . . .

I am not far from home. Once I cross Globe, there is nothing between me and my house except for a spread of prairie grass. The railroad bisects the area on a north–south axis until it begins its easterly curve, nearly parallel to my place. I cross the tracks, and I am no more than two hundred yards from home when I see a familiar truck backing out of our yard—the same '68 Chevy Robert and I will see in Lovington more than thirty years from now, when we have to clean up the disaster of a place that was once our home.

I am sprinting harder than I have ever run, thanks to a fear-induced rush of adrenaline. I hurl the cup from my hand, my first conscious act of littering. I begin to cry as I scream at the top of my lungs, hoping Mom will see me. I know she is heading out to find me, and I would rather the ground open up and swallow me whole, ending my panic.

Now, I *should* go home and wait for Mom to return. But in my ignorance and terror, I think I can somehow catch her! I see her drive down Hickory Avenue and then turn right onto E. Fortieth Street. I am running as hard as I can, foolishly thinking I can overtake Mom in the truck. By the time I arrive again at Harwell Elementary, Mom is emerging from the school building right as I stagger over to the parked Chevy. The folks inside were as bewildered as she was, and I could see the determination and fear on her. I want to be put out of my misery.

She unlocks the door and I get in. Mom is angry and in tears as we drive home. She tells me she thought someone had abducted me. (It happened just often enough to induce real albeit misplaced dread in the early 1980s.) She wants to know where I have been, what I've been doing. I tell part of the truth, which is that my friend had walked home with me but not before we stopped at the convenience store for a Coke.

"See, there's this thing you do with the Cokes where you get a little bit of everything!" But then I lie. I say we played video games at the store for the entire time, and she doesn't buy it. Mom has always detected bullshit like few others I have known, and I am no match for her. I'm a n00b and she's over 9000.

We are home within minutes. With the truck parked, I finally admit the truth, and it pours out of me: Little David, my friend from school, had invited me over to his house to play. I tell Mom that my friend had said it was no problem. See, it was no problem! But now I know he could not have been more wrong. There was a problem—a big problem. I know what comes next. Mom was inevitable long before Thanos.

I feel overheated from all the running as I sit on the couch in our living room. Mom closed the front door, that dark and heavy door intended for no family home, and much of the afternoon light is blocked out except for that which filters in through the curtains of the west-facing window. She and I are the only ones in the house, and I intuit that the climax of this dramatic piece is imminent. Mom has been crying tears of anguish and outrage. One thing to know about Mom is that she doesn't cry when she's sad; she cries when she's pissed off enough to bend sixteen-penny nails with one hand. Her tears tell me she is on fucking Jupiter with rage. She's giving off goddamn gamma rays of anger.

I have not been spanked much in my life up to now, but after today I will never forget this punishment. Seeing Mom cry is enough to ensure that I never do something this stupid again (wrong). But my own weeping, together with the feelings of guilt and remorse, is not punishment enough. And we both know it. I owe a pound of flesh, and Mom is as resolute as Shylock.

Mom has walked into her bedroom, where a belt her brother Juan had gifted her hangs on a nail. It is a tooled leather belt, the kind that has decorative etchings made with a heating element and a name burned into the leather. That belt was made for this day, steadily making its way to that moment. Like Anton Chigurh's quarter in *No Country for Old Men*. Only we didn't know that until now.

I am scared. Truly scared. I know Mom will not kill me (I think), but I do fear that she will hurt me somehow. I hyperventilate a bit as I sit alone on the couch. I am a small Brown boy with unruly hair who is nearly always good, and I have never been in trouble like this. But that's how Big Scary Brown Guys are forged, you see.

When it happens, it happens fast. Mom is suddenly standing in the living room with the leather belt in her hands. She pulls me up by my arm, and I hear Mom's voice but can't understand what she is saying. She is angry and crying. I am terrified and wailing as the belt crashes down on me again and again. Without intending to, I am counting every single blow I receive. I lose track after ten, but I am sure it is not more than twenty lashes. My back burns so much, I imagine the belt is angry with me as well, on fire and searing hot. When it is over, Mom retreats to her bedroom, and I stay on the couch to moan and sob. I stay there for hours, my face planted in the crease behind the couch cushions. And all I can do is think of running for home across the open field, my lovely field, with Mom driving the truck away from me, in search of me, a scarlet ibis, as I screamed for her to come back. I am humiliated. Not as smart as I thought I was.

I had to hear Mom's version of those events many times as I grew up. She would laugh as she told it, but I didn't. Was that her way of working through the epic beatdown she gave me or the unearned fear she endured? She never would have apologized for going so far, I'm certain of that. There may have been guilt there as well, and her lighthearted retelling robbed the actual moment of its seismic energy. Given the opportunity, she would tell the story to whoever happened to be in front of her. Her cue to a fresh retelling was always the phrase, "It's no problem," which is what Little David had uttered in convincing me to detour to his house.

She knew I had followed a friend to his house without permission, so that's why I got belted. I had mortified her (true, if unintentional), and in my family if you made Mom scared for or worried about you, you were also liable to incur her wrath. Mom—that is, Elva—was the one who doled out corporal punishment in the family. I never saw anyone other than me get spanked or beaten. Robert was so big by the time I was paying attention, maybe Mom would harangue and berate him more than beat him. Even after that, she never hit me much. Hers was a subtle knife, and its edge was mostly her sharp tongue. She could mock you and turn you into mincemeat with mere words.

After that, I tried hard not to provoke a beating, even when I learned, thanks to *Goodfellas*, that everybody takes a beating sometime. Even so, it was not long before I suffered what would turn out to be my last and greatest beatdown at her hands.

Chapter Twenty-Three

I was around the same age, in the second grade, when I took my next epic lashing, but I'm quite certain this was a bit after the Little David debacle. Unlike many kids who are a kind of walking disaster, I mostly kept to myself and was very mindful not to do anything that would cause friction. Mostly, I liked playing alone.

Rene was not in the house at this time either (she was already in Lovington), but suddenly I noticed I had a baby sister. A half sister, as we were told that we had different fathers. Weirdly, different people called this baby by different names. Everyone in the house called her Diana, which I thought was perfect and beautiful. It made me think of Princess Diana (whom I believe she was named after) and Diana Prince a.k.a. Wonder Woman. But cousins, aunts, and uncles called her Crystal—which was confusing to me because it sounded so close to Chris. And where did the name Crystal come from, anyway? Whenever I heard it, I was reacting before I caught the second syllable. Even now, I have no idea why this name, and I didn't question it. I had my own problems to sort out, both then and now.

As it happened, my sister had yet another name. Her birth certificate says Chencia—a made-up name derived from pop culture. Rene had watched a Cary Grant and Sophia Loren movie from 1958 called *Houseboat*. And in it, Loren played a character named Cinzia Zaccardi. Well, to Rene, Chencia was close enough to what she had heard on-screen. She had no access to IMDb back then, of course. But for her whole life, my sister had to explain the unwieldy name. Everyone outside of the family calls her Chencia. I still call her Diana. Mom and Rene always called her Danna.

Names are a thing in my family, y'all.

How Diana appeared one day in my home is probably the subject of its own book, and a topic I can only hint at here. For now, I envision my sister as a newborn, napping quietly in a white crib in Mom and Dad's room one afternoon when I came home from school. Mom told me explicitly to stay out of their room so as not to wake the baby. But I needed to get in there. I wanted to retrieve something that had rolled under the bed the night before, and I'd been waiting all day at school to get home and find it. It was either a tennis ball or a racquetball. A non-zero chance it was a baseball. Whatever it was, I had to have it at once. I'd grab it quietly and get out of there without waking the baby. Easy enough. Once I had sneaked in, however, it turned out I couldn't see a thing under the king-sized bed. I needed a flashlight.

But as I looked around, I saw a Bic lighter on the little nightstand next to where Dad slept. I'd seen enough movies to know a lighter could give you enough illumination when you needed it, and I felt pretty proud of myself for solving this problem. With the green lighter in my hands and my baby sister a few feet away, I got low and wriggled my way under the box spring like a ninja. Once in position, I flicked my Bic and felt like something out of *Indiana Jones*, using a small torch to light my way.

To my chagrin, the flame was weak, and I couldn't see much. When I finally spied what I was looking for, I had only an instant to rejoice before noticing that it was now much brighter under the bed. I also detected a lot of light. Too goddamned much. The gauzy covering under the box spring was going up in flames—and fast.

Did I alert Mom or Dad, the only grown-ups in the house, that I had set their bed on fire? Did I at least get my newborn sister out of the room as the smoke piled up? Did I call 911? A big negatory to all of these! Instead, I soaked a T-shirt with water and tried to use it to douse the flames under the bed. I did that twice—running for the kitchen sink to saturate the shirt, then back to the bedroom—before Mom smelled the smoke. On my first trip to the sink, I heard Mom say to Dad, "It smells like smoke." By the second round, I knew it was a lost cause and told her.

Mom. Sorry to interrupt your telenovela, but, umm, your bed is on fire. Actually, I don't think I said anything other than "There's a fire in the room."

She rushed past me into her bedroom and screamed for Dad. "Tome!" her sobriquet for Tomás, her husband, came out in a tone of sheer panic and got him to spring to action like he'd been catapulted. Soon a fifty-four-year-old Dad was dragging the flaming box spring through the house and onto the front lawn. He doused it with the hose and averted disaster, which is a kind of miracle. Imagine setting the box spring of your bed on fire right now, waiting in the kitchen a minute or two, then dragging that motherfucker out of your house. Now imagine the giant fireball not igniting anything else on the way out. No smoke damage at all.

That freak episode should have destroyed our house. It should have resulted in the tragic death of a newborn. It should have ended with me racked with unbearable guilt for the rest of my days. But instead, the anecdote survives as a curious chapter in my life and in my family lore.

Incidentally, many years later I would read Richard Wright's autobiography, *Black Boy*. Strikingly, one of the first incidents he relates is setting a broom, then later the diaphanous drapes in his home, on fire. He was younger than I was when he committed this act of arson. (He reports that he was four years old.) His house went up in flames, and he hid under the house. As I read his account, I remembered my own terror at setting a fire in my home (by accident, unlike Wright). At least I didn't burn down my house like he did (thanks to Mom and Dad).

He says of the beating he took: "I was lashed so hard and long that I lost consciousness. I was beaten out of my senses and later I found myself in bed, screaming, determined to run away, tussling with my mother and father who were trying to keep me still." I took a hell of a beating as well. Not from a stripped tree limb, as had been used on Wright, but with that goddamned tooled leather belt.

I sat in the backyard in the aftermath, waiting for my beating in the shadow of the house as the sun set behind my western field, having no excuse for my stupidity. I reaped many lashes for that one, so many that I could not count them all. And it was the last serious beating I would ever take. From then on, I might get slapped in the face for back-talking or being a smart-ass, but never again was I subjected to torturous punishment by Mom or anyone else.

Still, despite these black-letter days in my childhood, during those years in Lubbock, I enjoyed the house I grew up in and that implausible field to the west of us. For the rest of my life, I will consider that place my real home, and I view it as formative in my identity and sense of self. It is where I first understood myself as a Brown boy and as a Latino. I return to these days more frequently with each passing year because the answer to who I am resides in those early episodes of my youth.

The other day I mentioned to Robert that I would like to buy back our little plot of land that was once ours on the eastside of Lubbock, despite it now being a vacant lot.

"What for?" he dismissed, almost in disgust. "Chasing memories? What actually for? Let sleeping dogs lie."

Chapter Twenty-Four

After being mostly absent for many of my first years, Rene began showing up more and more. The intervals between visits grew shorter as her visits grew longer. Consequently, she was around more to give me what amounted to motherly advice.

For example, Rene had a go-to explanation for how we should identify whenever I asked about it. Her birth certificate proclaimed that she was "White," she would say. And that always seemed to be the end of the discussion until I prodded further.

"Okay," I would say when I was a kid, trying to follow the train of her logic. "So, you're white?" I found that hard to believe because even though she was very light skinned, her Chicana sensibilities and her Black affinities came out far too often for me to buy this idea that Rene was some white woman. Plus, my brown skin made the incongruity of her statement even more pronounced.

"Hell no!" she'd choke out like she had eaten some black licorice, which she hated, wrinkling up her face in distaste. "But I ain't no Mexican, either. And neither are you, *mijito*." It made no sense, but such was her way of looking at things.

This premise, while factually true, creates all sorts of problems when the average person tries to get to know me. It still trips me up and overloads my neural net. The most up-front people—almost universally they are white people curious about my identity—will simply ask, "What are you?" as if I were a dog whose breed needed to be sussed out so that they might be comfortable in their assumptions, and thus, justify everything else they might go on to presume.

ME: Ah yes, well, um, I am a bichon frise, thank you very much! A lovely breed once you get past the fluffiness and my powder puff nature. And you are?

WHITE RANDO: Oh, I'm white.

ME: Ah, all righty then! Carry on, old sport!

This question, as I have met it, is a racially coded challenge to your Americanness, as if your bona fides first must be cleared by this person who has no authority over you and who should mind their own goddamned business. "What am I?" If I say I'm Latino, they will respond without hesitation, "Wow! You don't sound Latino!"

When I have been asked this question throughout my life, I would often hesitate because it is more complex than this person is prepared to deal with. They want me to say I am Mexican so that their assessments of me might be confirmed or further called into question. They want a simple answer in much the same way someone who passes you in the hall asks, "How's it going?" when they for sure do not want to know how things are going. They want the uncomplicated answer, one that makes them feel like they have contributed something meaningful to society and to you. They want you to say, "Good!" or "Fine!" while they never break stride or give it a second thought.

In recent years, I sometimes get the question that asks, gingerly, if I am perhaps Black. It doesn't occur so often, but the query is informed by some physical attribute of mine, that is, my visual identity. Something in the combination of my hair (or lack thereof), the timbre of my voice, my diction, my build, and my skin tone sets off the Blackness detectors of some people when they first meet me. And, to make it perfectly clear, I have no claim to Blackness. Yet sometimes folks sense something that isn't there, perhaps spotting some vestigial affect that traces back to my mother. Not genetically, but maybe something akin to cultural contagion.

At any rate, I can appreciate the directness of that question at least. They want to know something specific: Am I Black? To which I can quickly and unequivocally answer, "No." When I get the question "What are you?" I could simply reply, "Well, I'm not Black, if that's what you're asking," but that isn't satisfying, even if it would shut people up and make things easier for me.

Anyway, Rene's answer was always confounding and unhelpful. It was obvious to me that we were not white. I clocked that by comparing us to our white neighbors, the Shues, and to every white person I ever saw on TV. So, her pronouncement that it says "White" on her birth certificate aligned with some antiquated ideas she was taught in school about there being only three races: Caucasoid, Negroid, and Mongoloid. (I swear these were the terms she used.) I can clearly recall her telling me this for the first time as we drove to Furr's Supermarket on the east side of Lubbock one day. I wondered how all people in the world could be reduced to one of only three categories.

"Orientals, Blacks, and Whites," she reiterated in a way she thought I could better understand. "That's all there are in the world." Today, I recognize this racial paradigm as one that supports white supremacist thinking, even among Latinos.

I said no more. My confusion was the result of her own confusion, I decided, and left it at that. But to complicate matters for me, Rene would often explain that we were not Mexican, because as far as we could tell, it had been a hell of a long time since any of our ancestors were born or raised in Mexico. I used to think this a stretch, but with the advent of certain for-profit genealogical databases, finding out where my ancestors came from has become a little easier. So, I searched for answers to prove or disprove my mother, and to settle my own internal debate. Because a part of me, thanks to Rene's occasional hyperbolic assertions, believed she was wrong about our not being Mexican. And if she were wrong, how much easier would it be to explain to people "what I am"?

But before I go on to what I discovered, it's important to understand why this is such an issue. When someone asks me, "What are you?" and if I want to give them what I believe to be a correct and, to my knowledge, honest answer, I say:

"Well, I'm from Texas. And my family has been in Texas for many generations."

That should suffice, but usually someone follows up with, "No. Where are you *really* from?" Such questioning often comes when I'm outside of Texas, though on occasion it happens even in my state of birth. I then recognize that the person wants me to admit that I'm somehow not American. "So, when did your family emigrate to the US from Mexico?" they might ask.

They are fucking determined to make me a Mexican against any obstacles or evidence to the contrary. Which shouldn't be a problem, as when people ask if I am Black, I don't take that as an affront or insult. But I grew up in a place where the word Mexican, always pronounced *Messkin*, was said with venom and hatred. The convergence of race, ethnicity, and nationality are always vexed in my identity expression. Like many Latinx people in the United States, I'm not easily categorizable by my skin color, my facial features, or my use of language.

Messkins was a synonym for what might be called "undesirables" in polite, but nonetheless racist, circles. If you were a Messkin, you were small of stature; you were unable to speak or understand English; you were unintelligent; you were meek and willing to be bullied; you could work so hard that you could be easily dehumanized and exploited; you were dirty and disease infested; you were a criminal, a drug runner, an ex-con, or a soon-to-be criminal; and you were a general nuisance except when it came to taking on maddeningly strenuous work. Mexican, to me, connoted all of this when I was growing up. Not because I had seen such stereotypes for myself but because white people were always saying these things about Messkins. It took me a long time to recognize this rhetoric for the racist hoax that it is.

It didn't help that everyone in my family, and especially Rene and Dad, had an extreme distaste for Mexicans and Mexican Americans as individual people and not the culture, of which we clearly partook. Hypocritical? Yes. I am at a loss to explain their contempt other than to say it was in large measure a function of a general societal hatred (at least in our part of Texas) toward Mexicans, and Dad was forever differentiating himself from the group despised by most whites here at the time.

In fairness, he wasn't Mexican, as I am not. He, his dad, and his grandfather were all born and raised in the San Antonio area. Yet they assuredly were most closely aligned with Mexican culture. That is, Mexican culture as it evolved in Texas. It's hard for me to acknowledge that he held these prejudicial views of people from Mexico who had recently made their way to the United States. But on the other hand, he also had a general dislike of most every group he came into contact with. I've said before that the misanthropy of my family was legendary. It's as if we were born to it.

Chapter Twenty-Five

When Rene said there were only three races, parroting outmoded theories she had learned in school, it highlighted something vital in our race discussions. Race is a social construct, which means that a given part of the world, based on its historical and cultural development, has views about race that do not translate to other parts of the world. An easy way to come to terms with this is to think about what it means to be Black in America—the history, the associations, the way it feels to be Black in America. And then look at how a nation like Nigeria doesn't think of Blackness in the same way as Americans perceive it. In simple terms, it must mean that Blackness is not immutable and universal, forever and ever, amen. Rather, it is subjective, even if we are talking about people who have ancestors who relatively recently originated in Africa. (All modern humans originated in Africa, but hopefully you take my meaning.)

Now, whether some people believe race is a construct is beside the point. Facts are what they are, conspiracies and false narratives to the contrary. However, facts are not of interest to many people, as the intransigence around the COVID-19 pandemic revealed. That's partially why some people who ask me the question, "What are you?" don't want the facts, which are too complicated for their easy and deliberate misunderstandings of identity.

And if you think it's difficult to explain my identity to white people, the process is even more fraught with Latinos. How troublesome it is for a Latino to understand that I can be Brown, speak terrible Spanish, and connect to a lot of the same cultural totems and tenets as they do—without identifying closely with a Latin American nation. To them, I might simply be an Americano or even a gringo, which lumps me, erroneously, with white American culture. Those Latinos with close ties to Latin America see me as having too much in common with a typical American not to be basically white, no matter my surname and melanin levels.

So, there is a situation, embodied in my intersectional existence, where Black folk may almost intuit a racial connection with me, Mexicans will not accept me as part of their group, and whites will insist on a default categorization of me as a Mexican. Sometimes I feel like Odysseus and want to answer that I am Nobody.

As it happens, Rene has a close affiliation with Black identity. Though no one will ever mistake her for being Black, as often happens to me, because she attended Dunbar High School, the "Black" high school in Lubbock, her views on race were strongly influenced at a tender age.

Attending Dunbar High School (which closed in 1993, the year I graduated from Lovington High School) shaped Rene's identity in ways that cannot be understated. During these formative years, she was steeped in Black culture—from music, dancing, and the teenage social forces and pressures that came from being a cheerleader. Her dearest friends were Black. Her boyfriends were Black (to her parents' chagrin), and ever since then she has more or less adopted Black culture as partly her own, even though she never pretends in the slightest that she herself is Black. Rene was at Dunbar in the first few years of the 1970s after the civil rights movement, when the historically Black high school was newly integrated.

Again, my mother most decidedly is not Black, and in my opinion, she has no claim to that culture. Yet she does have some clear affinity for it, in a way, as this was her social milieu during her youth. And often when she speaks, she will reflexively code-switch to AAVE (African American Vernacular English), and she will "sound" like a member of the Black community. And there are times when I find that I unconsciously do the same, to a certain degree. This kind of code-switching happens automatically if a Black person talks to me as if I, too, were Black. My daughters say I do this also when I meet someone who is from my part of Texas. I try not to be too critical of Rene when I see her do this. My annoyance stems from her penchant for assuming the vernacular even if it's the two of us alone in a room.

So, this connection to Black culture has influenced her identity in such a way that she is shaken by the injustices of racism and prejudice, not only against Latinos but against Black folk as well. Often, she would feel the need to speak on behalf of the Black community in our house, thus claiming that bond to the culture she identified with in high school.

Once, when I was watching ESPN, broadcaster Robin Roberts—a Black woman who later would go on to become a key piece of the show *Good Morning America* on ABC—used the phrase "Go on wit yo bad self!" in the style of the ESPN anchors who would offer witty commentary as the sports highlights played. Rene, who was standing in the next room and had not cared one bit about whatever Robin Roberts was talking about up to that moment, spoke up with indignation. "Who said that!" she demanded, upset because she thought someone not Black had used this phrase common to the Black community. Roberts had otherwise not "sounded" Black as she was delivering her lines.

It was as if someone had misappropriated the phrase from Rene's own people, and I still remember the glee I felt when I smugly pointed out that the announcer, Robin Roberts, was a Black woman.

"Well, she didn't sound like she was Black," said Rene. That was the end of that.

It was a moment for me. It made me realize that Rene believes she has earned her claim to Black culture. She's punched her ticket to the cookout, she'd say. She did spend many of her formative years among Black teens, yes, but it still makes me feel ill when I hear her unleash the N-word today. In her adult years, she no longer had such close connections and friendships, not only with Black folk but with people in general. She will say the N-word as someone from the Black community might—as a gendered idiom invoked among community and in solidarity. She talks in the same way, and I know it's not right that she does that. It upsets me when she does it around my daughters, and they are mortified when it happens. Yet, her affinity for AAVE and the invocation of the N-word is part of Rene's history in a way that's important to her. And because it is a part of her history, it necessarily influenced my own beliefs regarding race and identity.

My detractors out there who castigate me for being a radical leftist elitist may be surprised to learn that my household was a bit of a paradox, comprising not only extreme views that indeed align with the left (such suspect positions as thinking of undocumented persons as human beings and understanding that not all unemployed people are idlers wanting money for nothing) but also views that would deservedly get people into trouble today (characterizing the LGBTQ community in derogatory terms; employing cultural stereotypes when discussing most identity groups, even our own; freely lobbing misogynistic remarks).

And it wasn't "economic anxiety" or a similarly preposterous premise that explained my family's quite fucked-up ways of looking at people. We rationalized that we were assholes to everyone, demonstrating a kind of equality to which all could aspire. It was wrong to hate one group and meanwhile pretend that your own identity group was somehow inherently superior in all ways that counted. Rather, we mocked all groups across the board but were likely to feel compassion for their members as individuals. Didn't make it right.

Chapter Twenty-Six

I attended Christopher Harwell Elementary in Lubbock, Texas, through the second grade, and can recall not one single instance of racism from my teachers or my fellow students. I freely acknowledge that my inability to detect bigotry at that age doesn't mean it wasn't there, even in a school that was fairly diverse. My second-grade teacher, Ms. Johnson, was a lovely young Black woman who, as it turned out, had attended Dunbar High School with Rene. I could never ascertain whether they had been friends or rivals or even knew each other at all. Ms. Johnson was my first real, sustained encounter with a Black person, and I felt a great fondness for her.

After a good part of the school year had passed, Ms. Johnson chose a day of the week when she would allow her students to eat their lunches in the classroom with her. We could eat with the teacher! But it got even better. She had a record player in the room, and she encouraged us to bring a record so she could play some of it during the lunch period. Sublime!

I didn't own any records yet. Sure, I had all sorts of *He-Man* and *Star Wars* figures, but a music collection was another matter entirely. David and Robert, my uncle-brothers, had great music (mostly). David was my conduit for Kurtis Blow, Dazz Band, the Gap Band, Bootsy Collins, Parliament, and other funk artists. Earth, Wind & Fire, Journey, and Boston were perennially on the turntable. Those were mingled with Robert's fascination with Air Supply and Christopher Cross, and the soundtrack to the movie *Arthur*, which I tolerated. David, the middle and coolest of my uncle-brothers, had Michael Jackson's *Off the Wall*, and I would play that record without even knowing how to use the record player. Now I had an idea that I hoped Ms. Johnson would love.

"Ms. Johnson?" I asked one day during a break in our lessons.

"Yes, Chris."

"My brother bought Michael Jackson's *Thriller* the other day. Could I bring that for lunchtime when we listen to music?"

"You sure can, honey! I love Michael Jackson!" She wriggled as if she were already dancing to MJ's music.

The *honey* may sound stereotypical, but I clearly remember marveling at her use of the word. No one in my home used it that way, and the term of affection further endeared her to me. Ms. Johnson's enthusiasm confirmed for me that she was a lovely person and a great teacher. It's that watershed moment when a kid realizes their teacher is an actual person who does normal shit outside of work and doesn't live on campus, penned in at the school like some educator version of Miss Havisham. Ms. Johnson became real to me because she acknowledged the existence of Michael Jackson, a pop culture icon who was decidedly outside the purview of our classroom.

Now, MJ had not yet debuted his moonwalk, which was to come a few months later. His album *Thriller* had already spawned a megahit, "Billie Jean," that, as it turned out, single-handedly fully integrated MTV, which to that point had rarely aired any videos by Black artists. MTV had seemed very white in its infancy, even to me. I got to watch MTV because Robert was seven years older than me and at an age where he could appreciate music and music videos. I followed his lead.

But Dad had found MTV by accident, turning the cable box dial to the higher bands, where there usually weren't any channels. Suddenly, Kenny Loggins was singing "I'm Alright," which I knew as the gopher-dancing song from *Caddyshack*, a bit that Mom had found hilarious. But there were never any Black or Brown people singing that I could see. Like so much of the television I saw growing up, MTV was simply another venue of white pop culture, which equated to pop culture writ large.

That is, until Michael Jackson literally lit up sidewalk squares as he gracefully pranced about in a black leather suit, pink shirt and socks, high waters, and a red bow tie, singing about lovers, accusations, pregnancies, and something that a paternity test might have resolved without all the drama. Kind of risqué for a second-grade class to listen to.

But I didn't care. "Billie Jean" has a monster of a bass line that keeps the energy going. It sounds like it will never stop. MJ could have sung nonsense lyrics, and it would have been better than most songs on the airwaves. The video also captivated my imagination. I asked Robert if I could take his album to school, and I'm sure he said fuck no. But what did he know? I was glad he'd bought *Thriller* (at the Montgomery Ward) because I was tired of hearing "Arthur's Theme (Best That You Can Do)" thirty times a day! I was done with such cruel and unusual punishments from my big brother, who loved yacht rock before it was a thing and, even today, will play one song for days on end. (He single-handedly ruined the Weeknd's "Blinding Lights" for my whole family when he lived with us during the COVID-19 pandemic. He had it on repeat for *weeks*.)

I appealed to Mom, the ultimate arbiter of justice and fair play, and she ruled in my favor, but I had to be extra careful with Robert's record. And I was. And my schoolmates listened to the greatest album that MJ would ever release as we ate super-average cafeteria food in Ms. Johnson's glorious second-grade classroom at Christopher Harwell Elementary. (Okay, *Bad* may be slightly better.)

I still have questions, though. Did I decide to ask if MJ was a practical choice only because my teacher was Black and young? Would I have suggested it if my teacher had been white and looked like Aunt Bee from *The Andy Griffith Show*, one of Mom's favorite television programs? I feel that I would not have asked a white teacher for fear she might say something derogatory against MJ's music, or so-called Black music in general. Perhaps I felt that if any teacher could understand how that music made me feel, it was Ms. Johnson. And it is exactly because she was a Black woman that I knew she would understand.

Now, that is rather racialized thinking for such a young boy. But our understandings of race are formed early in our lives. Also, it puts the lie to that old chestnut about not seeing race. "Oh, I'm color-blind! I don't see race at all!" Yeah, sure. And I'm Lincoln's grandfather, as Tuco Benedicto Pacífico Juan María Ramírez famously said in *The Good, the Bad, and the Ugly*. We see race, okay? We see difference. I could clearly tell that Ms. Johnson was a Black woman. Her skin, her hair, her smell, her diction, and nearly everything about her were distinct from what I was familiar with. But though I knew she was different, I didn't yet know that there were some who might think that she was inferior because of it. I saw difference as merely another worthy expression of a person. I could recognize that MJ, too, was Black. I intuited that he and my second-grade teacher likely shared something that I couldn't put my finger on at the time. I didn't know how race and culture worked yet, which was fine. Forty years later, a hell of a lot of people still don't know.

As it turned out, Ms. Johnson would be the only Black teacher I had in all my years in public school, in two different towns in two different states, which makes me appreciate her even more than I did then. She is the only Black teacher I had, even including all my undergraduate college classes combined. It was not until graduate school that I had a professor who was Black.

Chapter Twenty-Seven

School would turn out to be where I gained a lot of practical wisdom about how my identity was perceived and policed by others. Rampant stereotyping among our standard social circles and cliques pervaded, and it seemed to me that everyone gave as much as they got in what amounted to a zero-sum game. Most everyone, boys and girls, tended to associate with their own racial, ethnic, and social class with the rare exception. This was the 1980s, and as on the world stage, mutually assured destruction held the factions at my school in check. I had friends across various social sets, and the students I disliked most were likewise distributed among all the groups. Some of the vilest kids I knew belonged to my own Latinx community.

But these attitudes of mine pertained to the boys. Girls were another matter entirely for me, as the fears of miscegenation that had given my grandparents fits now afflicted my parents' generation. My first heartbreak involved a young white girl named Tina and introduced me to how some people could not get past my identity as a Brown boy—or transcend their own prejudice.

Tina would ultimately serve as a prototype for the kind of girl I would often be attracted to: very smart, skinny, know-it-all white girls (later, women) with dark hair. My wife, Ginger, fits this profile except for her hair, which is a strawberry to dark blond. I guess everyone has a type, the sort of person they find instantly appealing. When I was ten, that person manifested for the first time as Tina.

By then I was living in Lovington, New Mexico, which looks like Lubbock in its topography and lack of distinguishing features but is much more rural and truly smaller. I was of an age where I didn't yet realize I liked girls in that way. Tina sat near me in class, and perhaps she didn't know how to handle the feelings she had for me either. She would tease me good-naturedly, calling me nicknames she thought were funny, like Chrissy Boy, and I would be rude to her, though I thought I was merely playing. That is how evolution has ensured the survival of humankind—with the inability to express oneself to a potential life partner in any way that captures the actual feelings themselves.

One day I was playing soccer during recess, and Tina, who was not playing, went out of her way to engage me so that I would notice her. Not only that, she teased me to try to get me to stop playing the game and literally chase her. *This girl is crazy*, I thought. My friends on the field mocked me relentlessly. "Hey, go be with your little girlfriend and get outta the game!" Maybe I should have been flattered to have a pretty if nerdy girl provoke me into chasing her in the middle of a pickup soccer match. Like, did I need an engraved invitation?

By the time I focused on Tina, I was irritated and annoyed, and I chased her out of sheer frustration. What was I supposed to do when I caught her, anyway? Soon, on the blacktop, I closed the distance between us and, in order to "catch" her, lunged for the first body part I could reach. Before I knew it, I grasped a fistful of long, pretty brown hair, which unfurled behind her like a banner.

And I hauled back on it the way a short-tempered horse rider might yank on the reins. I pulled Tina's lovely hair, and she stopped running; then she turned all her energy to crying, as though I had scalped her. She wailed with an intensity that scared me. I knew instantly that I had fucked up in a major way, and a few of her friends rightly stood up for Tina and menaced me.

I did my best to offer my contrition, and I even offered to let her pull my hair until I had suffered to her satisfaction. She declined, and soon enough forgave me. We were friends again. And we stayed friends for the next couple of years, despite my attending a different elementary the following year; for three consecutive years, I was enrolled in three separate elementaries in Lovington despite our family never moving house in that time.[3]

---

3 I don't know why it was the case that I attended Yarbro Elementary, Jefferson Elementary, and Llano Elementary respectively in grades three, four, and five. I lived so far out of town that it likely had nothing to do with districting. I seem to remember Rene enrolling me late one year, and I had to attend a different elementary than the year before. Perhaps she was so late every year that I would end up at whichever school had room for me.

Fortunately for me, we had both been invited to take part in a district-wide gifted and talented program. This meant that twice a week, I spent my afternoons at yet another school as part of a group of six students, one of whom was Tina.

By then, it was dawning on me that she liked me, and I liked her too. We laughed at each other's jokes, teased each other in a friendly and perhaps loving way, and not once did we comment on the other's race or ethnicity. In reality, I was the only Latinx student in my cohort, and that was utterly obvious to me. My gifted-program teacher, Mr. Gregory, was a kind and smart man, and I admired him very much. He drove out to our place to talk to Rene about the results of the test I had taken and why it would be beneficial for me to be in the program. Like everyone else who dropped by, he was not allowed past our front door.

After more than a year in the gifted program, on a lovely fall day, our cohort learned that Tina would no longer be participating. Other interests, perhaps music lessons or singing or ballet, were taking precedence, leaving her no time for our activities, according to Mr. Gregory. Honestly, the program was an opportunity to do very creative things like stage plays that we wrote or short films we directed. It fostered creativity and creative thinking. One of my final projects was making a stop-motion film using props such as *Transformers* toys and building miniature sets out of readily available materials. This short film was screened at my home elementary to the whole school, and I was mortified. But it was met with thunderous applause (as I like to remember the premiere), and I may be the first filmmaker in history to produce and direct a *Transformers* stop-motion animated film. It undeniably predated *Transformers: The Movie.*

Tina was leaving us, and I truly began to understand about absence making the heart grow fonder. Tina was gone! But then, to my surprise, she attended one last field trip with the group while I was in the program. Tina was suddenly there again! We may have gone to Roswell, New Mexico, to the Goddard Planetarium. On that field trip, I also figured out that my cohort was a tiny part of a larger program, which comprised dozens of students.

I didn't see much of Tina on the drive up or during our field activities. But on the approximately hour-and-a-half-long trip home, it so happened that Tina sat next to me on the bus, and we kept each other company, the details of which are more guesswork than memory at this point. But I remember feeling a growing confidence that Tina and I were made for each other. It had taken me a few years to get it, true, but now I was dazzled by the possibility of a very strong friendship—at a minimum. What I never would have guessed during that glorious ride home was that it would mark not the beginning of a beautiful friendship but rather its complete and absolute end.

Back at our school, when the bus let us off, we walked to the sidewalk pickup area in front of the school buildings. Tina and I were talking and laughing about something or other from earlier in the day. Maybe it was the over-the-top lunch Rene had packed for me. While students were buying parfaits at the Tastee-Freez, I unpacked a full-size grocery bag—picture the one Emilio Estevez's character busts out in *The Breakfast Club*, infinitely large on the inside, like a magical top hat. I was slightly embarrassed, but Rene had packed some good stuff for me, and I shared the bounty with my gifted and talented compatriots, who indulged without qualms. Thankfully, Rene had also given me a few bucks; like everyone else, I spent it on a parfait.

Anyway, we kept up a lively conversation while awaiting our rides home. An unfamiliar emotion had overtaken me: caring for someone *who wasn't family*. Middle school would be starting in a few months, but sixth grade seemed a long way off. And I fancied Tina more with each passing moment.

Someone pulled up in a small car the color of sweet tea, a man with a brown mustache at the wheel, whom I took to be Tina's father. She got in the car, we smiled at each other as we waved goodbye, and they left, the westering sun in their eyes and my own as I watched them drive out of sight in that golden, fading light of late afternoon.

Chapter Twenty-Eight

All through that summer of 1986, I could not stop thinking about Tina. I replayed our last interactions in my mind with such vigor that if they had been a VHS tape, I would have worn it out. A few times, I even dreamed of her (nothing untoward; she just appeared in the dreams). I had grown accustomed to her face! I had finally fallen for this little white girl, but I would never tell anyone at home about it. Their ruthless mockery would have reduced me to a quivering puddle.

When I saw Tina on the first day of the sixth grade, she regarded me with the eyes of an amnesiac. It was like she had gone from David Webb to Jason Bourne at a Treadstone summer camp for white girls, and she didn't give any sign of recognition. Had I changed so drastically in four months as to be unrecognizable? Perhaps the next day she would notice me. She'd come up to me and say, "Hey, Chrissy Boy! Where have you been! I was wondering when you were going to get around to catching up with me. Listen, sorry I didn't recognize you yesterday."

I cooled my heels and yearned for the arrival of such a next day. Garth Brooks later wrote a song about what might happen to love if we simply ran out of time. Well, tomorrow *never* fucking came, and over the next seven years, Tina did not speak more than ten words to me—total. At the close of our senior year, quite early one morning before class, we found ourselves roaming the same hall. Without slowing or missing a step, we walked past each other and shared our longest conversation in maybe seven years:

"Good morning, Chris."

"Good morning, Tina."

But way back in the sixth grade, I'd been left wondering . . . *Did I imagine the last few years? Am I in some dystopian future? Did I turn to the wrong page in my Choose Your Own Adventure novel? What happened?*

The next year, in the seventh grade, I sat behind a girl named Becca, who alternated between being insufferably nice and utterly insufferable to me. She had been a classmate of mine and Tina's in the third grade. One day, annoyed with me for some reason or other, this girl suddenly blurted out, "You liked Tina in the third grade!"

Like Peter in the Gospels, I would deny this before my seventh-grade Language Arts classmates no less than three times.

"No, I didn't."

"Yes, you did!"

"Wrong!"

Another classmate: "For reals?"

Me: "No way!"

But this blond harridan, to my sheer delight, had confirmed *something* between Tina and me. Becca had the receipts—in her own brain! I had *not* imagined it! Hell, this girl had caught wind of it a whole two years before I did. *I wasn't crazy.*

Left to pick up the pieces, I became self-aware, understanding that for some people, my Brownness was incompatible with whiteness. Something about me had changed in Tina's eyes, and I wondered if that last day when we were still friends, the day her father picked her up and regarded me, she'd been told not to fall for a Brown boy. I imagined the conversation that ensued:

TINA: Hi, Dad! That's my friend Chris that I talk about all the time. He's a dreamboat!

TINA'S DAD: That's Chris? He sure is Brown. Is he a Messkin?

TINA: I guess. But Chrissy Boy is different, not like those other Brown boys. I really like him. I think you would too.

TINA'S DAD: Stop talking to him. Don't ever talk to him again, understand me? When he makes eye contact, you look away. When he smiles at you, you give him a blank stare. You may never be friends with him again.

TINA: But, Dad!

TINA'S DAD: I'm sorry, my dear, but it's for your own good. You may think he's a Brown boy and that he looks harmless now. But someday he'll be a Big Scary Brown Guy, and he'll cause you nothing but grief. Believe me.

TINA: Fine. What's for supper?

I'll admit, there may be other reasons, legitimate reasons, why Tina stopped talking to me overnight. Maybe she lost interest, which was her prerogative. But did she have to crush me so utterly?

When I say that I was "left to pick up the pieces," I mean I had to try to come up with a rationale for the rejection, one that made sense to me. What I should have done was stop her in the hall and say, "Hi. Tina, right? I'm Chris, the guy who has been your closest friend for the last three years. Is there a reason you look at me as if I've had a face transplant? It's me, Chrissy Boy. Tina?"

But I was too chickenshit to take two minutes and perhaps change our lives forever. Not that I mean we would have ended up together as adults; I'm not *that* naïve. But I've been carrying this angst around for a good part of my life. I wasn't brave enough to confront her with the truth: whatever she was doing, it was inexcusable. And I was becoming too comfortable with being unacknowledged by Rene at home and Tina at school yet without the requisite courage to make myself seen, wanted, and loved.

Instead, I searched for reasons—daily, hourly—that explained how a girl could make me feel so invisible. Attempting to find some rationale for this consumed me. My thoughts were *always* on securing a justification for why I was now so unacceptable that Tina would not even deign to look at me. And what I continually returned to was the stark realization that I was a Brown boy, and she must either have been told by her parents that I was forbidden fruit that endangered her place in a White Eden, bringing shame upon her family, or she herself had concluded that going forward, this Brown boy was only going to be a goddamned nuisance.

Her actual motivations are, frankly, unimportant. I'm sure Tina went on to have a great life, never looking back—and I didn't turn out so bad either. For me, the devastating consequence of being discarded was that, in my bewilderment, I could only conclude that my ethnicity had been a bridge too far for my erstwhile friend. That I was worth liking or even loving—right up to the point that I was, alas, a Brown boy. Now that we were growing up, it was a dealbreaker. Even if this does not reflect her experience, the flat refusal to acknowledge me led me to question my worth and, perhaps, hate a core part of myself for a long time.

Chapter Twenty-Nine

That is what white privilege and white supremacy enables. It doesn't generally bother the person who is empowered and sustained by whiteness. On the contrary, an unfair and brutal system makes non-whites consistently agonize over why they aren't good enough, how they are not smart enough or beautiful enough, how they aren't white enough. If only they'd been born white, so much of this exhausting shit would be no more than a mote of dust floating in a sunbeam, since white people are not afflicted by such torment in the first place. Unfortunately, life doesn't work that way. Membership truly does have its privileges, I guess.

And every day until literally the day I graduated from high school (the first of several graduations Rene refused to attend), I thought that, surely, today would be the day Tina would reminisce about how meaningful we had once been to each other, and realize that I still meant something to her.

Like so many times across my life, I thought the problem was that I couldn't discover how to convey unequivocally my identity position in a succinct manner, clear enough to obviate the need for further discussion. My own anxiety over not knowing what I was to any great certainty triggered insecurity, imposteritis, competent fakery, and an ineptitude at discerning when it was worthwhile to take a chance and, as Lord Vader was constantly haranguing his son, fulfill my goddamned destiny. Only in more recent years have I begun to gain the supreme confidence of a mediocre white guy.

There were other girls who entered my life, of course, and we formed bonds that had outcomes typical of kid relationships. In the fourth grade, a Latina girl named Michelle wrote me a note to profess her love for me. Before I could formulate a response, Ernesto, a kid I was casual friends with, challenged me to a fight because Michelle, he claimed, was his girlfriend. Whatever. I didn't like Michelle one way or another, and as far as I was concerned, he could have her. I managed to convince Ernesto that fighting over a girl was colossally stupid. But it took a lot of convincing.

A red-haired girl named Loretta not so secretly adored me. Her hair was such a brilliant natural red that you could not help but fix your eyes upon it, and she was the first girl I knew in person who was covered in freckles. I decided that, while she was nice, she ultimately wasn't my type—my type being dark-haired skinny white girls. Loretta was a lovely thicc girl who never let up, and I grant her all the credit for letting me know how much she liked me. I was always friendly to her.

The point here is not to go through my rendition of "To All the Girls I've Loved Before." I only mean to say that I set no restrictions on potential girlfriends in terms of identity as I saw it.

Rene, however, had given me a kind of ultimatum, which is why I had thought it all too plausible for Tina's dad to issue an ultimatum of his own.

"Don't date a *mexicana*," she admonished, "or marry one. Marry a white girlfriend or even a *negrita*. But absolutely no *mexicanas*."

Again, this should not have surprised me, given Rene's hostility toward Mexicans, or Latinos, in general—even those with ancestries identical to hers. And while I ordinarily would have taken her advice with a K2-sized mountain of salt and outright ignored it, this sounded like one directive I should manage with care. But everyone in my family had disastrous experiences in relationships, so how could I do worse than them, no matter whom I dated? The short version of Rene's injunction was NO MEXICAN GIRLS, which I took as "no Brown girls." Even then I refused restrictions on whom I was permitted to fall in love with.

And that's right when Zinnia walked into my life. She had to be the prettiest Latina girl I had ever seen. Like me, she spoke English without a hint of accent, but her Spanish was light-years more advanced than mine. A freshman in high school, I still perversely held out a faint hope that Tina would come to her senses, though I admit that possibility faded a bit more every day. Zinnia was new to the school, and we sat next to each other in computer science class.

Even then, I knew she was one of our school's Eternals—a girl who likely wouldn't have any interest in a dork like me. But I was a dork whose latent testosterone was finally kicking in, along with my growing interest in fitness and bodybuilding. Yet this beautiful girl—with lovely brown skin that looked like honey, and light brown, almost blond hair—became my friend. I had no clue that such a pretty girl could stand me long enough to talk to me on a regular basis. That she was Latina—specifically, Mexican American—never entered my thoughts in those heady days of getting to know each other.

All that ninth-grade year, Zinnia and I grew closer as friends. The following year, we were in Biology together. When Valentine's Day rolled around, my school did what all schools did and allowed students to send a Candygram or something for like a buck to another student as a fundraiser. Solidarity manifested among the troglodytes and social lepers in the school, and they would get each other a Candygram so they might actually receive something from a "secret admirer" that everyone knew was your best friend but who cared? It was still pleasant to get one.

We watched Operation Desert Storm unfold on CNN on the classroom television that morning. An office aide delivered a vase of flowers to the class. It was Valentine's Day 1991. The aide handed it to the teacher, Ms. Spengler, rumored to be one of three lesbian teachers in the school, and Ms. Spengler called out my name like the coach she was: "González! These flowers are for you!"

It was the first time in my life that someone had spent money to buy me flowers, and I was genuinely surprised and slightly embarrassed. The boys around me jeered. It was a stellar arrangement of red roses and baby's breath. I'm not a flower person, but these were outstanding. They were the most glorious roses that had ever been delivered to a Brown boy in the history of Brown boys. I read the small card written in an elegant hand: *To Chris, Happy Valentine's Day. With love, A Secret Admirer.*

This incident and countless others like it have scientifically proved that you should *never* remain anonymous when you give a token of affection to someone. Take credit for that shit! It doesn't come cheap, either.

There I was, lugging a green glass vase with red roses around with me until I could get to my locker. Not that I wanted to hide them, but I didn't want them to get damaged during the day's hustle and bustle. And I tried, by process of elimination, to discover who exactly was my secret admirer. Of course, even I knew it wouldn't be Tina. That was too unbelievable even for an '80s John Hughes flick like *Sixteen Candles* or *Pretty in Pink*. Usually when something like this happens, the secret admirer is anyone you don't see yourself with, or to be blunt, a person you're not attracted to. That's why they want it to be a secret, owing to their fear of rejection. Finally, it was Oscar

Malagueña, my brother-in-arms in the iron game and a fellow Latino, who asked me if I knew who had given me the roses.

"Nah, man. I'm trying to figure it out."

He laughed. "You don't know yet??" He was hysterical. "C'mon, bro!"

"You know who it is?"

Oscar stared at me with this intensity I'd never seen before, even when he was trying a new one-rep max in the bench press. He smacked me on the shoulder. "It's Zinnia, *pendejo*!" He roared with excitement. "You're one lucky bastard, *ése*! She's fine, son!" (That was the term du jour for an attractive person. They were *fine*. A couple of years later, they would be *hot*.)

It might be the first time in my life that I experienced true vertigo. The whole hallway was spinning. Was this true? This beautiful creature who was always so funny and kind to me, this lovely girl who liked me, *really liked me*? I simply couldn't believe it. This was going to change everything.

I could already see us as a power couple in school, like a proto A-Rod and J.Lo but without the glamour and wealth. We'd look good together, no doubt. (To be sure, she was bringing the lion's share of our visual appeal, but her beauty would reflect on me.) I swooned with the possibilities but was also uneasy about the implications. Did I have to walk with her to every class now? Did I have to have lunch with her every day instead of with my Sweathog crew of misfits? No more pickup basketball after lunch? And I lived so far from town. Shit. How was I to see her after school and on weekends? And, oh God, how could I keep this a secret at home?

"So, when are you going to talk to her?" Oscar must have seen the anguish on my face.

"Today, if I can."

"Awesome, *ése*! Let me know how it goes!"

When I found Zinnia at her locker later that day, I approached her sheepishly but also with newfound confidence. She gave me the flowers, remember? I thanked her for the beautiful bouquet, and I had expected that at a bare minimum, she would be the same girl I had known to that point, but even better. Something was immediately different, however. She became almost comically shy around me. She could hardly look me in the eye. I said goodbye and that I'd see her tomorrow. But already, the bell was tolling out the doom of this relationship, not just the end of the school day.

"They were the most glorious roses that had ever been delivered to a Brown boy in the history of Brown boys."

Chapter Thirty

That night, I tried to come up with all the new things—responsibilities, to be sure—that I had to attend to, now that Zinnia was my girl. I loitered at her locker until she showed up that following morning, and I instantly picked up on her discomfort. This was the harbinger of what was to come. The more I wanted to do things for her and be near her, the more she retreated. She stopped talking to me altogether. I was getting annoyed, and in the recesses of my lizard brain, I felt that this was an elaborate practical joke at my expense. I couldn't figure out what had happened. Finally, after two agonizing weeks, I told her at her locker that I could no longer do this. I left her crying, but she still didn't talk to me.

News travels fast in a high school hallway. Oscar buttonholed me at the first chance he could, almost slamming me against the lockers. "What the fuck are you thinking, *ése*? You broke up with her?"

"She won't even talk to me! What kind of a girlfriend doesn't talk to her boyfriend?"

"She's nuts about you, dude!"

"Bullshit! She's giving me the cold shoulder at every turn, like she don't want me around. What the hell am I supposed to do?"

Oscar looked puzzled. "That don't make no sense."

"No shit."

"You want me to talk to her?" he asked, now suddenly an expert in matchmaking and conflict resolution.

"Nah, forget it. It's over, bro. *Se acabó*." Leave it to me to squander this chance. I was sure I had screwed up somehow.

And it was over. But my friendship with Zinnia was over as well. She turned hostile toward me. She soon picked up another boyfriend and went out of her way to flaunt him in front of me. When I had a moment alone with her after several of these incidents, I said the last words I would ever give her.

"I'm so happy you have a boyfriend that you're comfortable with. I tried, but I guess I wasn't good enough." I sounded like a terrible power ballad. More Winger than Guns N' Roses.

I left the beautiful Zinnia in my wake as I resisted the temptation to be "borne back ceaselessly" into my past.

Somehow, Rene had learned of this debacle through an unnamed *chismosa* parent she knew, and she unloaded on me with both barrels of buckshot. "Didn't I tell you to stay away from *mexicanas*?" she brayed one day out of the blue. "They are crazy and will do the most bizarre shit you can think of. They are trouble."

I shook my head. "This was different. I think I fucked it up somehow." (Lest the reader get the wrong impression, I had been allowed to cuss in conversation with Rene from a pretty young age. But never *at* her.) "She liked me before all this, but once she got me the flowers, she changed. But maybe I changed too."

Zinnia would not be the last Latina of Mexican heritage whom I would date, but the relationships all ended horribly. I never heeded Rene's exhortation to avoid Brown girls. I wondered how many parents still forbade their children from dating or falling for someone from a specific group. At other times when I ran across this, the incompatibility was religious rather than a matter of race or ethnicity.

And what did I ultimately find when I went digging for my ancestry using several websites billed as these great resources for discovering who you are? In the genealogy commercials, people are all like, "Wow! I had an ancestor who came over on the *Mayflower*!" Congratulations, I think. Your ancestors would go on to contribute to a lot of terrible shit to come without ever being seen as nothing other than good, God-fearing people who founded the greatest nation in the history of everything. Be proud of that terrible shit as well! Or they say, "I'm related to Thomas Jefferson!" . . . Nah, that's such low-hanging fruit I'm close to stepping on it.

What I discovered was that, as far back as I could find, my ancestors were indeed born and raised in Texas—in the San Antonio area, to be specific. Furthermore, two identifying descriptors are often attached to the names of my ancestors, either by census takers or government officials filling out marriage licenses, birth and death certificates, and other documents.

My ancestors are labeled as "White" or "Mexican," despite not being either. The indeterminacy of something that ought to be so clear ripples through the generations. Dad hated eating out when I was a kid, and I later learned that he had been forced to pick up food at the back entrance of restaurants or was refused service by fine establishments that proudly displayed signs that proclaimed NO DOGS OR MEXICANS ALLOWED. My own discomfort in settling on an identity influenced how I interacted with people, even if it wasn't an overt factor in our relationship. And my daughters now must contend with Latinx kids telling them they're not Latinas, and white kids seeing them as Brown girls all day long.

For those unambiguously white people who are frustrated by all of this, asking why they have to hear non-white, non-majority people interrogate identity perpetually, the answer is that, for people like me, every aspect of life is rendered through the filter of identity, not because we desire it, but because that filter is applied to and imposed on us whether we want it or not. People ask me, "What are you?" not "How are you?" The people who complain, "Why is everything about race?" or "We're all the same! Quit dividing us with race!" act as if we who are affected by this accident of birth and heritage were the ones who created the very social order that disadvantages us unremittingly. Zora Neale Hurston was exactly right when she said, to paraphrase, if you don't say shit when people fuck you up, they'll point to your silence as proof you liked it. (Hurston was much more elegant in her phrasing.)

Now when someone asks me, "What are you?" I say, "I'm a Texan." Sometimes, "Tejano." Or, more broadly, "Chicano."

"Oh! Texan!" they say with excitement and wonderment in their eyes. "You don't sound like a Texan!"

Chapter Thirty-One

There was a time when my destiny seemed written in the living rock, like the Decalogue, etched by a hand of fire, and it lay before me in a clear path—the way a farmer's son knows, at some point, exactly what he'll be doing for the rest of his life. If his dad was a dirt farmer, then he was going to be a goddamn dirt farmer too. In my case, I was expected to continue the tradition of cockfighting, which had been a part of my family for generations. It may sound like a joke now, but it was only going to be a matter of time before I set the cockfighting world on fire. Legends aren't born, they're made!

Someday I would breed prize gamecocks and lord over a cockfighting empire, but I had to work my way up the ladder in order to fulfill this great destiny. First, I would learn the easy stuff by doing the drudgery: feeding the animals, giving them water, cleaning their pens, holding them while their spurs were trimmed, that sort of thing. I wonder what people who have labeled me an ultraleft elitist would make of my literal blood-and-guts origins. Chicken shit on Winner's Choice shoes from Walmart and blood-covered tees must be both savage *and* elitist, I guess. Anything is possible in the good ole US of A.

Cockfighting is now illegal throughout the United States, but when I was a kid, several states continued to defend their residents' God-given right to participate in the sport, as they had since the earliest days of this nation. Those states—Arizona, Louisiana, Oklahoma, and New Mexico—promoted the long-standing tradition as an expression of cultural heritage, it seems. It was as if the states were defending the honor of this beleaguered blood sport, probably for much longer than was reasonable. If some founding father had included the right to bear cocks and fight them to the death in well-regulated arenas, chances are cockfighting would still be practiced today. It sounds like the kind of thing a far-right conservative or a libertarian would support—the type that has no compunction about slaying a wild elephant or giraffe, say, for the fuck of it. No government is gonna tell me that I can or can't fight some roosters! YOU CAN PULL MY COCK FROM MY COLD DEAD HANDS! I mean, the slogans write themselves.

The writing was unmistakably on the wall with respect to cockfighting long before I was born, and it was only a matter of time before the sport was made illegal in all fifty states. The only things left to be resolved was which state would be the last holdout, and when it would finally capitulate. That would be Louisiana, ladies and gentlemen, in 2008.

I'm certain that for most readers, cockfighting is a gruesome and disgusting abuse of animal rights, and I'm not trying to change anybody's mind about it. It is bloody. It is indeed gruesome. The roosters often die or are horribly maimed. At times, you have no choice but to put the animal out of its misery by promptly wringing its neck.

You should also know that I spent many years with these animals, raising them, caring for them. I almost came to see them as pets. This was a disaster waiting to happen, and farmers who raise livestock rightly caution their children not to get overly attached to the cow, turkey, or hog that will be putting meat on the table for many suppers to come.

Caveat: I feel that anyone who goes to the local supermarket and purchases chicken breasts and drumsticks or perhaps goes to their favorite restaurant and orders chicken salad is taking part in an inhumane industry. Hens and roosters are raised to supply capes, saddles, and hackles for pre-made fly-fishing flies. And I'm not trying to guilt you into abstaining from chicken, pork, or other animal products. I'm simply saying that, before you declare how abhorrent and disgusting cockfighting is, make sure you're not polishing off some Buffalo wings midsentence. There is plenty to be up in arms about when it comes to cockfighting, and it's not only the brutality of the fighting itself. The recklessness of degenerate gambling, the drugs at the periphery, and the bloody butchery of the birds' extraneous flesh all are excellent justifications to bring cockfighting to an end.

And, yes, free-range and organic chickens will have fewer bad days than those mass-produced animals that supply the lion's share of restaurants and grocery stores. But even the most conscientious chicken eaters (vegetarians and vegans can assume the dais of righteousness and good karma) are contributing to an industry that is arguably more inhumane than the blood sport of cockfighting. I am not here to defend cockfighting or to say that it should still be legal. When I took part in cockfighting, I was a kid, and it was legal in New Mexico.

When I became aware of it, cockfighting had turned out to be a part of my family for many generations, and I was expected to carry on the tradition. In my youth, I remembered seeing a black-and-white photograph that showed Dad and his dad, each holding a rooster. It is a photo that does the same kind of work as when someone poses with their car or some prized possession. It conveyed the idea of legacy and provenance. *We have been here a long time, and this is what we do*, the picture said to me.

In addition to the familial lineage of *galleros* (a much more elegant title than the English *cockfighters*), it is worth noting that cockfighting has strong cultural ties to Latinx cultures around the world. The sport is illegal in the United States, currently and probably forever. As president, Donald Trump extended the ban on cockfighting to include all US territories in 2018. It's ironic that for many in Puerto Rico for whom cockfighting is a way of life, their very livelihood was taken from them by a man they can't even vote for or against. Many of those countries where it still is legal happen to be Latin American, and some, such as the Philippines, are Asian. In fact, the standard fighting roosters are sometimes known as jungle fowl because they originated in tropical parts of the world. (You can already see the kinds of problems that might arise in bringing them to live and die in a semiarid land like West Texas.)

Honestly, I've never heard any Latinx person complain about cockfighting at any point in my life. It was always white people and, even more specifically, white women. When people would cry out that they were disgusted by the idea of cockfighting, I took it as a personal insult because I associated it with my family and my culture. I suppose there are Latinx peoples who hate the sport as well; cockfighting is illegal in many Latin American countries, for instance. Such Latinos have just never happened to be in my orbit. And this subject of cockfighting shows the difficulties in trying to tell cultures different from your own what practices are morally and ethically wrong. How we treat animals, unfortunately, is not a universal, and like so many other things, the mores around animal welfare are socially constructed.

When I heard mostly white people say only cruel barbarians participated in cockfighting, I always felt like they didn't know what the fuck they were talking about. My family revered these animals, even at the expense of their own well-being. Contrary to dogfighting, in which we never participated, we generally saw fighting cocks as a way to work with the fowl's genetic predisposition to fight. For us, the birds held a kind of allure and were worthy of adulation. Our dogs invariably took on the role of house pet or a kind of guard dog. My complaints over how my family might have treated those dogs traced back to their ignorance in keeping them constantly tethered to a chain or penned in an enclosure that was far too small. We would never do that today.

Anyway, in a number of countries, cockfighting is still a proud pastime and the source of much-venerated cultural traditions. Because many Latinos in the United States still have close and strong ties to their nation of origin, cockfighting continues to be a significant aspect of Latinx culture. And even though it is illegal to own or breed fighting roosters in some states, or even to own cockfighting paraphernalia, it still occurs. For instance, while it is a felony to fight roosters in Texas, you may raise and sell gamecocks to your clientele who, what, don't fight them?

As one might expect of the many things that were once legal and then made illegal, cockfighting has gone behind fences and out of sight. Texas made cockfighting illegal many years ago, and it, like other states, is constantly tweaking the laws, which are inconsistent at a national level. States' rights, I guess. So, back in the day, my family, I assume, took part in these underground groups that would fight roosters at people's homes, in their backyards, and at other unadvertised venues. In the right circles, word traveled quickly.

A huge part of cockfighting is, no surprise, gambling. While there is pride and bragging rights in having roosters that can win, frankly, it's a form of gambling like dog racing, dogfighting, horse racing, and other betting events that involve animals. Even when it was legal in New Mexico, I remember attending cockfighting tournaments, which are called derbies (horse racing has derbies as well—think of the Kentucky Derby), and at specific locations that were chosen for these tournaments, I remember quite clearly the large signs that unambiguously would insist that wagering on the fights was illegal:

UNDER NO CIRCUMSTANCES IS ANY FORM OF GAMBLING PERMITTED AT THIS LOCATION! It all seemed to me such a farce because everyone was obviously gambling.

You would place your bets, sometimes before you had even entered the arena—the cockpit—and the moment you entered the pit with a rooster and your opponent, shouts from the crowd would cascade from the cheap bleachers, wagers that would typically go something like this: "I got twenty-five, twenty! Twenty-five, twenty?" Meaning they would take your twenty-dollar bet and entice you to take their twenty-five. They win, you pay twenty dollars. But you win, and they pay you twenty-five. That was so confusing to me as a kid. And people would outright say, "I have fifty dollars," on this particular bird and, "Who wants to take that bet?" "Five hundred dollars on that red bird!" And so, the bets would be placed.

The gambling was all quite out in the open; nothing hidden about it either. So as a kid, I never understood the purpose of the signs. Of course, now I understand it was CYA (cover your ass) so that the proprietors of these arenas could claim that they had posted signs and they were shocked—*shocked!*—to see any gambling happening in their establishment. Everyone ignored the signs, and though my family took great enjoyment in our roosters, there is no question that the major allure of cockfighting was the opportunity to make money, but with the pride associated with gambling on one's own birds. It was the opposite of Pete Rose, who may have bet on baseball but never bet on his own team, he claims. In contrast, we were betting on our birds to win it all.

"I got twenty-five, twenty! Twenty-five, twenty?"

Chapter Thirty-Two

When I was a child in Lubbock—I lived there through my second-grade year, after which I only visited a few weeks at a time at most—I remember there being two roosters in our backyard. Each had its own coop, and often someone (probably Dad) would put each rooster on a tether, with one end fixed to a leg and the other end tied to an anchor—kind of like the ones you can get at a pet shop to temporarily tether a dog.

I had learned the hard way not to get too close to these roosters. Unlike goofy Foghorn Leghorn caricatures, these roosters brooked no bullshit whatsoever. If you got too close, their hackles—that is, their neck feathers— would flare out and the roosters would lunge toward me. They were mean and I disliked them immensely.

I didn't see many roosters until we lived in Lovington, New Mexico, which is about a hundred miles, or a little under two hours west of Lubbock. Rene was getting settled in Lovington, at the time booming in large measure due to the oil industry of the early 1980s and its proximity to the Permian Basin, a great reservoir of oil hidden deep within an otherwise forbidding land. Of course, ranching was the other major industry in the area. Today, Lovington is not known for much beyond being the hometown of NFL Hall of Famer Brian Urlacher, who was a freshman when I graduated from high school.

Rene had purchased a trailer house on ten acres of land about seven miles north of town, and she used the trailer as a means of enticing first her younger brother, Tom, and then her parents to move away from Lubbock. Tom joined her, and then we all moved, keeping up our small Lubbock home as best we could from afar. What we should have done was rented it out, but I guess we weren't savvy or trusting enough to do that. And not long after we made the move for good, little complexes of chicken coops and rooster pens started to show up, until we had dozens upon dozens of birds. I guess I was too small to pay attention to the changes as they happened, but unexpectedly it seemed to me that there were all these roosters and chickens and chicks and pullets and hens and stags on our land. And I noticed the roosters were the mean kind—the kind that loved to fight.

What I learned rather quickly was that not all roosters were inherently mean-spirited. Many would as soon run away from you if you approached—they are chickens, after all. But a few would not hesitate to charge you, even though they were all of five or six pounds. These were known as manfighters. One might think a manfighter would be the best kind of fighting rooster. But imagine this animal with razor blades or spikes on its spurs impulsively turning on its human handler, and you can quickly reckon the outcome. Just deserts, some might say. Definitely, it was a hazard that came with the occupation.

Tom and Dad were passionate about cockfighting. Like many hobbies, it cost a great deal of money and required huge portions of your time. David had shown interest at one point, but it turned out he was more interested in getting married and having children. Robert was always a blunt instrument and lacked the finesse needed. Plus, he had a sadistic streak with animals that was at times too intense for the rest of us, so it was no wonder that he was not much interested in cockfighting. I watched him once defy Mom—who'd asked him to take a stray kitten for a ride, which was our phrase for taking an animal many miles away (probably to the dump) and leaving it there—with disastrous results.

This kitten had made our home its home. I'm sure it was only about six to eight months old. It was a dark male tabby with big green eyes, and it had a funny disposition. Cute but mischievous, which describes almost every kitten out there, I suppose. We generally liked cats around because they were mousers and kept down the vermin on the farm. But we also didn't want the cats killing the chickens—especially the little ones.

Unfortunately, while we had a menagerie of animals, sometimes the cartoons are correct in showing that putting them close together is not a good idea. This little tabby had gotten a taste for feathers, and it had already polished off a few chicks on the property. We knew what happened to animals—dogs or cats, that killed chickens or roosters. They didn't last too long. Mom herself had seen this kitten pounce playfully on a chick at least once, and she wanted it gone rather than have its little life end through no real fault of its own except for stumbling into our house of horrors. She ordered Robert to go on a mission. I was in my early teens by then, so Robert had to have been a legal adult. The age matters here, I think. Robert was no kid at the time.

The trouble was that Mom and Robert were already beefing about her having told him to do something several times, and he hadn't done it yet. Arguments and beefs happened so regularly in the family that it could have been almost anything. I don't think Robert had been doing his part around the house, and Mom jumped on him for it. Whatever it was, I was going to have to help him. And in this specific case, we had to go take the full burn barrels to the dump. We burned our trash on that property because we didn't have trash service so far out. We had several fifty-gallon drums that we used to burn our trash. Eventually these would fill with compacted ash, and we would have to take them to the dump. These barrels were heavy, heavier if it had rained recently, and it was always a multi-person job.

Well, we had to do it, and Robert had been putting it off. He's the guy who loves to talk shit but hates it when he's the butt of the joke or object of scorn. He gives it, but he can't take it. I was rather enjoying watching Mom ream his ass for being a lazy fuck, which wasn't something we could always say to him, because he often did work hard and could do hard work.

Now he was annoyed, humiliated, and angry. But it's Mom, so what could he do? I went outside, shivered in the crisp cold of November dusk, and waited for him to come out so we could get this shit over with. It was getting dark, and the sun had already set. We had maybe half an hour before we would be doing this with flashlights and headlights, and no one wanted to be out in the middle of nowhere emptying barrels full of ash without enough light.

The dump was literally an expansive caliche pit about five miles to our east that people in the area threw their garbage into; it wasn't an actual municipal landfill run by a town department. Rene would get in trouble shortly thereafter because not all the trash had been fully burned, and remnants of junk mail with her name on it were discovered by state environmental people. We would go there for fun sometimes to see what other people had tossed out, or to use wrecked appliances as target practice. Now Robert would drive us out there memorably one more time.

As he was walking out, Mom added from within, as a cherry on top, "Oh, and go take that fucking *gatito* for a ride like I goddamned told you a hundred fucking times!" That wasn't a problem or any added burden. Why? Because we were going to the fucking dump anyway! We would leave the kitten there and drive off. I was sure that, before long, the kitten would come back, even though the dump was several miles away.

But I saw that look in Robert's eyes and knew trouble was brewing. And the kitten! Of all times, it decided to come right out and stand before Robert. I saw it happen in an instant before anyone even moved. I knew what he was going to do. He always had a perverse streak with animals.

He reached down to snatch the kitten, lifted it as high as he could, and slammed it onto the cinder block sidewalk with all his might. The little tabby gave one plosive shriek, and it was silent forever after. It amazes me how certain sounds can imprint on your memory for all time. I will never be able to forget the last sound that kitten made on this earth. That is my curse for not doing more to try to save it.

That may be the first time I ever screamed, "*No!*" like in a movie. I think I even threw my hands up into the air, hoping he would stop. When it was over, I cussed him out: "You sorry motherfucker! You goddamned fucking bastard!" I tried to come up with as many combinations of curses as I could muster. "You fucking dumb cocksucker!"

Mom heard the commotion and stormed outside. I didn't wait for her to ask. "HE KILLED THE KITTY! HE . . . HE . . . HE JUST SLAMMED IT!"

Robert was too big for Mom to spank or beat, but she had other ways to castigate and humble a person. He was a grown-ass man still living with his parents and sister, so he wasn't as much of a badass as he thought. I could tell Mom was furious, and when she was furious, she got quiet and might even cry. "You're going to pay for that," she said as she squinted her eyes and ground her teeth, but in Spanish: "*Lo vas a pagar.*"

"You wanted the cat gone. Now it's gone."

"*Cabrón,*" she whispered. "God will punish you. He won't forget," but in Spanish. "*Dios te va a castigar.*" Then she went inside.

That shut us both up. I picked up the broken kitten, and I felt a piece of me was broken as well. It wasn't even my kitten, merely a little tabby that didn't deserve what had happened to it. It was so soft, and still warm. I refused to put it in the barrels full of ash. I placed it in the bed of the truck, away from the barrels, and when we got to the dump, I hopped out before the engine had died and carried the kitty to a place where I thought it might rest comfortably. Then I helped Robert with the barrels as fast as I could, though I could not seem to work fast enough to get away from him as swiftly as I wanted.

A few years later, Robert was head over heels about Rottweilers. That's all he could talk about. He wanted one, and he had to find a breeder. Still living at home with us, he found a breeder in Lovington, an older Black gentleman Rene knew. Robert named the pup Brutus, and he was as tender with that animal as anyone has ever been with a dog. He didn't want it to use for fighting or anything like that; he simply adored it. It was interesting to watch, especially since I had witnessed a lot of animal cruelty at my uncle-brother's hands.

But Mom's old curse came back in force when Brutus got sick, and nothing Robert did—visits to the vet, spending every waking hour with Brutus, even praying—helped that dog. Robert cried real tears for Brutus, which showed that he wasn't a total monster. It surprised me because the only times I'd ever seen him cry was when he was binge drinking mescal or Presidente brandy.

"Sorry about Brutus," I said one bright afternoon as Robert finished refilling the hole he had dug for the dog's grave. I tried to be careful with my words, but I also wanted to be sure of what I was about to tell him. "I think it's true what they say. What you take from others will be taken from you. You weren't always the friendliest to animals, and now an animal you loved was taken from you. Funny how that works." I walked away before he could register what I had said and hit me with the shovel.

So, of course Robert wasn't going to be the keeper of the cockfighting flame. That left little ole me to take my rightful place as the one who would carry on the family tradition. Only I didn't know it until I neared puberty.

Chapter Thirty-Three

Once I understood the birds were neither pets nor livestock for our own consumption, I quickly came to admire them. You can instantly tell a fighting rooster because it will be dubbed; that is, freed from its coxcomb (that iconic piece of flesh atop a rooster's head) and wattles (more seemingly extraneous flesh where you might imagine a rooster's jawline). A dubbed rooster is magnificent to behold, and one wonders why they were not thus designed or did not evolve this way on their own. The removal of those fleshy features gave the bird a sleek profile, more like a raptor and less like a cartoon. Only the turkey with its snood tops the chicken for such a ridiculous bit of unnecessary flesh on its head.

There is a practical reason for removing this flesh from the rooster. In a cockfight, the roosters use their beaks to latch on to their opponent, which gives them leverage to shuffle and use their spurs to puncture the other bird and cause serious damage. The coxcomb and wattles make for excellent things to latch on to. Without them, it becomes harder for a rooster to "take hold" of its rival. The rooster's natural spurs are trimmed to a blunt edge about half an inch long (these would be measured), and the specific weapon would be slipped over the rooster's trimmed spurs, which are wrapped in a very sticky kind of electrical tape. The weapons are secured at last with waxed twine.

Other than my first experiences feeding chicks and frequently giving them fresh water, my initiation into the cockfighting world was holding the rooster during the dubbing process, as well as during the spur-trimming sessions. Holding the rooster was an art form that required courage, a high tolerance for pain, and extraordinary stoicism. If I could have turned into stone while holding the rooster, I would have done my job perfectly.

First, even the gentlest rooster has an affinity for pecking and biting. When you hold one, you kind of hold it as you would a football—in the crook of your arm so its body rests on your forearm, and with its head almost lying against your lower biceps. The rooster, annoyed at being held, will peck and bite you unceasingly. Think of the rooster's beak as a pair of sharp, strong tweezers or, better yet, pliers. Yes, that's it: needle-nose pliers. If the beak opens wide and it grabs a healthy amount of flesh, then you are likely good to go. But if the beak does not open wide, it will sometimes grab only a small bit of flesh, which is agonizing.

For days, I would have these bruises along one of my arms (usually the left), and they never, ever, gave cause for a girl to ask me what was going on with my arm; nor did they make me more alluring as a kind of bad boy. I probably looked more like some freak crackhead or heroin junkie.

Further, the birds were often undergoing a procedure that required no small degree of care. When I held them, I had to be uncompromisingly still. I got better, but it was damn well a struggle when I was starting out because it fucking hurts to be pinched in the arm by needle-nose pliers. You probably have some lying around. Give it a try and see what you think.

Without question, the most gruesome aspect of cockfighting wasn't the fighting itself. It was the dubbing, which entailed cutting whole chunks of flesh from a rooster's head while the bird is not anesthetized. That means they had to feel the pain of that procedure. Quentin Tarantino's iconic torture scene in *Reservoir Dogs* is a nice analogue. Cutting off a coxcomb must be like severing a human ear. Sure, you may not strictly need it. But it's a large piece of flesh taken from the head, no matter how you want to look at it.

There I would be, holding the poor devil of a rooster as steady as I could. In doing so, you have to hold its body, keep its legs steady, and secure its wings to keep them from flapping. Tom would take the extraneous flesh in one hand and trim it away with extremely sharp scissors. With fucking *scissors*! I still remember them. Later he got fancy surgical-style scissors, but for most of my youth, he had a small pair of Fiskars with brown handles. He was livid once when I cut some paper with them, and rightly so. The brown-handled scissors were to be used only for dubbing.

Tom was like a barber of old, performing bloody butchery on our jungle fowl. Those moments were my first real sustained experience with blood— the tang of its smell, its stickiness after mixing with the air. For a time, the blood was overwhelming, but thankfully, I was unmoved by the sight of it, even my own. And I saw plenty of blood, even though dubbing roosters was almost seasonal in that you did it intensely for a week or two and then you wouldn't have to worry about it for a while. My experiences might have been different if I had graduated to being the bloody butcher himself and not the rooster holder.

Chapter Thirty-Four

Tom was actually Tomás González Jr., Mom and Dad's firstborn son and younger brother to Rene. As with all Rene's brothers, I thought of Tom as my own sibling. But he was almost old enough to be my father, so he was this intriguing mix of father, uncle, and brother. He would joke about our strange relationship and say that he was my uncle-mother's-brother's-fucker, and we would all laugh when he said it.

He was the brains of all the boys. Never formally trained in anything, he was a crafty jack-of-all-trades, excelling in such disparate pursuits as fine art, bricklaying, carpentry, electrical, plumbing, sculpting, jewelry making, agrarian efforts, animal science, genetics, and, of course, cockfighting. He was also Mr. Fix It, the one we all went to if something was broken. In that sense, he was a kind of Renaissance man, and I can say that in the truest sense because he was, at his core, an artist. He would draw and paint beautiful, intricate works without having pursued formal studies. When I was a kid, I always saw Tom first and foremost as a visual artist. In my kid's parlance, he could fucking draw.

Tom was also a roving Gargantua, with a wide belly and a great black beard, very much in tune with his hedonistic side and indulging it whenever he could. He is still the fastest drinker I have ever seen in person, with essentially the ability to open up his throat and pour beer and wine down the hatch as fast as it could issue from its container. He "could consume mass quantities," as the Coneheads were fond of repeating, and it was through him that I learned of life's most salacious and forbidden things. In that sense, he was like a father but mostly like the favorite uncle who shows you naughty pictures or lets you drink whiskey straight from the bottle, smiling proudly when you take a huge, big-boy swig.

Honestly, Dad was already too advanced in years (and not in the best of health) to actually be like a dad to me. He was more of a figurehead, someone to look up to, but he was never going to come out and shoot hoops with me or talk to me about how to practice safe sex. I'm being deliberately coy about this, but Tom was the one who overtly modeled a kind of machismo to me—how to view and treat women. As you might imagine, it made for a skewed and unhelpful example. His sage advice that you simply had to pull out during sex right before you came, because the air "neutralized" or killed the sperm and thus you couldn't get a woman pregnant . . . was typical of the howlers he often preached. So, even as a kid, I had a healthy suspicion of all the advice on love and sex imparted to me by Tom—a guy who never married, never had a long-term relationship, and whose experiences with women always ended in disaster.

Once, a woman almost shot and killed him. He was with some woman he was working hard to date, showing off a prized handgun while driving down Thirty-fourth Avenue in Lubbock one summer. This event was surely laden with meaning and symbolism. I saw the bullet hole in our truck's passenger seat and the exit hole underneath the chassis of the Ford F-150 after it happened. He had a devil of a time explaining this to Mom and Dad because it was their truck. But I had seen the woman, and she was quite attractive. I understand how easily Tom had lost his reason and nearly gotten himself killed. As they were driving, Tom thought it would be a good idea to take out the .45 and let this woman handle it. She didn't know it was loaded, and while they sat at a red light, she lifted it toward him. He slammed the gun into the seat, and it went off. *Bam!* Tom was often so close to catastrophe when it came to women, and this moment was almost his last and best example.

But with roosters, there was no greater authority than Tom. Dubbing was a bloody mess of an undertaking, and it was always unpleasant, even if the result left the roosters looking beautiful and striking once their scabs had healed. Yet it was always straight butchery, until Tom took to digging into the knowledge of animal husbandry. He began reading farmer's almanacs and other publications like *The Gamecock* for ways to make cockfighting more of a scientific pursuit.

In one of these almanacs, he discovered that during a certain phase of the moon, the blood of the rooster was mostly in its feet. (Even to my preteen brain, that seemed impossible—like talking about human health in terms of the four humors.) At such times, and especially by the light of the moon at night, if you dubbed the roosters accordingly, they would hardly bleed at all. Though I wouldn't outright mock Tom about anything concerning roosters—he had become the resident authority for a reason—I was certain this was complete and utter bullshit. Literal lunacy, because we had to now do this complicated and gruesome task by fucking moonlight—as if we were reading moon letters on an ancient scroll in Tolkien's Middle-earth. What we were doing felt *that* antiquated and fantastical.

He had been raving about this technique, building it up like it was major news. I was in the fifth grade, and even I was doubtful. We observed the phases of the moon with the awkwardness of ignorant stargazers, even though his copy of the *Farmers' Almanac* told him exactly, almost to the hour, when he should do this operation.

It was dark, but we had the benefit of a large sodium-vapor lamp at the northwest corner of our ten acres, which is where the bulk of the rooster pens were. The bluish-white light was barely enough to see by, and it felt like the kind of skulduggery you'd read about in a Sherlock Holmes story. Maybe something like "The Case of the Bloody Cocks by Moonlight." Tom had his kit, which included his trusty scissors, peroxide, and something to stanch the blood, like crushed chalk. I was ready to hold these birds as I always did, expecting nothing to be different from before.

"Well, let's see what happens," Tom said simply enough as he began to cut into the first bird of the evening. He was nearly done cutting the coxcomb, when I saw the top of the wound looked pale, the way the fat on an uncooked steak looks white and gristly. I stared at it—we both did—and to my utter amazement, the amputation bled only a few almost-imperceptible drops.

"It fucking worked?" I blurted out in wonder.

"I told you, kid. I know what the fuck I'm doing."

"Well, let's see about the next one." I was big on the scientific method at the time, thanks to my school lessons, and I knew once didn't prove a goddamn thing. Or as Sir Mix-a-Lot said, *One time's got no case.*

But with each rooster we dubbed that evening, we noticed there was virtually no blood. Now, that's cold comfort to those roosters that endured the pain. It had to hurt them. If someone cut off my ear, I'd be in agony for weeks. But these birds would look like normal almost as soon as we were done with them.

From that night on, Tom was the undisputed mage of the cockfighting business in the Llano Estacado, and soon people from all kinds of identity groups came to the property to learn from him. When I saw this, my respect for Tom grew immensely.

Chapter Thirty-Five

I learned all sorts of things as a cockfighter in training. I would come home from school, and I'd have to go check to see if any eggs had been laid. I had to keep them organized and clearly marked. For the first few days, I would rotate the eggs in their cartons; then at some point, they went into an incubator in our trailer house in Lovington. The middle room came to be devoted solely to the production of baby chicks, and it lost all functionality as a bedroom. Another reason why most of us didn't have a room of our own.

I learned about genetics before school introduced me to Punnett squares, how certain breeds could be crossed with others, hoping for inheritable traits, and more. For us, nearly all tendencies and personality quirks were inheritable. If a rooster tended to run headlong into the fight, that was inheritable. If the rooster had a style of shuffling their legs and thus spurs—maybe they shuffled low or they broke high and shuffled while elevated in the air—that was all a trait that you could perfect through breeding. This idea was so intoxicating in my family that we believed genetics could account for all aspects of an individual's personality. It was our version of the Myers-Briggs Type Indicator, and it, along with an unswerving belief in astrology, sun signs, the horoscope, made all of us into easily reducible types that robbed us of free will and agency. See, you were destined to be X because of your genetics and how the heavenly bodies were aligned at the moment of your birth. I have always hated that shit. Fatalism, to me, is like giving up on life.

I learned that a chick hatches in a blazing twenty-one days, and Tom showed me how to check for bad eggs by putting a shoebox with a small hole cut on top over the bare bulb of a lamp. I'd set an egg on this makeshift light box and marvel at the egg's microcosm. We would check the egg every few days, and it was amazing to me how the chick developed so fast.

We would mark them almost as soon as they hatched by piercing the webbing between their toes, with certain combinations indicating the breed or cross for that season. As they matured, we could then figure out the genealogy of the roosters and chickens by referring to the markings on their feet.

Some would develop into roosters that were destined to fight, if they were good enough. And how would you distinguish a rooster with good fighting potential from one that didn't have it? Well, you sparred them! (Cockfighting picks up a lot of terminology from boxing.) Sparring the roosters took up the bulk of our time. And whenever we had interested family members or friends visiting (or Tom's acolytes paying a call), we invariably had to spar roosters and show off. Naturally, Tom and Dad loved it. Me? I'd rather be playing *Castlevania* or *Ninja Gaiden* on Nintendo. I was killing it on *Metroid*. But I'd have to help, and they saw sparring as an opportunity for me to learn how to "handle" roosters.

Here, handling has a very specific connotation. The handler was the guy (almost *always* a guy) who literally carried and handled the rooster during a fight. He usually was the one to affix the weapons, have the bird weighed (as in boxing, roosters of the same weight were matched against one another), and they were the ones who had to master every rule and strategy available to them in order to win. The handler is almost as important as the rooster in winning fights. They can also cheat, so other handlers are compelled to keep their counterparts honest.

One thing I must clarify is that cockfighting never made roosters want to fight. This again had to do with breeding. Either a rooster is born a fighter, or it isn't. Unlike dogs, which must be abused to make them fight and be aggressive, roosters are made that way. We never abused a rooster in order to make it more aggressive or a better fighter. Yes, the dubbing is awful, but that happens with many other domestic animals, even dogs and cats. Ears are trimmed. Tails are cut. Claws are pulled. But I've heard journalists report on cockfighting, and imply that we beat or abused the roosters to get them to fight. I've seen baby chicks mimic fights, and they've never been near an adult fight in their short lives. It is a defining trait of these fowl. If you put twenty roosters in a cage with no human in sight, it would be a bloody battle royal.

Anyway, when we sparred roosters, we would slip what looked like tiny boxing gloves over their spurs. The sparring was evaluative, but we also didn't want serious damage to come to the roosters. Typically, the sparring session would be very quick—less than a minute.

I came to be fascinated with these roosters, and as they got older, we would give them names. I remember Pretty Boy, a Democrat (that was the breed name; I assure you he never voted), who had maroon-colored hackle feathers and white legs. He was an elegant chap who won often and lived into old age. And the Harold Brown, who bore the name of his breed, named after some guy called Harold Brown. Many breeds are named after a person, ostensibly the one to innovate the breed—Kelso, McClanahan, and so on. Other breeds like Hatch, Roundhead, Brown Red, and Grey all had unique physical characteristics. Hatch always had such a fighting, indominable spirit that it became a shorthand for gumption or courage. The Grey variety was instantly recognizable, thanks to its bright yellow hackles, as if it were blond. In Spanish, we called Greys *giros*. And thus, when David had a son whose mother was white, a son who was fair skinned and blond, he was given the nickname Giro, and much to his chagrin, that's what the family calls him today.

The Harold Brown was large and had a pumpkin-colored neck. He was mean and I didn't like him. They kind of had names like professional wrestlers, which probably isn't so surprising. One was called the Maniac, because he was another one of these goddamn manfighters. He was the rare white rooster with black spots. He won us a lot of money because no one bets on a white rooster—its color was said to betray cowardice and a tendency to run soon after the fight started. But the Maniac was a winner and lived until old age. He, along with hens of the same breed, produced beautiful chicks that were silver in color. We called them Silver Bullets, and I took ownership of these white roosters because even though they won, everyone was conditioned to bet against them. Their defiance against expectations resonated powerfully with me, as I always resisted scripts that didn't apply.

Chapter Thirty-Six

Once I turned twelve and was old enough to be allowed into the derbies, I became a greater help to Tom and Dad during the fights. We lost a lot, but we won enough to keep alive the fantasy that this was something that could sustain the family in perpetuity, like some sort of business. Tom was always in charge, and with a big black felt cowboy hat on his head, he was a great handler to my uninitiated eyes. We often competed in gaff fights (where the roosters have curved spikes on both their spurs), and later, Tom did more with what they called slasher fights (the roosters had one short, curved knife like a razor on a single spur).

The fights themselves varied wildly. Sometimes they would be over at the first engagement of the roosters. The referee would call "Pit!" (that's like saying "Go!") and the handlers had to release their birds on a line scratched into the dirt at a precise distance from the other rooster. The referee was there to tell the handlers when they could grab their roosters—typically when the gaff or knife was stuck. The handler whose bird was impaled had to remove the opponent's weapon from their own animal to ensure no further damage was inflicted by a cheating handler. Other times, the fights dragged on forever, and usually at least one of the roosters was on the brink of death, if not both. These fights would be moved to a drag pit that was much smaller than the main pit.

Not all birds die quickly or instantly. So, how are winners determined? There is a count system, and points are awarded by the referee. These are known as Wortham's Rules, and they are like the official rules in something like boxing, like the old-timey Queensbury Rules. The last rooster to make a legitimate hit on its opponent before the fight must be handled. (Meaning, when the roosters' weapons are hung up and the birds are essentially clinched, the ref will cry out, "Handle that!" and the handlers will, indeed, handle it.) One bird will have the count (having made the last hit), and the ref counts to twenty. As he is counting, the handler is working his rooster like the corner men for a boxer. He puts pressure on wounds to stop bleeding, he rubs them in a way that seems to reenergize the rooster, or maybe he puts his mouth on the bird's neck or back and breathes on it the way someone would warm their own cold hands. I once saw Tom lick a rooster's eyes to get dirt and grit out of them. (It worked!) When the twenty seconds are up, they place the birds on their respective lines and let go when the referee calls out, "Pit!"

Now the strategy, for the rooster that doesn't have the count, is for it to break the count, which is done by the rooster making a fighting move or strike against the opponent. This can go back and forth for an excruciatingly long time. The rooster that can successfully make it to three consecutive counts is declared the winner.

This kind of system allows for some weird shit. For instance, I've seen the following, which isn't that rare: A rooster, mortally wounded and fading fast, will make a desperate attempt at its opponent, gaining the count. The other rooster is hardly scathed and is by all accounts about to be the winner. But the lively rooster is no longer interested; it thinks it has won the contest. But the dying bird has the count. Imagine the handler desperately trying to get his rooster to engage and hit the dying bird one last time. But, nope. It's no longer interested. The essentially dead bird will die a winner.

Among the ghastlier sights at a derby are the infamous barrels filled with dead roosters. Most reports that position cockfighting as a menace to society typically fixate on the weapons and this ubiquitous barrel where dead roosters are deposited. Sometimes the reports emphasize that some of the roosters are still alive. While I have never seen that, it may be that the roosters are so close to death that the owner doesn't bother tending to their wounds.

I once watched Tom go through a backbreaking fight handling a bird he was quite fond of. When he lost, he refused to throw the rooster's body in the barrel. That bird at least deserved to come back home with us, was Tom's thinking. And it did.

As it happened, I never got the opportunity to be a handler in an actual derby. I didn't want to do it, and I think my reluctance finally became obvious as I was doing better and better in high school track and field. My path was going to lead me away from home and from the roosters. My destiny had been altered, and I was the one who rewrote it.

That didn't deter Tom, who seemed to replace me with protégés who hung on his every word. As it happened, they were white guys desperate to get into cockfighting. This shook me because I had grown up believing the sport was a Latino thing. All the Mexican movies about cockfighting had led me to conclude this. Vicente Fernández and Antonio Aguilar were like cockfighting superheroes—patron saints to a grueling and undoubtedly controversial endeavor. To see these white guys so into cockfighting was as confusing to me as seeing Anglo-Americans rise in the ranks of *lucha libre*. One of them had ridden the school bus with me daily and was a few years older. (He had a younger sister about my age who was so far out of my league she was in fucking interstellar space.) They essentially took my place, these white boys, and Tom kept fighting and, often, winning. He took on the entry name Pig Money, which had nothing to do with pigs or hogs. It simply meant "dirty money," or that "money for nothing" Dire Straits sang about.

When I left for college, Tom continued the cockfighting game, always trying to get better, with White Boy Steve and White Boy Brian at his side. Later, it would be David's oldest son, Eric a.k.a. Giro. Giro almost became a son to Tom. For a guy who never had kids of his own, he sure gathered some foster sons to him and was in many ways more of a father to me and Giro than our biological ones.

I didn't mind that I had been supplanted, usurped; it was better than being the reason my family gave up a tradition that had been a central fixture of our identity for generations. Tom continued even after Dad died in June 2001, and right up to his own death in February 2004. He was buried in a T-shirt with lettering on it, the kind that is hot-pressed onto the fabric. It was a shirt he had worn often at derbies and elsewhere. It said, THEY CALL ME MR. PIG MONEY!

A whole lot of knowledge went with him when Tom died, and his death made our history of cockfighting exactly that: a thing of the past. I was happy to see it go. But did it have to take my brother's-mother's-uncle's-fucker with it? Of all my family members who have died, he is the one who went far too soon. He, too, was a Big Scary Brown Guy, and a lot of me—the good and the bad—is a credit to him, because we Big Scary Brown Guys have to stick together.

Book III

Chapter Thirty-Seven

When I was a kid, and Robert and I would go out in public, he always made me talk for the both of us. Mind you, he's two months shy of being seven years older than me, and he has always been bigger. In our youth, the size disparity was even greater. He was probably six feet four inches and 285 pounds in the ninth grade. I've never been 285 pounds in my life.

One of the more significant differences between us is that he has hazel eyes, bordering on green depending on the light source, and very fair skin, such that many people mistake him for being white. I've never been confused for a white guy, at least not by white people, and if anything, people might mistakenly assume I'm Black. Robert's "whiteness," which he uses whenever he can and reminds me of often, precludes his membership in the Big Scary Brown Guy club. And he's fine with that, as am I.

My uncle-brother had always been Bobby to all of us in the family, but today he prefers the more adult-sounding Robert. (We'll sometimes call him Bobby or else Bob, which also sounds kind of mature, because old habits die hard.) Named after Senator Robert F. Kennedy, assassinated a few months before his birth, this guy—literally born with blond hair, basically an Infinity Stone for Latinx people—could not find the courage to speak to strangers—any strangers, even Latinos. Sometimes if they spoke Spanish only, he was *especially* uncomfortable around Latinos.

It used to be that if we went to the store to get something and needed help from an employee, he'd say to me: "You talk to them."

"No. You do it." In my mind, he was older and therefore should've taken charge of the situation.

"You talk to them," he would insist. "You're smarter." Very likely true, but I hate how he played that card so often. We all had our own burdens to carry, so why did I have to take on Robert's as well?

I relented every time: "Fine. Fuck it," I'd say eventually.

And lest the reader get the wrong impression, Robert speaks far better English than Spanish, so it's not as if I needed to translate for us. But in a way, having to speak on his behalf all the time allowed me to get over any innate fear of public speaking I myself might have had. It's not always easy for a Brown person to speak up in public. As I got older, I found that I excelled in public-speaking situations. Perhaps I became better at it because Robert so often refused. So, who's winning now?

That's the way it always was, though, and sometimes I had to talk us out of a bind because Robert would freeze as though Medusa had given him bedroom eyes. Like the afternoon we were lost in Albuquerque, minutes before one of the biggest moments of my life (to that point):

The New Mexico 3A and 4A
High School Track and Field Championships
Albuquerque, NM
May 1993

I had already accepted a full ride to Blinn College in Brenham, Texas, eight hours from where I lived. At that time, Blinn College, a community college sandwiched between Austin and Houston, perhaps improbably, had one of the greatest assemblies of collegiate talent in American track and field. While at Blinn, Samuel Matete had won the World Championship in 1991 in the 400-meter hurdles and, later, an Olympic silver medal in the same event in 1996. James Beckford of Jamaica, who would go on to take the Olympic silver medal in the long jump behind Carl Lewis in 1996, was in my cohort of incoming freshmen—as was sprinter Tim Montgomery, a troubled future Olympian and onetime world record holder in the 100-meter dash; and Eric Thomas, a future Olympic 400-meter hurdler. I hoped to show the Blinn coaches what I could do in my event of choice, the Boys' AAA shot put competition at my state meet, where I was heavily favored.

Unlike Robert, who won the selfsame event four consecutive times when he was in high school, I was looking at my best chance—my only chance, my last chance—at being state champion. I'd squandered my opportunity the year before, taking home a silver and a bronze medal, and I wanted to prove that I could win at the state level. I had worked so hard to win this specific competition, and Robert had become my de facto event coach by then—to the everlasting annoyance of my actual coach, here named Coach Clement. Having already broken Robert's own school record twice in the last few weeks and setting the district shot put record (both of which still stand as of this writing), I was aiming to break the state record once and for all.

For all Robert's precocious and preternatural strength and ability, this state record had eluded him, and I had been the designated champion to rectify this unfortunate circumstance. But what it had boiled down to for me was that I never had a real chance at four consecutive state championships; I could best Robert only by breaking records that had always remained tantalizingly close but forever beyond his grasp. My strategy would be to lay claim to what he couldn't, and it was working so far.

As it was, Robert could not (and still cannot) keep from mentioning how great a champion he was in his high school days. Whenever he goes on about it, I say to him that he's Al Bundy from *Married . . . with Children*, who often bragged about his glory days, when he scored four touchdowns in one game and won the last city championship trophy for Polk High. In this respect, Robert also peaked in high school (albeit a hell of a peak), having never had a meaningful competition after the age of eighteen. At least that's my rejoinder when he constantly brings up his high school championships and his All-America accolade in his junior year. He always mentions that he is an All-American, to this day. Even though I had farther throws than he did and ranked higher nationally when comparing our respective best years (my senior and his junior year), he has a plaque that states he was All-America. I don't.

The problem, as I outlined before, was that Robert and I were currently driving aimlessly in Albuquerque. We had left the stadium with plenty of time before the shot put competition. The plan was to get out of the heat and find some needed distraction. So, we were off to pick up shit that I didn't need: Gatorade, granola bars, fruit, who knows what the fuck. Maybe it was simply diversion. I had been in the stadium too long and I needed to clear my head. The pressure was on, not only to win but to crush that long-standing state record besides.

Truth be told, I don't know why we left the stadium in the first place. Yes, I could feel the heightened expectations, but I had made great strides in handling pressure the entire season. A few weeks earlier, at Ruidoso, New Mexico, one of my warm-up throws blasted past the sixty-five-foot line—had it been launched in competition and not in warm-ups, it would have been among the farthest throws in the nation that year. In my junior year, I had choked in the shot put competition, allowing myself to get beaten in what was something like an out-of-body experience. I was better than these guys! What the fuck was I doing? It was a strange sensation, as if my body had forgotten what it needed to do. Like those dreams where you run in slow motion or can't seem to move as normal, only this was real life. And though it's not the same at all, I'm reminded of how Simone Biles described her case of "the twisties." She could no longer trust her body to perform movements that had been nearly automatic. My problem didn't risk life and limb as it did for Biles, but I can relate to the challenge posed by your own body not following what it has been trained to do.

I had the best mark in the state in our AAA classification in my junior year. But nothing I did seemed to shake me out of whatever funk I was in. I ended up in third place, which in my house was not worth a goddamned thing except to serve as a reminder that you weren't good enough. Third out of all AAA competitors statewide wasn't bad, actually. Still, I was crushed and worked like a berserker all year to ensure that never happened again.

Robert pulled over at a convenience store not far from University Stadium. He had made the drive to Albuquerque to help guide me to victory. I was grateful for his presence. Coach Clement, my actual coach of record, was less appreciative.

We went in the store, got whatever it was we thought we needed, then had every intention of driving right back to the stadium. But it soon became obvious that we were nowhere near where we had been before. Lovington was a tiny town, and Lubbock was big but easy to navigate. Albuquerque, however, conquered our asses in no time. As we drove, my Spidey sense was screaming: *I should be back at the stadium preparing to warm up for the competition!* Instead of warming up, I was sitting in the passenger seat of our truck, looking out the window, hoping Robert knew where he was going. Mind you, this was long before Google Maps and GPS.

"Um. Where are we?" I finally blurted out, as if it were the most ordinary question ever. See, I tried to remain calm because I knew Robert became an anxiety-ridden hulk under pressure. "Shouldn't we be close to the stadium by now?"

"I don't know," he said. "We should be there already."

Well, no shit! I thought, but I knew better than to say it. If he melted down, I'd never see the stadium again. And was it possible that, if I shamed him, he'd keep me from the competition on purpose? The thought crossed my mind.

I let him drive aimlessly as I nervously kept checking my Timex Ironman watch. Every second was excruciating. Already I was thinking about the fallout. What would my coaches say, especially after what I had said to Coach Clement the morning the team left Lovington for Albuquerque? (More about that later.) How would my teammates ever look at me again? For the rest of my life, I would have to talk about how I should have been the state champion, but instead what happened was that my brother and I had a fateful joyride in Albuquerque, where we got hopelessly, utterly fucking lost because we were hapless dumbasses. My present self was already embarrassed for my future self.

"We should stop somewhere and ask someone." That's what I said. But what I meant was, *Stop the fucking truck when you see the first human being who looks like they live here and has a pulse.*

All I got from Robert was silence.

We drove past what looked like a golf course. This was not the first time we had passed this very golf course in the last few minutes. We were going in circles.

I saw an older man on the sidewalk. He seemed like a man out for a daily walk because his cardiologist recommended it. "Stop the truck. Let me ask this guy."

Robert, surprisingly, pulled near to the sidewalk. I knew I must do the talking because I always did. *I better get this right*, I warned myself.

"Sir, do you happen to know how we can get to University Stadium from here?" I tried to sound calm and disinterested, like I was asking him where the nearest post office might be. And I knew I had to be as nonthreatening as possible for this man to help me.

"Sure!" he said. I wanted to hug him.

The man proceeded to give us directions. I did my best to listen, repeat them back, and then we were off. I was telling Robert where to turn, but I wasn't sure I was right. I couldn't bear to imagine if I was wrong.

Miraculously, I spied some familiar landmarks, and suddenly I made out the stadium. I was out of the truck before Robert could even stop. I could already see my competition gathered in the shot put area. I arrived just in time to begin my warm-up and check in.

I won, but I did not break the state record—and I blame being lost in Albuquerque.

Chapter Thirty-Eight

Although you couldn't call my household outgoing, we imagined ourselves a family of athletes. That is, we did from Rene's generation to mine. I suppose she began things by being a cheerleader—ultimately, the head cheerleader—at a mostly Black high school. Her ascent to head cheerleader was not easy, and even now she draws upon those experiences to explain her resiliency. I suppose she figured that if she, a light-skinned Latina, could be the head cheerleader at a Black high school, the rest of us could and should work hard to be great athletes as well.

Tom went to Dunbar High School also, and he had been a solid football player. Unfortunately, his many severe knee injuries at a young age barred him from pursuing any serious football past high school. David played football at Dunbar, but then he dropped out because he assumed he was going to get married. Mom and Dad thought otherwise, but they couldn't get him to go back to school.

Rene made it possible for David to enroll at Lovington High School, and he played football like a man in a Mark 3 Iron Man suit. He destroyed whoever was in front of him. He had been playing Texas high school football at a Black school, took a year off, became a man, then played at a small New Mexico high school populated with mostly white and Latinx kids. David shone as if he were from a high-gravity planet where they played real football. He received college offers to play and was voted one of the top defensive players in the state his last year in high school. Instead, he got involved with a white woman who was already married. When she divorced her husband, she married David. She was several years older than him. His life as an athlete was over, but he was still basically a boy.

Robert was probably the most naturally gifted athlete of the family, me included. He has always looked like an NFL lineman or WWE wrestler. His passion had been amateur, Olympic-style wrestling, and while attending

Atkins Junior High in Lubbock, he was proving to be a natural. His size was such that he practiced wrestling with the grad student who was a coach in training because no one else matched Robert's size. When we moved to Lovington and learned there was no wrestling program there, Robert turned to the shot put and discus, in which he had also excelled in Lubbock. Coaches wanted him for football, naturally, but he didn't dig team sports, so that was never a long-term possibility. Instead, he carried on his shot put and discus ambitions at his new school.

But he had one ill-fated athletic flaw. (Okay, maybe more than one, but that's not the point.) His greatest flaw, as I see it now, is that his early success came so easily that he was probably the laziest four-time state champ in history, or if we're being as understanding as possible, let's say he was among the most complacent student athletes that passed through New Mexico. He rarely practiced. He was preternaturally strong, and he never put himself through an actual training regimen. And though he'll talk today of having settled on a shot-putting technique that worked for him alone, the truth was that he had no real technique to speak of. He kind of shuffled his feet, turned, and the shot would sail farther than everyone else's. He was the high school kid coaches prayed for. Of course, he was destined to be a shot-putter and discus thrower. His frame and size screamed either football lineman or shot put and discus. He was made for it.

Not so with me. When Robert was beating competitors three years older than himself at the state level, I was watching *Dungeons & Dragons* and begrudgingly learning how to be a cockfighter. For a kid about to enter middle school, nothing about me even hinted at being an athlete. Instead, I was looking forward to enrolling in band classes. I thought the saxophone or trumpet would be right up my alley. I had always been enchanted by the idea of playing music. We never had a real instrument at home that I could practice on.

One day in the school year, I was given a form to take home so my parents could sign and give their permission for me to be in the band. A modest cost was central but not prohibitive, and I mentioned that I was interested in sax or trumpet. I wasn't sure what a French horn was, and I didn't think I was coordinated enough to be a percussionist. By a process of elimination, I had settled on a handful of choices and was sure everyone would go for it at home. I recalled David had played bass in orchestra years before, so I didn't even imagine what might possibly be problematic about this beyond cost.

When I handed Rene the permission slip, she read it quickly, then gave me an expression of doubt or distaste, I wasn't sure which.

"Do you really want to do this?" It didn't sound like an actual question. Her tone was saying, *You don't want to do this.*

"I think I do," I was quick to reply. This would be a turning point in my life, but I didn't know it, of course. I could see myself making music, being in a band, maybe even parlaying that into my real desire: playing the piano. We could never have afforded a piano, obviously, but I thought a keyboard would be the next best thing. I'd pore over the cheap Casio keyboards in the Fingerhut catalog for hours.

Rene continued to stare at the form, as if searching for something that only she could find. "What would you play?"

"I was thinking saxophone."

"Ugh!" She sneered in exaggerated disgust, as though she had found a spider in her spaghetti. "That's what your father played."

"So? I don't know him."

She paused. When she wanted to, Rene could be a wordsmith and a great salesperson. "We're not musicians. We're athletes. You're going to be an athlete. The music may be a part of you, too, but it's a part of you that you shouldn't look to encourage."

She handed the permission slip back to me—unsigned.

I was angry with her, and I left the room with tears in my eyes. Even then I felt she had robbed me of a chance that would never pass my way again. For some reason, I didn't take my case to the highest authority in our home, which was Mom. Maybe I presumed she, too, would turn me down. Rene's denial of my request felt final, and I would resent her for years because of how often she would arbitrarily cut me off from various opportunities. In this case, the sticking point was not necessarily financial, as I had anticipated. Instead, it was simply that my playing music would be too powerful a reminder of my biological father.

I knew only the smallest scraps of information about the man:

He was a Latino whose family had been exceedingly close to Rene's. It turns out that both my grandfathers had been childhood friends, and my birth ultimately led to an estrangement of nearly twenty years. I feel sorry about that, though it wasn't my fault. Meaning, even though this rupture was a result of my birth, I'd had no say in the matter.

There is at least a happy ending there: Before I graduated from high school, all four of my grandparents would gather together again as they used to before I came along to wreck the arrangement. When they passed away one by one, until my paternal grandfather and maternal grandmother remained, they stayed in touch. When my father's father passed, my grandmother spoke of him in kind and loving tones. This is an ultimate sign of respect from Mom, a woman who would brutally mock whomever she felt deserved it. Both my grandfathers, as it turned out, were kind and generous men.

Chapter Thirty-Nine

When I was younger and before I hit twenty-five, I favored Álvaro, my father, according to Rene—who frequently harped on the resemblance, as though it were my fault. "You have those same sad eyes Álvaro had."

As a child, I was an enduring, unwitting reminder of Álvaro for Rene. Their split was beyond acrimonious (one of their last fights ended with Rene bashing Álvaro's head with a frying pan), and owing to the small detail that they were never married (I guess that was coming later?), I learned at the age of fifteen that I was not only one of those sarcastic, too-smart-for-his-own-good bastards but also a literal bastard to boot. Not a bastard out of Carolina but rather Texas. (This was before Jon Snow made it somewhat cool to be a bastard.) When I had my first extended conversation with Álvaro—one of only two in-person conversations we ever shared—he contradicted my understanding that he and Rene had been briefly married.

I learned a lot that night in this stranger's truck in an empty Target parking lot in Lubbock. Still confused about what this meant for me, I then took this news back to Rene. When I told her what Álvaro had said, she burst into tears and admitted that, yes, I was illegitimate. It pained Rene to admit this to me.

For my part, I didn't give a good goddamn about my bastard status, and my surname had always been Rene's family name, González. (She later married and divorced a man with the last name Foster, a name she kept.) I believe I cried in sympathy when Rene confessed her anguish to me. But I truly didn't see the problem over being illegitimate. Was this feudal England, where the rights of primogeniture obtained? Not by a damned sight. Was Álvaro a Steve Jobs who would deny me his wealth and empire and name as the tech magnate did to his daughter Lisa? No. I was an absolute nobody, and lived a long airline flight away from any reasonable center of power or metropolis. Why the fuck would I care that I was a bastard?

I'd been more infuriated in middle school, when, because of Álvaro—no, my mother's *memory* of Álvaro—whom I had not yet met at that point in my life, I was not allowed to learn and play music. The musicians in my genetic pool had clustered on Álvaro's side, and apparently my paternal grandfather could play a mean accordion. When I mentioned my desire to play music, my González uncle-brothers would tease me about it and say they wouldn't let me play the accordion in marching band. I guess they thought playing an accordion was fodder for mockery.

The González clan were not musicians, David's foray into orchestral music aside. All the Gonzálezes stood out in sports because they were stronger, bigger, and faster than nearly everyone else around them. They were all highly gifted in athletics, but they never seemed interested in perfecting that natural talent. David, who might have done something notable at the collegiate level with his football talents, decided to chain-smoke his way into a marriage that most of the family didn't approve of. Robert was probably the best chance for any of us to go pro in an athletic endeavor, and he taught me more than he ever intended to about all of this.

Though he was a big guy, Robert was also tremendously explosive, a term used in sports to describe the combination of strength and speed (what physicists call power). So, he was powerful—literally. These athletic exploits seemed to come easy to him, and he also had the misfortune of having no competent or able coach within a hundred miles. There he was with Tom and David, trying to devise a homespun technique for putting the shot. And it worked. He was beating other shot-putters with much better technique without much of a challenge. But what if he had learned a proper technique?

At the end of his junior year in high school, at age seventeen, Robert was diagnosed with severe hypertension. He was quickly placed on a medication regimen, and it wasn't long before his blood pressure was within normal parameters. But he claims the treatment had a significant side effect: it put him through a major albeit undiagnosed depression. If he had been unmotivated before because he was so much better than his competition, now he didn't give a damn about much of anything. He sleepwalked through his final year of high school track and field. He won his fourth shot put state title, but it was a lesser throw than the previous year. He had peaked in the eleventh grade.

At the time, I had no inkling that I, too, could be a shot-putter, to say nothing of surpassing Robert. He was this huge guy throughout my childhood, and I was always destined to see myself as a runt among a family of giants. Since I wasn't allowed to be a saxophonist or trumpeter, I was looking for my entrance into a world of sports. I knew that at a certain age, I would be expected to play football, though Robert again set a precedent by playing football and then becoming so dissatisfied with it and the coaches that he walked away from it, literally, during a game. He got into an argument with a coach (let's call him Coach Barr; we'll see him again soon), and he walked right off the field in the middle of the game, into the locker room, and then homeward. And he was as good as his word, never taking to a football field ever again.

His dissatisfaction with football—a game "where you can be great and a loser at the same time"—made the same possibility available for me, if necessary. Rene was an advocate for my uncle-brothers, and she was constantly at odds with our schoolteachers and principals. She would pull us from any extracurricular school program at a whim, feeling always that their loss was worse than ours.

My problem was that I was nerdy and uncoordinated, and I didn't have much in the way of inherent athleticism. My cousin Colo, whenever we gathered, was smaller than me and always so quick and agile. And I wasn't comparable to any of my classmates who could be called athletes. I was middling in those end-of-year Field Day events, though I did win an egg race, in which I had to balance an egg at the end of a spoon for about fifty yards. I may have placed in the three-legged race, and I did terribly in the sack race. These were my accomplishments as my uncle-brothers were winning state medals.

In middle school, bereft of dreams of band glory, I looked for a place to discover my physical talents. At that time, there weren't the kind of youth club sports that dominate today. I thought basketball might be an option, but never found an opportunity for it beyond pickup games with other nerds. In junior high, the basketball coach passed me in the restroom and encouraged me to try out. I was too scared to follow through, but I was flattered. (In high school, years later, I would play basketball in the few minutes before the end of lunch and the next class, and I was like Defensive Player of the Year against some of our actual varsity basketball players. One of those guys was so mad that he literally threatened to fight me. Such are the fragilities of the young male ego!)

In the ninth grade, I tried out for football. I was good at *John Elway's Quarterback* video game, and I had three uncle-brothers who were basically experts. I thought I would be a natural. Two-a-days came, and I wanted to cry. I was still clumsier than I thought I should have been at my age (a few months past fourteen years old). The helmet felt oversized and uncomfortable, and I had not yet discovered the miracle of the contact lens. I had huge glasses, and I couldn't wear them under the helmet, because they were cheap and my only pair. I was a menace at practice, seeing only blobs of color—and we all wore basically the same colors. We were running plays, and not once did a coach tell me what I needed to do. No coaching whatsoever, yet I'd get screamed at for fucking up. I was a thinker, and if someone would tell me what to do, I would execute.

"Hey!" I groaned to a teammate and friend as we walked back to the locker room after practice one day. "Can you tell me what we're doing?"

"What do you mean?"

"When we are running plays. Like, okay, what does 'strong side' and 'weak side' mean?"

He paused. He was a good friend, and he probably didn't want to embarrass me. He whispered, as if he were divulging national secrets during the Cold War. "Watch the tight end or extra receivers." Maybe I still looked confused. "The side of the offense that has more players is the strong side."

"Is it right or left?"

"Depends on the formation."

We went into the locker room, where the coach (in the normal course of the school day, this was my PE coach, but here he wasn't the same guy) harangued us like we were puppies who had pooped on the white carpet. I found I didn't like getting yelled at when I didn't know what I was supposed to be doing.

Most of the other kids had already played for a couple of years, and so they had the basics down. But I knew football only as something on television, and back then we didn't have Tony Romo explaining the plays before they happened. A few more practices over the next few weeks did not suddenly reveal any hidden talent within me, and I was feeling hopeless.

Here things get blurry for my football story. Rene had done what she always did and confronted the coach about something. Maybe I had complained because I didn't feel that the coaches were *coaching* me—instructing me—and I was frustrated. But instead of letting me speak up for myself, Rene used my discontent as her own excuse to ream the coach, with whom she had some unsettled score (from when he coached her brothers in high school). I had asked her to go easy because I knew how she liked to carpet-bomb school employees who had the misfortune of crossing my path. When I saw her that afternoon, she said she had pulled me from the team, as if telling me we were having frozen pizzas for dinner.

"What!"

"Fuck them. You don't need them."

The next morning, the coach sought me out before I even got into the building. He, like me, didn't know what had happened—but could I reconsider and be on the team?

I couldn't understand why he wanted me on the team at all. I was half the size my uncle-brothers had been at that age, and I was more or less a liability on the field. Once or twice, I had made an excellent play by pure luck. Had that been enough? I seriously doubted it.

"Sorry, Coach. My mom said I have to quit the team." And that was that. My glorious career in football was over, having lasted far longer than my career in music.

I remember a teammate, a guy I never came to like, sidled over to me one day between classes and asked why I had quit the team so suddenly.

"It's a long story."

"C'mon, man. We need you."

Bullshit, I thought. I had been nothing out there, and no one ever tried to help me get up to speed. "Sorry. I can't. Talk to my mom."

Chapter Forty

Months went by as football season ran its course without me. One weekend, I sat on the floor of my living room on a lazy Saturday. It was late afternoon, and I found a book on track and field techniques that one of the guys had gotten. I read it and wondered if I could do the long jump. I went outside and tried, but it seemed complicated—certainly more was involved than simply running as fast as you could, then jumping. With that failed experiment, I headed back inside, when suddenly I noticed several shots lying in the backyard. Maybe I could throw one of these?

It was stupid. I was lanky and shot-putters were humongous, or at least heavyweights. But then I recalled the 1988 Olympic shot put final—a legendary competition for students of the event.

I still remember when we saw the broadcast, and Robert had been quick to record it for posterity. What I remembered at the time, and then over a year later when I thought I might be able to put the shot, was that the seemingly smaller, lankier putter had beaten the other hulking competitors. That smaller guy was Ulf Timmermann from East Germany, and though now I know he is a large man, by comparison he looked impossibly small to my young eyes. What Timmermann lacked in bulk, he made up for in speed, agility, and power. I pulled out the tape, put it in the VCR, then watched it over and over until I had memorized everything about the recording and Timmermann's technique.

Before long, I was outside trying to emulate him. I thought I was doing well and measured off the distance. After asking around, I realized that I was throwing as far as the best shot-putters in junior high in my part of the state. It's not that I was a prodigy; it's that every other kid doing it wasn't that good.

Specialization had not yet reached the shot put, if it ever did outside of me. Shot-putters my age came from the ranks of football players, and they did it for only a few weeks every year. What if I trained for it year-round?

When Robert found out what I was doing, after I'd been sneaking about for a few days, I thought he would ridicule me into oblivion. Instead, he began helping me, which was the biggest shock of all. He had never offered to help me in anything that would require this level of commitment.

You may be wondering what Robert was still doing around the house at twenty-one. It's a fair question, and it calls for a quick explanation. In your typical Latinx household, you will find that children are not so eager to leave home after high school graduation. And if they are, they often can't overcome their parents' pressure to stay a few more years. Commonly the kids are expected to work and contribute to the family coffers before moving out and making their own way in the world.

Rene had basically stayed home with her parents, or she had brought them to live with her, it's hard to say. Tom never had his own place. Never had his own apartment or house that wasn't also shared by another family member. David and Rose had left home, but their departures were always a result of being estranged from the family for some length of time. Robert had no real motivation to leave, and so he stuck around. The year before, he and David had competed for the New Mexico Junior College track team, but it always seemed like they were killing time until the next adventure.

Robert helped me a little in those early days, which was more than enough and more than what most of the coaches knew as well. I had watched Timmermann and the other throwers enough to recognize that shot-putters did not throw the metal ball the way you did a baseball or football. That is, by first moving it backward then forward, starting with the elbow. Instead, you pushed the shot in a motion similar to how you do an incline bench press. What complicated this was that you started by facing the opposite direction, you had to move backward, then at some point you turned, timing the push correctly. All of this was done in the blink of an eye, inside a seven-foot-diameter circle or ring, with a funny little curb or ledge at the front called a toeboard.

I took to the concept of pushing the shot instantly, and somehow, I instinctively latched on to the principle that your legs generated the bulk of the force for your throw. In simple terms, it felt like I had to jump into the throw first before pushing.

I joined the track team with a confidence I had lacked in football, earlier in the year. I knew exactly what I wanted to do, even if the coach didn't. When the coaches saw me, they saw a potential hurdler or high jumper, and for a while they tried to get me to do several sprinting events as well. I had one day of hurdle practice, and I was so bad I was never invited to do it again. I did pick up the companion event to the shot put, the more elegant and classical discus throw. The two events are like fraternal twins, like Apollo and Artemis—clearly related but quite different on many accounts.

Thus began my love affair and obsession with the shot put. I emulated Timmermann as I practiced and competed, and it worked. I found that my body was able to do what it needed to do, technically speaking. My problem was that I wasn't strong enough. And this fault was largely a matter of needing to grow more.

To everyone's surprise, I won the district junior high championship in the shot, beating a kid who had always won it, including the year before. He was sloppy but strong. When he realized I had beaten him, he was furious. I must have sent him into early retirement because I never saw him again.

All this time, I was throwing a junior high shot that weighed four kilograms, which is the implement girls and women also use at all levels, even the Olympics. For you imperialists, that shot weighs eight pounds twelve ounces. But once I moved up to varsity, I had to throw a high school boys' shot that weighed twelve pounds. A three-and-a-quarter-pound increase in shot may not sound like much, but the upgrade feels astronomical. You're now slower, and your deficiencies in strength are harder to compensate for and mask. I knew I had to throw over forty-seven feet with this heavier weight to qualify for the state meet, and I fell just short. Robert had not only qualified for the state meet as a ninth grader but won state! I couldn't even qualify.

Despite this setback, I felt I had found something worth pursuing. I was soon convinced that my problem, other than a lack of experience, size, and strength, was that my technique needed to change. Timmermann brought me so far with the glide technique and more esoterically the O'Brien technique after Parry O'Brien. Timmermann had likely perfected it, but I felt it wasn't dynamic enough, and I needed all the help I could get. And that's when a guy from West Virginia, a Texas A&M University alumnus, caught my attention. His name was Eric Randolph Barnes, but he went by Randy Barnes.

A few weeks after my ninth-grade year had ended, Barnes broke Timmermann's world record in the shot put. It was sweet revenge for Barnes, who was the guy Timmermann had bested in that legendary 1988 Olympic final. We recorded this competition as well, and it would serve as a great learning tool for much of my career as a shot-putter. I resolved that I would throw the shot the way Barnes did, with a discus-like rotation rather than a glide down the center of the ring.

I was mostly alone in this switch in technique. Tom and David got jobs in construction that took them all over the place for months at a time: Texarkana, Barstow, Nashville, Odessa. It was good money, and they left. The money was so good, they told Robert to get on a plane and join them, so he did. I was about to be a sophomore in high school, and I was going to be my own coach, mostly, by emulating Randy Barnes.

Chapter Forty-One

I became a kind of man of the house. Dad wasn't in the best of health, and so I did as much work around the property as I could, so he wouldn't have to. I also recognized that the key to my success would be in weight training. I bought muscle magazines and tried to figure out how to get stronger. GNC started to be a thing, and I jumped into the supplement zeitgeist with both feet. I paid what seemed like a fortune for a kit called Cybergenics, a cool name for about six different supplements. It came with a VHS tape and booklet that described the workout regimen exactly. The crazy thing was that it worked, but I doubt the expensive supplements had much to do with it. (They turned my piss the color of orange Gatorade, though.)

I convinced Mom to buy me an Olympic bar and accompanying plates that totaled 315 pounds from Sam's Club. Someone, perhaps Rose, donated an adjustable bench. I was about to turn fifteen, and my body must have finally opened the testosterone spigot. That undoubtedly helped. But I also did this workout from the Cybergenics program that emphasized something called the "negative" muscle contraction or part of the exercise lift. Basically, the muscle is contracting while elongating—what's known as an eccentric contraction. In most lifts, this is the part when you let the weight down. I had never paid attention to that part of the lift before.

The second thing this program emphasized was time. (Today they call it *time under tension.*) In lay terms, you had to count as you raised and lowered the weight, something like five seconds up and five seconds down. A set felt like an eternity.

The final thing featured in this program was an idea called failure. *Failure,* in weight lifting terms, simply meant going until you couldn't complete another rep. But this demonic program demanded you go to positive and negative failure. Keep in mind that your negative is stronger than your positive. For instance, you may not be able to complete another repetition by fully lifting the weight, but you can still lower the weight with excellent control. It's a safety design in the human body. Well, this unreal program advised going to negative failure. In the bench press, this would mean you would go until you could no longer stop the bar from crushing you. An extremely dangerous situation, as one might imagine. Especially if, like me, you were a novice working out alone where no one could hear you cry out for help. More than once I had to find a creative way to get myself out from under a barbell.

But I was ignorant and thought the program knew better. I never was able to complete a workout as described, because it was so difficult, and this was six days a week. My body was in such agony, but I soon saw real results. Years later, I would try a different program, sans supplements, which also emphasized negatives and time under tension. In four weeks over a Christmas break, I got so big that I'm sure my teammates and coaches thought I was on some chemical enhancer, juice, or gear. Nope. Only these madman workouts that weirdly seemed to work for me. But I did them on my own only because coaches created our strength programs, and they were supposed to know better.

Anyway, when I went through the Cybergenics program, it was around the time when I met Álvaro and his family for the first time. My uncle-brothers would soon be gone on construction job jaunts, and I resolved to be a state champ like Robert. If I could throw over sixty feet, I was sure I'd get a scholarship to college. For most of my sophomore year, I coached myself. I was left to my own devices in the fall, and in the spring my field event coach, Coach Clement, was more interested in flirting with the girl athletes than coaching us throwers.

Today, I'm certain I derive much of my determination to get things done from this formative year to year-and-a-half period of my life. With no one around to help me, I did what was necessary. Unfortunately, my academics suffered. My father seemed to welcome the idea of me but then thought better of it, which hurt. Rene sued him for paternity and won, which was traumatic. My uncle-brothers were away. And my shot put idol, Randy Barnes, failed a drug test and would be suspended for two years.

Every year, I improved—and I suddenly became known for something at school. I got cocky as a junior and blew great chances to be a state champ. In my final year, Robert became my de facto coach, coming to every practice to help me and the other throwers. Coach Clement was allowed to play more grab-ass with the girls' team, so he must have been okay with it.

I know I dog on Robert in this book, and he has earned all that he gets and more. But he also gets credit for doing a lot of the coaching and mentoring I needed after my junior year. We cracked the code, and now all sorts of records were in sight. When I wondered if I could go to college on a scholarship, he was the one who mentioned Blinn College to me.

He had seen them when he competed that one season for NMJC, and he was impressed. He said I should go there if I wanted to be a better thrower. Yes and no, as it turned out. Once I got on Blinn's radar, it all seemed like a matter of time. And how did I get on its radar? I listed Blinn as one of the schools where my ACT scores should be sent. None of my coaches ever bothered to help me get the attention of any track programs, to say nothing of a scholarship. It was a happy accident. Which is frustrating because how many people aren't lucky enough to have a happy accident?

Robert would come to my meets and coach me. At one meet, he ran into Coach Barr, the guy he had walked out on during the football game all those years ago. The man, now a coach for a rival school, had a vise for a handshake, and he caught Robert unawares when they saw each other once more. They had let bygones be bygones, but that grip pissed off Robert like he had been publicly slapped.

"That bastard had a strong fucking grip. *Pinche güey.*"

"I guess you ain't that strong, then," I shot back, to see what he would say.

"Oh, I'll fix his ass next time I see him."

When they saw each other at the next track meet the following week, Robert unloaded on Coach Barr, and he made him cry out in agony. They laughed, and it was like Robert was an actual coach out there and not some volunteer. He was certainly appreciated, until the morning we were set to leave for Albuquerque, a few days before we would get lost. Coach Clement caught me outside one of the school buildings before class.

"I just got off the phone with your mother," he spat. "She said she wants Robert in the photo for the *Lubbock Avalanche-Journal.* And not me!"

I tried not to laugh. The Lubbock paper, the one Mom read religiously, wanted to stage one of those pictures where an athlete signs a letter of intent with coaches and administrators and parents around them. I was okay with the idea, but I wanted Robert in the picture as my events coach. He had earned it. "But, Coach, he should be in the picture. He's been the one coaching me for like two years, not you. Why shouldn't he be in it?" I thought I was being obvious.

I'd never seen this man so enraged. "But he's not your coach! He's your brother!"

This was one of the first moments in my life where I felt I had every right to raise my voice and rebuke someone in a position of authority. Perhaps my confidence swelled because my days at this school and this town were numbered. Maybe it was that I knew this man had no real power over me. Whatever it was, I felt my size and confidence swell, then roll down like waters on that pathetic excuse of a coach. Robert had done all this work, stayed up late and gotten up early, spent his time helping me get to the brink of something great—and this guy was going to rob him of the credit that was Robert's and Robert's alone?

"Coach, you care more about flirting with high school girls than you ever did about me. I looked for you, and where were you? Come to say hi, then you leave! That's what you do every day. Robert has been there when you weren't, and you don't care about the work he's put in. You oughta be thanking this dude! I sure as hell am!" I put my finger right in his face and lowered my voice to almost a whisper. "He's going to be in the picture with me. Not you. If he's not in it, I'm not doing it. It's bullshit." I left him standing there and never said another unnecessary word to him.

Coach Clement was not the head coach, a guy who had been around for years and one that I liked well enough. He understood our position, and it didn't hurt that we weren't excluding him from the picture. But, look, why should Clement get the honor of riding my coattails when he had never given a damn before? What did he think was going to happen? As it turned out, the staged picture never took place. All that aggravation for nothing.

When I returned to visit a few years later, Clement had moved to another school, where he apparently was still steaming about what I had done to him. I'm sure a Brown boy had never stood up to him before, and the confrontation must have left a mark on him. He may be credited with instigating the first appearance of me as Big Scary Brown Guy, which was an accurate description at that moment.

For all his faults, Robert is the one most responsible for putting me on a path to college, to academics, to a hall of fame, to a PhD, and even to the woman I married, which necessarily leads to my children. Even if he got us lost in Albuquerque and made us excruciatingly late to the competition, he was the right person at the right moment in the right place. And it makes me wonder about how many people are not so lucky as to have a Robert in their corner, and instead must rely on the incompetence of a Coach Clement.

Chapter Forty-Two

I speak of Álvaro in the past tense because for me, that is where he currently resides, as a kind of living ghost robbed of the power to terrorize or frighten. Not unlike the spooks in the Haunted Mansion amusement ride at Disneyland—dusty, antiquated, of a bygone era, and liable to break down before the day is done or while you're still buckled into your seat.

Álvaro liked cars and knew how to take them apart and put them back together again. He had a fondness for martial arts and, naturally, Bruce Lee, and he served in the military at a time when the Vietnam conflict was over for US soldiers. I met him in the summer of 1990, a newly minted fifteen-year-old, and he must have been around thirty-seven, making him a decade younger than I am as I write this.

Time works in strange ways. Now that I have children about the age I was when I met Álvaro, as a father, I feel like fifteen years are a few chimes on the clock tower. He seemed old to me then, but thirty-seven isn't *that* old. I guess what I'm trying to say is that fifteen years for him should have felt like a couple of years, and maybe it did. I'll never know. He must have imagined me as a tyke and not the teenager who was already as tall as he was.

Something was in the air for a meetup. Things were coalescing, like how conceptual artists show stars going from dust until they are bold enough to start a fire in their cores. Rose was in contact with one of Álvaro's sisters or sisters-in-law, and there was interest on both sides. I imagine it was like setting up a meeting in *The Sopranos*, only with less fear of death and dismemberment.

Incidentally, Rose was adopted by Mom when her own sister didn't want this girl as a newborn. Rose was a middle child who was adopted. Wrap your head around that shit! Like, *Oh, I don't want this kid, you take her*, and then, *Hey, let's have another and keep this one!* My observations growing up were that this happened enough that it wasn't strange, and I think it was viewed as a better alternative than abortion. Give the child away, but only to someone whom you knew or were related to. That way you could still kind of see your kid grow up under the auspices of a trusted relative. In a way, that almost happened to me, except Rene never officially gave me to her parents. Mom thought I was hers the way Rose had been hers. It was a huge point of contention between them when I was growing up, and I had to hear about it anytime they went after each other.

For my first few years, I thought of Rene as my big sister, and everyone in the family also went along with this fiction. I called Rene by her first name, as I still do today. Since everyone called my grandmother Mom or Amá, it was logical for me to call Elva the same thing. But as a kid who was already butchering language (boys seem to suffer from childhood speech impediments more often than girls, it seems), I couldn't say Irene. Instead, I called her Rene. A few of her younger cousins called her Reenie. This early arrangement in my family, a pact that everyone decided upon without my consent, has so marked my identity that—even now, as a forty-seven-year-old man—I still call my mother Rene, and refer to my grandmother and grandfather, both now deceased, as Mom and Dad.

Now that I am a parent, I understand at a personal level how demoralizing and devastating this must have been for Rene. When my daughters met Rene for the first time, I had to confront this confusing arrangement in their behalf. Rene would be Big Mama, and Elva became Little Mama. (Mom always resisted being called any variant of the word *grandmother* because it made her feel old.) The first time Rene heard my daughters called her Big Mama, she wept unabashedly.

"They called me Mama," she wheezed through convulsive sobs, huge tears staining her plump bulldog cheeks. And then, a sharp dagger for me: "No one has ever called me Mama." I mean, what was I supposed to say? And who was responsible for that, after all?

I often wonder at questions for which I will never have an answer. Why did Rene go along with the fiction that I was her baby brother rather than her baby boy, at least initially? Why did my grandparents practically adopt me? The actual events that precipitated this situation are unclear because the parties involved, Rene and Mom, have different versions of what happened and what was agreed upon between them. Rene claims that their agreement was that her parents would care for me until I reached a certain age, at which point I would be told the truth. In the interim, because Rene was pursuing a career in the computer programming industry, it would be best for me to have someone to care for me full-time rather than for her be a single parent.

Mom remembers it differently, and she told her version during practically every argument she and Rene had that I was privy to when I was growing up—after the truth of my parentage was made known to me, of course. Mom would repeat to her last days that their agreement was that Rene gave me to her when I was born. Clearly, this was unofficial and not legally binding.

I remain troubled by all of it. You mean to tell me my mother put me, a babe in swaddling clothes, in another person's lap and walked away, but only a few steps away? Like, she stayed in the house and said, *Here, have this child!* I understand many people do this for many reasons, and wonderful children find love in the arms of adoptive parents all the time. It confuses me, however, because Rene never truly left home. Except for a few years in my childhood when she lived elsewhere, Rene lived with her parents for most of her adult life. Until recently, she and Mom lived together, the two of them alone; they stubbornly refused to have it any other way. So, was she going to live in the same house where her mother was now mother to her child?

All the scheming and secret pacts made for a crisis of identity for me nearly from the start of my life. I don't know what the truth is, even today. Any stories they would weave for my benefit would be riddled with inconsistencies and bedeviled with suspicion. I have toggled between the two women as my mother for my entire life, but never at the same time. Elva is Mom, and then Rene is mother. I hate explaining the relationships in my family to others because of this setup, so I often commit lies of omission for simplicity's sake. Though I don't see Rene as my sister any longer, I view her brothers and her adopted sister as my own. When people ask if I have siblings, I say yes, but in my mind, I'm thinking, *Not exactly. But you don't wanna know.*

My discovery of my parentage is shrouded in an air of mystery too. Mom would say that Rene flat-out violated the agreement and confessed to me one day who she was and who my birth father was. In this version of events, Mom sees this as a betrayal. Rene believed someone in my extended family, perhaps her aunts and uncles, blabbed around some of their grandkids (who, incidentally, were in the same position as I was, thinking their grandparents were their parents!), who then babbled to me. I must have been utterly confused and resistant to their revelations. Rene has further argued that it was then that I sought her out and asked if what I had been told was true. Her version seemed to me most plausible.

To her credit, in that ugly kitchen in Lubbock, Rene told me the truth of who she was. She could have simply convinced me that my cousins didn't know what the hell they were talking about and that I should forget it. Instead, she decided to be honest with me, something that has never been natural for her. Perhaps it was a moment of weakness; her only son asks her if she was his mother. What monster could lie to their own kid's face? Well, Rene decided she wasn't going to be that monstrous, and she told me that, yes, she was my mother. I believe Mom wanted her to honor their agreement and lie to me. Ever after, one of her favorite ways of insulting Rene during an argument was to tell her that Rene had "fucked up his [my] life." And one wonders why cusswords come as naturally to me as breathing.

Often, I was the rope in a tug-of-war, both Mom and Rene vying for my filial love. "And who do you love more?" I was sometimes asked. "Who do you think of as your mom?" It was my version of the Kobayashi Maru test for Starfleet cadets in the *Star Trek* universe—a scenario that reveals something of your tendencies and instincts within a no-win situation. I suppose they split the difference—Rene, my blood mother; Mom, my surrogate mother, who stepped up to the challenge when she didn't have to. Mom was the one who thought I had been abducted on my walk home from school at a time when the panic of such kidnappings in the early 1980s wildly outpaced the number of actual documented cases. But she was also the one who gave me a beatdown of epic proportions.

Mom's fear, which manifested in her belting me with tooled leather, was proof of her love, as she saw it. On the surface, there's a kind of perverse logic to that, so even if I can't condone her actions, I understand her motives. For her generation, spanking with whatever was convenient—the back of a hand, a belt, a *chancla*—was how you deterred such dumb behavior in the future. *Let me beat you with a wooden clog now so that it saves your life in like three years.* Mom was always the disciplinarian of the family, and all of us had felt her wrath at some time or another. But, as often happens in a family, the older children generally get the worst of it while the younger siblings benefit from a growing laxity in house rules and standard operating procedures.

If Mom spanked me infrequently albeit intensely, Rene hardly did at all. She was not a firm believer in corporal punishment, no doubt aggrieved by the harsh treatment she had received at Mom's hands years before. Rene's method of child behavior modification was either to ignore a transgression or talk about it. As a preschooler in Lubbock, I once screamed at her in the grocery store that she was the literal devil, outraged because she was refusing to let me have something or other. I dropped to the cold industrial tile of Furr's Supermarket, our grocery store of choice at the time, and thrashed about wildly as I yelled with all my might. *"Youuuuuuuu deviiiiiiil!!!!!"*

Rene paid for the groceries and nonchalantly pushed her basket toward the exit. I suppose I realized my gambit had failed, and my fear of being left behind in the store superseded my desire for whatever candy or trinket I had wanted so badly. Rene got the last laugh, as she tells this story about my fit in Furr's multiple times a year, as if she has never told it before. Of late, I will follow up by asking, "Was I wrong?" She sneers at me. Says, "You asshole."

Some years after the "you devil" episode, and after Rene had bought what I would later designate as the main trailer house in Lovington, I recall being at her side in the kitchen. She was on the telephone, and I was desperate for her attention, for reasons unknown to me today.

It must have been an urgent call, likely work related, and Rene had finally had enough of my pestering. Incensed that I would not mind her, she grabbed me by the arm and threw me across the kitchen. I had a feeling of weightlessness as she hurled me, and then I crashed against the counter cabinets, my head knocking hard on one of the wooden doors.

That scared me terribly, for Rene never put hands on me, either before or afterwards. It was one of the anomalous times when it was the two of us alone, when she would whisk me away from Mom and Dad for a few days or even a week or two. Whenever I felt that I had her all to myself, I would become too clingy and often panic if she left my sight. But with this incident, I experienced my first real distrust of Rene. She had shaken my tenuous confidence in her, and I was no longer sure that an adult in my family always had my best interest in mind.

Chapter Forty-Three

Now, I can usually rationalize a lot of weird shit, but there is no fucking excuse for throwing a child across the kitchen and into a cabinet door. If I did that to one of my daughters, I'd be divorced and probably in jail, rightly so. An adult could kill a kid like that. Doesn't matter that they didn't mean to harm the kid. Mom beat the hell out of me with a goddamned leather belt, but at least I could see why she had done it. Rene threw me across the kitchen with a pro wrestling Irish whip because I had done what all kids have done since time immemorial: bug their parents when their parents are working.

For many years, I thought maybe I had imagined the episode, but I've always had a good memory. When Rene lived with me during the pandemic, she mentioned it. I said that I remembered it, and she laughed. But I found nothing funny about it, then or now. And I wonder if my relationship with her didn't change the moment she picked me up and slung me across the kitchen. I know one thing for certain: Rene wouldn't have done that shit in front of Mom or Dad.

Lately I've read books and attended lectures on how our bodies are literally changed by the stress we endure, and how this stress can remain long after the stressor is removed. It makes much sense to me.

I am unsure about what happened next after I overcame the shock of it. Rene likely apologized, probably explaining to me why I couldn't do what I had done. That the phone call was significant, and that we should always be quiet when someone is on the phone. That it was my fault. That I had made her do it. Four decades later, I still go deathly quiet when someone is on the telephone, lest they are unable to hear whatever important business is being conducted. Plus, I don't want to be launched across the room again.

Ironically, despite this one colossal abuse of power, Rene was also much more protective of me than Mom, whose philosophy was that your circumstances would make you tougher. If some kid or teacher bullied you at school, it was up to you to handle it. If you got hurt owing to someone else's negligence, it was your own fault for being stupid enough to get yourself involved with the people who hurt you. In other words, don't be a *pendejo*. If you are, serves you right. And then, on top of whatever it was that had happened to you, she'd beat you for good measure.

Rene was often the archetypal mother bear, but to the extreme. She yearned for a reason to tear into someone for anything that might have hurt me. Around the same time she tossed me across the kitchen in Lovington, I recall some people had pulled up to the property from the highway and banged on our front door late one evening. People clamored outside, screaming at one another, and I got the distinct sense it was a domestic dispute that had spilled out onto the front of our trailer. Rene threatened them, ordering them to leave, to take their bullshit somewhere else. She reminded them that our neighbor to the east was a county sheriff, which was true.

I was terrified, but Rene patiently explained that though the people outside were crazy, she was going to protect me. Again it was just the two of us in the trailer house, one of those times she had taken me with her and before she was able to convince the rest of the family to move to Lovington. I felt so very far away from town and anyone who might help us—even though I knew a police officer, our neighbor, was only a minute or two away. Normally we would be suspicious of cops.

"Don't worry, *perrito*. I'll protect us."

After saying this, she showed me a small pistol, likely a .22 or a .380. In movies, I had seen how guns could kill and protect, depending on who had them. I had full confidence in Rene, and I watched her put the pistol underneath her pillow. I still feared the gun in such proximity to me. This is not good gun safety protocol. What if it went off while we slept? What if it accidentally hurt one of us? Despite these questions, watching Rene wield a gun with such composure made me believe that she would do anything to protect her family and me from anyone who might do us harm. It also seemed to underscore her independence and readiness to get into a fight if it came to that. Rene's fearlessness and eagerness to quarrel would serve her well throughout her life, especially many years later, during her time in prison.

What both these women lacked in their dedication to corporal punishment, they more than made up for in verbal aggressions, taunts, and chastisements. They could hurt you with words and expressions of disdain, and they were the enforcers of family discipline and order. Their word was law, and the power and influence they exerted were proof of the power of women in a patriarchal Latinx culture. Yet of these two, I ultimately saw Mom as the authority in the family, while I regularly watched Rene do things counter to Mom's directives.

Rene would drink, more than occasionally smoke marijuana way before it was legal in places, and bend the rules and the law to her whims. And whenever Mom caught her, they would argue and then quickly return to the status quo. No matter how angry these two women—mother and daughter—would get at each other, they never fully pushed the other away. Unlike members of our household who may have been excommunicated for familial transgressions, Rene always remained. For all my mother's failings, her talents earned her a place at the center of our family.

I went to Mom if I needed lunch money or permission to do something. I went to Rene if I needed a parent to go to a school function or explain life's mysteries to me. They performed distinct iterations of motherhood, and for most of my youth, they exhausted enormous amounts of energy trying to displace each other, often at my expense.

But into their old age, Mom and Rene held fast to each other, distrustful of the world and even of their family. Even of me.

Chapter Forty-Four

Back in 1990, Rose had been living in an apartment complex in Lubbock, recently released from her long-suffering husband (unnamed here because he's been through enough), and we would gather at her place because the complex had a pool. Rose was always living the high life compared with us, and she would visit often enough to remind us how well she was doing and how pathetic we were. This was Rose the entire time I've known her:

ROSE (showing up unexpectedly after a few weeks away): What is there to eat?

ONE OF US: Well, not much.

ROSE: Really? I was craving some Long John Silver's.

ONE OF US: We haven't had that in a while.

ROSE: And, you know, I was gonna bring some! I thought maybe about stopping to get dinner, but . . .

She never would finish why she had considered getting something and taking it to her mom and dad—and then thought better of it. What made her think, *Now, that might be a good thing to bring to them on my visit, but . . . nah, fuck 'em*? Rose was always talking about how she had been thinking about treating us to something or other and then decided not to, until finally, Mom told her to stop. I think she got off on seeing us go without and be miserable.

At some point, when I was like seventeen, Rose had a serious falling-out with Mom and Dad, and was run off. Persona non grata. She left, and no one saw her for years. When Dad died in 2001, Rose suddenly showed up at the funeral home like a prodigal daughter. It was poor form to show up after Dad had died. She could have saved the tears and shown up while he was still alive, we all thought.

As a child, I saw her as a bringer of hand-me-downs and the beta tester for white culture, the person who might take me on a special trip to McDonald's to buy me a Happy Meal. But once Rose visited to take Diana to McDonald's and get her a Happy Meal, and she didn't invite me or bring me something back. I was probably, like, nine years old, and I'm not sure if that's still in the Happy Meal age range. When Mom realized how hurt I was, she destroyed Rose for her dumbfuckery to get one kid something and the other kid nothing. Before my sister Diana appeared, Rose would come whisk me away for a few weeks during Christmas break, and I loved it. I got to watch TV, eat different take-out food (she was and probably still is a terrible cook), and hang out with her husband—he was blind in one eye and super mechanically gifted. I would observe that man solve a combination lock while he watched a movie. Because she would care for me from time to time, Rose was like a junior mother in my life. That is, until she got a kid of her own.

At this moment, she was the pool keeper. I could not swim, and everyone was taking turns trying to teach me. Somehow, I had gone fifteen years on this planet before anyone thought it might be a good idea for me to learn how to swim. Tom, David, Rose, Rose's boyfriend at the time, some friend of Rose's, all of them tried. And every single one of them failed. For some reason, I am not as buoyant as I should be. Even when I try to relax, I sink like a marble statue in ancient Atlantis.

The day had arrived, and Rose announced to me by the pool that Álvaro would be stopping by suddenly and, because he had other things to do, quickly. I was nervous and unsure what to do with myself. Minutes turned to a few hours, and I began to forget that he was supposed to drop in at all. I was too busy trying to do something as simple as float, and failing. Dead bodies float. Elephants can float. I couldn't.

The apartment complex was gated, and you had to buzz in or enter a code to gain entrance. For some reason that I cannot remember, I had to leave the pool area and go outside the gate. Perhaps I had to retrieve something from our truck parked outside. It was early afternoon and already hot. I went out the gate and saw a man standing there, an average Brown guy you might see everywhere in Lubbock. He looked at me, and I said hey as I passed him because he kept staring awkwardly. When I returned to the gate, he was still there.

Does DNA entail a sort of cosmic connection? Can siblings who have never met know if, by accident of fate, they suddenly happen to be standing next to one another? Can a child somehow intuit the presence of a parent she's never known?

In hindsight, our mutual recognition can readily be explained: we each knew the other was in the area. I can only affirm that I knew for certain it was Álvaro, and at the same moment, he knew it was me. We hugged and cried. He repeatedly said that he was sorry. I cried so hard that one of my new contact lenses popped out, and we both laughed as we struggled to find it on the concrete pad where we stood.

He said he would see me later, and then he left. Our first meeting had lasted no more than three minutes.

I met with Álvaro twice more over the next few weeks. First in the Target parking lot, where we sat in his truck while he told me much of his side of the story. Rose dropped me off at the Target next to her apartment after it had closed. Before she left, she delivered a threat: "If you hurt him, I'll fucking kill you." Álvaro laughed like it was a joke, but I believed her. Despite Rose's peculiarities, I found it reassuring when she called for a vendetta should harm befall me.

In the truck cab, we spoke awkwardly, comparing stories. While mine were secondhand and from a somewhat untrustworthy source (Rene), his accounts were firsthand. Mostly our stories aligned, except that Álvaro claimed he and Rene had never been married. It clearly pained him to tell me that. I think we both cried here and there, and we hugged each other a few more times. We drove to Taco Villa, and for once in my life, my father bought me dinner. (It would not happen again.) I found out he was an engineer and good with numbers. I confessed to being terrible in mathematics. Rose came to get me, and I debriefed her and Rene back at the apartment.

I thought the meeting with Álvaro had gone well, but things were unraveling fast. I saw him a second and final time at his home. I had to see him because I soon realized my very existence was threatening his relationship with his then wife, who sustained a murderous rage toward me. The idea was to tell them both that I wanted nothing from Álvaro except for the chance to get to know him. Tom agreed to drive me there, and he was also on hand to bear witness. And let's be honest, he was there to make sure nothing bad happened to me. It's likely that Tom was packing heat. He was the man with all the guns, always.

We found the address as dusk had blanketed the sky, and I went up to knock on the door. I could see and hear little girls running around inside with the TV on, hard at play and without a care in the world. Álvaro's wife, a small woman with dark skin and dark hair, opened the door. I knew that her name was Esther.

When she opened the door, she did not know who I was. Then I asked if Álvaro was home, and Esther was savvy enough to figure me out. Angry as all get-out, she roared, "Get the hell away from here!" I might have been some wild beast she was trying and failing to scare off.

I stayed calm. "I just want to talk to him for like two minutes. I need to tell him something."

"Fuck you and go to hell. He's not here anyway."

Now I was annoyed and plenty angry myself. His truck—the one in which we shared our first, and ultimately longest, conversation ever—stood in the driveway. "Go get him and tell him to come out here," I ordered in defiance of her anger.

He must have heard the commotion from somewhere within, and he soon came out, wearing shorts and a towel around his shoulders. He had just taken a shower. We walked away from the front door, leaving Esther cussing us both out.

About halfway down his driveway, I said, "I came to tell you that I don't want anything from you. I want to see you sometimes. To get to know you. But I won't be talked to like she talks to me."

"I know." He was trying to be sympathetic, but he was the one who had to live with her, not me.

More was said, and Esther came over to where we were and shouted us down. She was brazen and should be ashamed of her behavior toward a fifteen-year-old. Tom observed it all and didn't say a thing, like fucking Uatu the Watcher eyeing the folly of humans. Álvaro spotted Tom at last, and it was like he had seen a ghost from *chingaderas* past. His mind was obviously reeling.

"Why don't you leave with him and get the fuck out, then!" Esther bleated at Álvaro.

What he said next rattled me to my core: "Maybe I will."

Yo, man, what the fuck? Come with me? Where you gonna sleep? With Tom on the floor of the living room? Does that mean I can call you Dad? Now my mind staggered, beset by all sorts of ideas, tantalizing and fleeting.

Esther continued her blue streak, and I said I would leave now—because why bother at this point? They kept arguing, and I went over to Tom, who leaned on the fence at the front of the property.

I walked away from Álvaro that day, and I never saw him again.

Having children of my own now, I do what most people who had absent parents must certainly do when they bring children into the world, which is to wonder how a parent could do that to their kid. After a lot of deliberation, I have concluded that some adults would rather not dwell on the abandonment, and Álvaro was one of these.

He refused to look back. I'll never know how this is possible. If I let it, the curiosity would kill me. If I had turned out to be an incel or a murderer or a conspiracy theorist, a Holocaust or Sandy Hook denier, then I could see why my father might want to steer clear. But having met me, having seen his progeny doing well, why not claim some small part of that? Why disappear? Only he can say.

Chapter Forty-Five

As a kid, I had to come to grips with Álvaro's absence. Fortunately, in my household, I never wanted for examples of manhood to emulate or learn from. The uncle-brothers, in descending birth order, were father figures and brother figures: at times sharing their insights on how to be a man; at other times giving me hell, the way brothers do. And there is that mysterious family icon known as the uncle—the guy who can confidently slide between paternal and fraternal roles. I had three of them in-house at various times, and they all gave me models of how to be and what to avoid.

Tom, being the oldest, was most like a father figure to me. His age and experience allowed him to impart the kind of worldly wisdom that is the purview of fathers. Car can't start? Well, it's the battery, the starter, or the solenoid. He taught himself to weld, do electrical work, fix plumbing. He is the one I would go to when I needed something repaired or a problem solved.

He bought my first car and delivered it to me, a 1982 Oldsmobile Delta 88 that looked much older than its thirteen years. I was in my third semester at Blinn College when my uncle (and savior) drove that car from Lovington, New Mexico, to Brenham, Texas and flew back to Lubbock after I drove him to Houston Hobby Airport. Five years later, Tom would help me dispose of it after we had stripped the 88 of its remaining valuable parts. It was a temporary car, after all, a stopgap.

Tom never had kids of his own, and he became a surrogate dad to a number of young people in his periphery—a dad unencumbered by the many long-term concerns that might engage a parent. Tom gladly exposed me to quite a few things a kid probably shouldn't see until society inevitably draws back the curtain . . . and a kid named Tyler in seventh-grade social studies class tells you what *69* means. My family refused to let you find out from the world what you should have learned at home first. Your first sip of beer, your first swig of whiskey, your first joint, your first deliberate understanding of sex (from watching porn, of course), and more were a part of what the family allowed as an eyes-wide-open understanding of the world. We may not have grasped as much as we could have, but we would sure as hell be worldly-wise and pragmatic. Not *won't get fooled again* but, rather, *won't get fooled at all.* And if I were to engage in low-stakes teenage rebellions, I'd drink that beer or otherwise "wild out" at home, accompanied (okay, supervised) by my uncle-brothers.

Tom was also slow to anger. Not that he wouldn't get angry, but the few things that agitated him sometimes didn't seem worth getting upset about. He was quick witted, the guy who whipped out an instant joke or humorous comment, even in serious moments. His best jabs were directed at family members, and he had a way of joking around that didn't get people mad. (Well, most of the time. On occasion, he would piss someone off.)

I was always learning from Tom, and he would confide in me, a kid. He was a born storyteller who couldn't shut up, even after the lights were out and people were snoring. Rest often seemed optional for him, and he had the quirk of sleeping on the floor, directly in front of an air conditioner vent, lying on his side with his head propped up similar to Rodin's *Thinker*, except his wrist would support the side of his head rather than his chin. Time and again, I asked why he slept in such a fashion, and he would always answer that no other position was comfortable, given several injuries he had suffered to his neck and back.

He had the gift of gab, and I would see Tom chat up anyone who gave him even the faintest sign of interest. No reservations ever manifested in his interactions with people he hardly knew, and more than the rest of the family, he never knew a stranger. Effortlessly code-switching, Tom would slip into a country twang when speaking to a rural white person (what we would call a *gabacho*) or speak Spanish to a guy who'd recently arrived in New Mexico.

Make no mistake, Tom was a Big Scary Brown Guy. Though he wasn't as tall as the rest of the men in the family would ultimately be, he was broad shouldered with a large belly and deep brown skin. He might talk shit after a confrontation, but Tom always came across as respectful and rational to bosses and coworkers. His humor was a coping mechanism, as it is for me, a way of placating people who might fear us or be intimidated by our presence. I believe I may have picked up this approach from him.

Humor has a sizable disarming effect, and I'm always quick to try to put a person at ease if I meet them in a public space after dark. A quick joke or genuine smile lets people know I'm not out to get them. Tom often made such conciliatory gestures, and I would wonder why he was "overdoing it," at least to my young eyes. Now that I am older than he was when he died, I fully understand the performative quality of his outside-the-house persona.

Big Scary Brown Guys are often funny guys, I think, because they must constantly put others at ease. But the funny factor is inversely related to the respect factor, naturally. The funnier you try to be, the sillier you seem, and silly people are never taken seriously. So, you amp up your comedic repertoire, and soon you're dropping jokes and choice cuts (good-natured insults) with ease. You quickly become known as the funny guy, but then you turn into Joe Pesci in *Goodfellas* when someone starts breaking your balls and insults you a little bit. They tell you to go get your fucking shine box, and soon it's night night for Billy Batts. Because you're being funny to get people to relax, not to be a goddamn clown. If they don't see that, then you feel unappreciated—because you went through all this horseshit for nothing.

Tom was always cracking jokes at people's expense, but he didn't like to take that fire from others too much. He'd get upset if you eventually crossed the line, especially with me, because I didn't know shit from Shinola (an expression Mom was fond of using), and I was a young punk trying to drop insults on men who were my uncles, remember? I was put in my place all the time, deservedly so.

I'd forget that these guys were my uncles, and I'd mess with them as if we were actual brothers. I crossed the line often, and they would physically and verbally remind me of my place in the pecking order, which was pretty goddamned close to chicken shit on the ground. In concert, Tom, David, and Robert imperfectly filled the void in my life created by Álvaro's absence. I did have a father archetype in Dad, yes, but he was generally more of the elder who wasn't going to tell me about life or actively father the kid who was biologically his grandson.

And what does it mean to be a father, anyway? I think about what I have to be for my kids; then I think about who did that for me. For instance, my kids will come to me, eventually, if they need help with some homework. (I say eventually because they try not to ask me, because they know I'm a professor and they don't want to look stupid in front of me. Little do they know that they often are the ones teaching me.)

But I couldn't seek out Dad for help with my schoolwork, because he was illiterate. He could reckon with numbers, and as a bricklayer, he knew measurements almost intuitively. He calculated figures in his head but could only write and sign his name when called upon to do so.

This is not to say that I wasn't close to him or did not love him as a father. My first "job" as a little kid was taking off Dad's shoes at the end of the day. I'd untie them (he'd wear dress shoes—never sneakers), then I'd remove the shoe, then the dress sock, ignoring that his feet, like the feet of most people who work for a living, smelled. I always did this modest act of filial piety, even into my high school years. I was proud to do it because I knew it gave him relief and made him comfortable, and the gesture humbled me in a good way. And it's not that he was lazy or anything like that. He merely couldn't remove his shoes easily.

Dad was a Big Scary Brown Guy—the original one, as far as I was concerned—but in my lifetime, he was never in great health. As he was diabetic, I'm certain that by the end of the day, his shoes were bothersome and uncomfortable. In a strange way, I looked forward to performing our ritual. His mood lightened once he was unshod, and I was privileged to make that happen.

Chapter Forty-Six

I couldn't always relate to Dad, because of a large age gap that affected almost everything. Except for boxing and wrestling, that is. He loved those sports with a passion, and he was always asking for us to tune the TV to a wrestling or boxing match. If you went through the channels without finding anything, he'd grouse that there *had* to be boxing or wrestling on. He just knew it. If you couldn't find it, you weren't looking hard enough.

The good thing is that I also enjoyed these matches, and I especially connected to professional wrestling. I grew up in a time before the nationally televised matches of the WWE (then WWF) and WCW. This meant I often had the chance to watch matches in the regional World Class Championship Wrestling, or WCCW. It had originated as Big Time Wrestling (a much cooler name, in my opinion), run by Fritz Von Erich, the patriarch of a wrestling dynasty.

The WCCW was an organization whose territorial epicenter was Dallas–Fort Worth. Even as the WWE surged in national popularity, WCCW always felt right to us because they were relatively local (if you can call a five-hour drive distance "local"). The Von Erichs were these wrestling dynamos. Kerry Von Erich was a statuesque wrestler destined for tragedy. His brother, Kevin, was one of the rare breeds, like Jimmy "Superfly" Snuka, to always face his opponents in bare feet. King Kong Bundy, Mick Foley (as Cactus Jack), Eric Embry, Jake Roberts, and many others seemed to always be on our television screens, and Dad was a huge fan of these local matches.

We would sit around and laugh at their antics, but also rant about how the heels cheated and seemed to get away with it. It was a joy to watch wrestling matches with Dad, even if we knew they were scripted. When people would complain to me that professional wrestling was fake, I'd tell them to quit watching their soap operas and favorite shows because they were fake, too, and if we didn't want to watch fake stuff—well, let's go all the way then. Am I supposed to think that KITT is real? I wish! That Thomas Magnum was even remotely a reality? I'd squash arguments in defense of professional wrestling all day long. We never thought professional wrestling was a sport in that sense, sure. But we sure as hell knew that you can't fake the pain of falling ten feet onto a concrete slab. You try faking that.

Dad loved boxing, too, and it did not take me long to become a fan in my own right. I remember we watched the monumental middle heavyweights like Sugar Ray Leonard, Roberto Durán, Marvelous Marvin Hagler, Tommy Hearns, and others. These were such terrific matches, and then came one Iron Mike Tyson. He was so good he almost took the fun out of watching these bouts with Dad. Tyson would come out and bully his opponent, and then before we had even settled into our chairs, the fight was over. One match ended so fast, Dad stared around confused. "It's finished? *Pos, cómo hijos de la chingada . . .*"

We looked to other contenders to give us entertaining boxing rather than spectacle. A boxer with whom we could identify. If they were still alive, I have no doubt that Dad and Tom would love Canelo Álvarez. Fortunately, we had Julio César Chávez, and his magnum opus was a fight against Meldrick Taylor on March 17, 1990. If you have never seen this fight, please watch the last two minutes of round 12 on YouTube. It is worth your time, and for my money, it's the most thrilling end to a fight in sports history. After twelve grueling rounds, the fight ended with only two seconds left.

I had already begun my track career, and I finally felt like a fully fledged if nascent athlete and thus a part of the club. The buildup to the Chávez–Taylor fight was staggering, and Dad, Tom, and I were looking forward to watching it. The analysts, while respectful of Chávez—who was undefeated—mostly commented on how this was basically the end of his career. Though their tone was laudatory, it was also weirdly elegiac. He was being eulogized and lionized by anyone and everyone, and we took this as disrespect because the fight was still ongoing. Dad was angry at how they were insulting a living legend. Tom was more hopeful that this older guy was going to knock the piss out of the young fighter. As for me, I was swept up in the enthusiasm of my elders. If they said Chávez was going to win, then dammit, I believed it as well.

All during the fight, *HBO World Championship Boxing*'s Jim Lampley (who has a great voice but with whom I often disagreed) and Larry Merchant (whom I disliked more than most of the heel managers in professional wrestling) could not seem to shut up that it was so sad that Chávez was going to meet with inevitable defeat. It seemed that Father Time had finally dealt the one knockout blow Chávez could not deflect, and these older white men were so goddamn faux mournful of the great Mexican champ. I was certain they were internally and infernally gleeful at the prospect of seeing this living legend of a Brown fighter on the mat for ten seconds for the first time in his entire career. Sugar Ray Leonard, the third man on the announcing team, was less eager to prematurely proclaim his demise. As the only commentator on the broadcast who was a decorated fighter, he likely knew better than to count out any contender before fight's end.

The fight wore on—a true grinder—and I grew increasingly fed up with the commentary. "They say he's losing!" I groaned. "How? What fight are they watching?"

"It's bullshit," Dad said. "They don't want him to win."

"It's not over yet. *Este cabrón Chávez es peligroso.*" Tom was the most optimistic of the group.

My eyes were not trained like other audiences and viewers, because I was so young—not even fifteen. But I could see that Taylor's face was beginning to resemble a jack-o'-lantern still moldering on a Houston porch come Thanksgiving morning: a swollen, mushy mess. Meanwhile, Chávez hardly looked worse for the wear. Yet these experts kept telling me that the Mexican hero was ascending the gallows toward his inevitable defeat. I couldn't stand it.

The last round I will never forget. There we were in Lovington, huddled around a small color television in our trailer house. Our satellite dish gave us all the cable channels despite being so far from town, and when it wobbled in the wind, static appeared on the screen. I'm not talking about a small DirecTV satellite dish; I'm talking about a dish the size of the ones you used to see at television stations. It had to be eight to ten feet in diameter, and when we first got it (a hand-me-down from Rose, naturally), you literally had to crank this thing to get it to turn. Later, a motor was retrofitted so that we could turn it without going outside. Praise be!

Going into the last round, I was nervous. I felt that if Chávez lost here, it would somehow reflect on all Latinos. I know that's not fair, but that's how the media positions underrepresented groups. Despite his perfect career to that point, this one loss would make Chávez a loser forever. (American boxing experts didn't want to give Chávez credit for so many wins, saying that many of his fights were in Mexico and thus suspect.) I wanted nothing more than for Chávez to win in the final round, but I didn't think it was going to happen. I knew those incredible boxing finales were the stuff of *Rocky* movies. Lampley and Merchant, in their best Statler and Waldorf routine, stressed repeatedly that all Taylor had to do was stay away from Chávez, and they had almost convinced me. This was in the bag. And they were right. And yet, here was Taylor, mixing it up with Chávez. In the lizard part of my brain, I appreciated what Taylor was doing. He wasn't going out like that, running and hiding. He was going to stand toe to toe with Chávez, the probabilities and statistics be damned. There must be some happy medium between defending a lead and continuing to play aggressively. Taylor was too aggressive.

It proved to be an all-time mistake. In this, the final round, in its waning seconds, Chávez caught Taylor with a perfectly timed right, stunning the younger fighter, who stumbled toward Chávez, making him look like he had barged the Mexican. He probably should have backed off at that point, but instead he stumbled forward right into the trap the older, more experienced fighter had set for him. In an explosive series of punches, Chávez turned Taylor into the corner and summarily knocked him to the canvas.

You've never heard three Latinos scream in delight the way we did in our trailer that evening. When he finally stood up, Taylor was out on his feet—a term of art meaning he was effectively knocked out while standing. Referee Richard Steele continued his count to the mandatory eight, then asked Taylor if he was okay and could continue. Steele peered deeply into Taylor's puffy eyes and must have concluded that Taylor, keeping himself upright by holding on to the top rope, was now sitting comfortably somewhere in the next week. The referee threw his hands into the air and called the fight in Chávez's favor with two seconds left. It was over.

Pandemonium ensued. We couldn't believe it, and neither could Lampley or Merchant. They immediately wondered if Steele had been too quick to call the fight for Chávez. "You're gonna watch Lou Duva [Taylor's manager] *go crazy now!*" Lampley shrieked. We watched the last round again and again (we had recorded the fight) and tried to understand what had happened. Tom gloated because he had called it already. Chávez was dangerous, he had said, and even with one second in the fight, he could win. He was correct. Turns out Chávez had a second to spare, even.

When Merchant interviewed Taylor in the ring after, Taylor had felt cheated. He said he was "throwing flurries," a sign to him that he was still in the fight. But it was so clear to us. Never count out a Latino who has gone more miles down the road in Reverse than you have in Drive. As far as I know, Tom coined that expression. It's one of my favorite sayings. We were proud of Chávez. His indomitable spirit made the *galleros* in us say he was *puro Hatch.*

Throwing flurries thus became a shorthand between me and Tom, and for years afterward, we often marveled at how that fight had ended. "I was throwing flurries, Larry!" Tom would say apropos of anything we had overestimated or screwed up. It meant that you had deluded yourself into thinking you were doing far better than you were. But we also used it with reference to Chávez— people can proclaim your inevitable defeat even while you still have a puncher's chance—so the phrase had a double meaning for us. Other improbable sports moments have come and gone, but Chávez defeating Taylor with two seconds left spoke to us in ways that are perhaps hard for many to understand.

I had no father in my life, true. I did have men, however, who were flawed and integral to my own development. Fatherhood is a dicey game, and no doubt there are all sorts of permutations of it that influence how each of us has managed to face the world. I had imperfect women who stepped up and prepared me in the only ways they knew, even if those ways were harmful and hurtful. Sometimes you think you're throwing flurries when you're out of the fight. But sometimes you're winning even when everyone is writing your obituary.

Chapter Forty-Seven

When I left for Blinn College, my place and standing in the family were over and done—though I wouldn't realize it for years. Crisito, with all the smarts and potential, had flown the coop, had effectively escaped the temple of doom, and he was now out there amid the flotsam and jetsam of the wider world. Now that I was living and sleeping under different roofs, I was decidedly outside the circle of trust. As far as my family was concerned, I was over.

Well, that's not fair. Dad always remained proud if a bit sad that I had left for college. The man had claimed successes on my behalf before anyone else, like some prophet, and part of his pride for me was in his ability to foretell that I would be exceptional at something that involved my brain. He would tell anyone who would listen, perhaps after a phone call with me about how things were going at college, that I was going to "make it." I think he meant that I would be independent, out of trouble, with some level of success in whatever field or career I selected. Self-sufficient. But he also would say it in a way that more than hinted that I was able to do this while others could not. Plus, I was his first grandchild, first grandson, and much more like a son. Perhaps he above all others wanted me to do well, even if it meant my leaving home.

But because I was his grandson, and he ultimately viewed me as such, I don't think he felt possessive of me, as Rene and Mom did. He didn't require my presence in the same way as he did his three sons. I'm not hurt by that; it makes sense to me.

My uncle-brothers also supported me in various ways when I left, intrigued by what I was learning and the experiences I was having. David was living outside of Houston, not very far away if I needed something. Robert was going with me for a time to make sure I was settled, but he would also stay with David and work with him (to send money home, naturally). Tom understood I had to go, and he supported me always, even though I wasn't going to be around to assist him with the roosters anymore. He had plenty of helpers and was doing fine. Diana, in middle school when I left, would thrive as best she could, especially when she, too, found athletics. Like Rene, she pursued cheerleading.

The truth was that I was done as far as Rene and Mom were concerned. They would offer minimal encouragement once I left, though they always reminded me to be careful and not get into trouble.

I received modest financial aid because my family didn't have much to spare to begin with. Being on a "full scholarship" generally meant there were few things I had to spend my money on in terms of tuition, fees, and books, but I was on my own for any other spending dollars. Food always seemed to be a problem for me (what we call food scarcity at today's university). The dining hall served three meals a day, crammed into about ten hours, meaning we had dinner around five thirty. For students routinely up past midnight, eating dinner so early was trouble. On Sundays, Blinn offered a single meal—lunch—and that was it.

Any extra money I could get was spent on snacks and food. With no refrigerator and only a communal microwave in the dorm to prepare hot food, I ate a lot of peanut butter sandwiches and instant ramen noodles. I left the beer buying to the older, international athletes on the track team. In turn, I edited and sometimes heavily rewrote whole class papers for them. It was a trade that worked for everyone, and it came easy to me. I'd put in minimal time and effort, they'd get a B, and I'd get beer or a few bucks from Swedish or Ukrainian teammates.

During my first semester, Rene sent me two large care packages. Whole boxes of Post Toasties, bags of trail mix, beef jerky, and other snacks that Rene thought I'd like. I appreciated it immensely when they arrived. Food was food.

But I had not expected to mean something different to my family after leaving home. Even if I had seen them run off other family members before—people like Rose and David—I didn't think that shit applied to me too. I was leaving to get an education and pursue this sports dream I had, not to get married. That sports dream, unfolding steadily as a pleasant reality in the form of an athletic scholarship, gave me a sense of purpose and direction. The work I had completed, and was preparing to embark on, was real. The accolades and attention I garnered were real. Going to college was the next step in a natural progression. And it, too, was real.

Only it wasn't so natural as I had imagined. From that moment on, I became more and more of an outsider to my family. Everyone's attention and love turned toward the remaining children under their roof—Diana and Giro. When I visited during breaks from school, Rene would rave about them and how they were so good. And she would remind me of how I had always displayed a tendency toward selfishness, of which my college adventures were proof positive. "You were always so selfish!" she'd say whenever she could fit it into conversation. What I should have done, according to her and Mom, was stayed home and worked, giving most of my income to the family. Perhaps after seven years or so, I could leave home with their blessing.

I had already been doing that for years, though! All my efforts working those onion fields and in cockfighting usually earned me twenty bucks here and there. When I heard that I had to stay and contribute to the family even into adulthood, I thought of Disney's *Sleeping Beauty*, when Maleficent mocks Prince Phillip's future as a broken-down old man. He was finally allowed to leave his dungeon cell on his old nag, a shell of his former glory.

Rene would describe that tradition of self-denial and dreams deferred as if it were both immutable and logical. But couldn't she see that it never worked out that way? She and Tom, in fact, had never left home. While she viewed their decision to stay as akin to earning treasure in heaven for honoring their parents, I saw it as unreasonable, unnecessary sacrifice. Ultimately, to leave the family without drama or trauma was impossible.

Another major problem with waiting for years before leaving home was that athletic talent is on a timer, and scholarships don't sit around on a shelf for years. NCAA rules also limited how old you could be and still compete. Rene was smart enough to understand this, but she was also stubborn enough not to care.

I don't know if I was aware of what would happen to me once I left. I had not received much guidance beyond the generic notion that having a college degree would make you more employable. Honestly, I was focused only on my throwing. I had an inkling that I might be able to compete on the world stage, but I knew early on that even the best throwers in the United States weren't earning what run-of-the-mill NFL or NBA athletes were making.

Most of all, however, I had the desire to make enough money to help my family. They might have wanted me home longer so I would hand over my paychecks to Mom or Rene and contribute to the household, but I fantasized about paying *all* their bills. That was my castle in the air for winning the lotto. Discharging their debt would make me a good son in their eyes, at long last.

For much of my upbringing, it was painfully obvious that we had no money sense. I would tag along with Rene on a run to Bob's or Furr's when, after what seemed like weeks without proper food, we suddenly were able to buy groceries. I learned about the booklets of government food stamps that looked like a cross between coupons and currency to my young eyes. These were exchanged for tangible relief: food in the house.

In one act of desperation, I was put to work licking and affixing S&H Green Stamps into different booklets. The trading stamps were a light green color with the stylized *S&H* in bright red. Nearly extinct by the second half of the decade of excess, the convoluted premium program had come down to us from a bygone era. After we bought groceries, the cashier would turn a wheel on a device that resembled a rotary phone dial. The device would spit out a strip of gummed stamps, which you were supposed to take home and add to your collection. When you had collected enough, you could redeem the stamps for merchandise. It was essentially a rewards program.

We had trash bags filled with these stamps, or so it seemed. I was licking stamps until I was practically in the same danger as George Costanza's fiancée on *Seinfeld*, who perished from licking wedding invitation envelopes and ingesting all the glue. God knows how many booklets I filled. Visions of what we were going to get with these stamps danced in my head: Video games? A TV? For sure something electronic. No goddamn doubt.

But when we went to redeem a mountain of stamp booklets, we could hardly get anything. The items were so underwhelming, whatever we got, I cannot even remember them. It was humiliating. I didn't blame the Sperry & Hutchinson Company, though. It was merely another lesson in expectation versus reality.

We were always behind on some payment or other, no matter how one looked at it. And I ached to live a life free from the oppressive thoughts that surrounded our lack of resources. I thought the aim of a college education, beyond pushing my athletic ability and talent to their full potential, was to get a job good enough to allow me to get my family out of debt and pay their monthly bills. That was it. I saw professional athletes doing that, and rappers like the Notorious B.I.G. talked about indulging their mothers in a lavish lifestyle after a lifetime of hardship. Their families didn't have to worry about anything anymore.

I wanted to do that.

I wanted to save my family like that.

I wanted to save Rene like that.

But it annoyed her that I left Lovington. It was a betrayal. And with every milestone I reached and accomplishment I attained, the more distant we became. The closer I got to positioning myself to help her out financially, the greater her revulsion at the very thought.

Chapter Forty-Eight

I received a full scholarship to be on the Blinn College track team, which was as serendipitous as winning a small lotto jackpot, even if Rene didn't see it that way. My high school coaches had not bothered to help me with recruitment for whatever reason, despite the fact that I was a highly ranked thrower nationally in two events. The Blinn coaches ultimately contacted me because I had taken the ACT college entrance exam, scored fairly high (my verbal score, English and reading, was like in the 30s; my math and analytical scores were far less impressive), and was allowed to send my scores to three schools. One of the places I had my scores sent was Blinn College because I didn't know any better. Unbelievably, the coaches there contacted me via Rene.

She approached me seriously one day after track practice, wearing a shirt two sizes too big and sweatpants to match. "Chris, someone called me from Blinn Junior College today. He said he was a track coach. They want to talk to you about a possible scholarship to go there or something." Her tone was reserved and did not evince the kind of excitement you might associate with good news.

For a moment I was confused because Rene never could seem to pronounce *Blinn* as one syllable. She would say, *Beh-LYNN*, which left me wondering because there is a Belen, New Mexico. I wondered why Belen High School had called her.

Robert overheard, and his enthusiasm in my behalf was palpable: "Blinn? Hell yeah, dude! Now you're on your fucking way! I told you!" He was a true believer in their program and the reason I even put Blinn down as one of the schools to receive my scores.

Early in my senior year, Robert had proposed Blinn College as a suitable venue for my track talents. In his one year at New Mexico Junior College, he saw the Blinn athletes and was mesmerized by their performance. If I wanted to be a part of something significant, then Blinn was a logical choice. They clearly had some secret training program, outstanding coaches, or both—so why not go there?

I had piqued their interest, confirming that I was as good as I hoped I might be. Across several calls with Coach Napoli, I was offered the opportunity to join an outstanding track and field team and have college paid for. Coach Napoli, in his role as recruiter and salesman, urged me to commit soon because they were also considering recruiting two brothers in Mission, Texas, and Blinn couldn't take us all. I knew of those brothers. They posted slightly farther throws than I had that year in the national rankings. Napoli did his job well because the thought of losing this chance if I didn't act quickly compelled me to get on board.

The coach also mentioned a guy from Carlsbad, New Mexico, crushing it in the javelin, who was coming to Blinn. Though Carlsbad was relatively close to Lovington, and we often competed at the same track meets, it was a larger district, and I never had paid it much attention. Carlsbad had no shot-putters or discus throwers to challenge me. That guy Napoli had mentioned was named Justin Gurney, and he would end up being my first college roommate. To this day, from his corner of Florida, Justin is my dearest friend and like a brother to me.

Anyway, I was sold easily on the idea of Blinn College. Texas Tech University, the natural choice for me in Lubbock, was overly close and would feel like I'd never left. One of my uncles on my father's side was attending Texas Tech, and he hosted me one weekend when I was fifteen. He and his girlfriend treated me to a football game at Jones Stadium against the University of Miami. That was fun, but the university had no special allure for me. I often think of this—that for many years of my childhood I was less than ten minutes away from Texas Tech by car—yet it seemed as far as the other side of the state to me.

I had never considered it a place to go to college until recently, when colleagues, finding out I'm from Lubbock, assume I went to Texas Tech. They say, "Why not?" And I reply, "I'm not sure, other than I needed to get away from my family." Today, Ginger is convinced that if I had attended Texas Tech, I would have been urged—likely forced—to return home, and my chances for a degree or the career I have now would never have materialized. "You would have gone back and you would have been another Tom, giving your life to your family in exchange for their approval."

Indeed, I longed for a break from my family, not because I didn't love them (as they often insisted afterward) but because I wanted to discover something beyond my immediate confines. The Llano is beautiful, but there isn't much there if you're not involved in agriculture or oil. I'd seen both industries up close and knew I wanted nothing to do with them.

When Ishmael opens *Moby-Dick* by narrating his own overwhelming desire and near obsession with going to sea, I recognized something of myself in that sort of mania from what seemed like a kindred spirit. Unlike one Ishmael, I had a desperate longing not for the sea but for a change in scenery. Anyplace away from the 806 and 505 area codes. I had been a dreamer since my earliest memories and imagined going off and living in faraway places. I would not be able to travel to the stars or Ceti Alpha V, true, but I had to go somewhere. Though I thought of leaving, I never wanted it to be forever. Deep down, I always imagined I'd return.

My first trip to a major city outside of New Mexico or Texas was that glorious Second City to compete at a national track meet called the Keebler Invitational, where I placed third. I was actually in Chicago the night the Bulls clinched their first three-peat, beating the Phoenix Suns in Arizona. Since they won the series on their opponent's home court, it took a bit of the glitter off the celebration as it concerned me. I longed to be in the city as the home team won a world championship. I wanted to feel a part of a winning tradition, and though I was never a Bulls fan per se, I was, like millions of others, a mega fan of Michael Jordan.

As I walked through O'Hare Airport early the next morning to board my return flight, Chicago Bulls commemorative shirts and memorabilia were everywhere. I picked up two overpriced shirts to take back to a girl I was friends with but never dated (her mom and Rene were friends for a time). She loved the Bulls (who didn't at that time?) and had asked me to bring a little bit of Chicago back to her. I bought those tacky championship shirts because I was too inexperienced to know what she might have wanted. But evermore, my feelings for the city were those of a first love: sweet and naïve and overflowing with devotion. Even though I was there for a national track meet, my movements strictly chaperoned so that I only went from the hotel to the track and back in large charter buses, I loved the idea of being in Chicago. Now, whenever I hear people talk shit about the Windy City, and there are plenty of those motherfuckers to go around, I want to bloody up some mouths. I enjoy Chicago every time I visit. I would live there if I could ever make it work. If Chicago would have me.

Chapter Forty-Nine

I am a blatant, biased flatlander, yes. And it's easy to see how we are prisoners to the limited places we know best, like people with ugly children who are proud of their little ones. If you grew up near mountains or sandy beaches, a place like the Llano Estacado looks boring or even forsaken. You would see me and people like me and think, perhaps, how sad or pathetic to have grown up in such a forbidding place. People with such attitudes, too, would be wrong.

The Llano Estacado is a beautiful geological formation of flatness that consistently shows its charm and no-bullshit attitude, and it tasks its inhabitants to respect it. To search deeply for fortitude. It is largely rural, and many people are connected to agribusiness or the petroleum-based industries that dominate the region. Characteristic of the Llano is a lack of water, which comes mainly from underground via the Ogallala Aquifer. The vast yet finite source of fresh water likely dates to the last ice age, and directly affects the farming industry. Agriculture is as integral a way of life on the Llano as it is across most of the Great Plains, which relies on the same immense store of underground water. Beneath this tableland are parts of the gigantic Permian Basin, which energizes the oil economy of the region.

These resources allow people to live in the Llano, thanks to modern technology. Without such amenities, it's no wonder that early visitors to this area were so quick to disparage it or speak of with foreboding—people like Charles Goodnight, Randolph Marcy, and, of course, Francisco Vásquez de Coronado. But as flatlanders continue to drain its subterranean cradles of water and oil, we are relentlessly moving to a time when the Llano will again live up to its reputation as inhospitable for human settlement. We are but temporary visitors; the Llano Estacado will transform and move on without noticing we were ever there.

Loving the Llano enough to leave it paradoxically made me pine for its flat, sere horizons. Or, at least, I romanticized it even as I do in this memoir. But that is fine. The Llano Estacado has so many detractors, so many people who hate it, there ought to be more folks glamorizing it as a sort of correction. (Apologies to Larry McMurtry, who famously chastised Texas writers to stop romanticizing the West.) Watch the movie *Hell or High Water*, a neo-Western film that does a great job of capturing the Llano. The classic film *Hud*, a favorite of mine (based on a McMurtry novel!), does as well—in gorgeous black and white. People want to call the Llano an armpit or whatever. Fine. Maybe it is. But maybe there is always a place more scenic, beautiful, entertaining, or livable than the one you are in at any given moment. There are worse places that I can think of. And maybe someone loves those places too. Maybe you live in an armpit relative to other places.

I'm proud that Buddy Holly is Lubbock's favorite son and that Dad met Holly. The rocketing rock star was having a house built for his mother, as a good son should, and he wanted to meet the man who had built this one brick mantel and fireplace he had seen. Well, it was Dad who had designed and built it, see? Holly is like a godfather of rock and roll. Without him you don't have Roy Orbison (also from the Llano Estacado). You don't have the Beatles. You don't have the Rolling Stones. Oh, we may have had rock in a different form, thanks to so many Black musicians who worked in relative obscurity. But Buddy Holly changed the game. And he was from Lubbock, and Dad had met him not long before the music died. So how about a little of that respect and nostalgia after all?

Brenham was a welcome change, but it was likely too much, too quickly. The late summer stickiness was so overwhelming I thought I could see the humidity as mist or even fog. Like a malevolent spirit that refused to go away. Not long after I moved there, someone told me that you can never adapt to a humid place unless you were born and raised there. Well, then I was properly fucked, seeing as I came from an arid land of wind and dust. My anonymous sage was proved correct because for years I bemoaned and begrudged the humidity in that part of Texas. In my naïveté, I had assumed I would get used to it, that it would recede to background noise. Hell, it gets hot on the Llano, and the sun can scorch skin the way a magnifying glass intensifies heat and light to burn through grass and ants. Surely I could handle a little humidity.

But I was overwhelmed before I had completed my first practice. Even navigating the line in Old Main to register for classes (ah, the good old days!) was a nightmare. That old building, crammed with eighteen- and nineteen-year-olds and their corresponding odors on all levels, even stairwells and landings, was insufficiently air-conditioned. I was utterly miserable. After a few hours, I was ready to sign up for any course so long as this shit could be over and I could deposit myself before an air conditioner vent before I melted beyond all recognition.

After I had registered for classes, Robert drove me back to David's home in Katy, over an hour away, for the weekend. Robert stayed there for at least a few weeks, working with David in a job that did patio and deck resurfacing. It would be my last weekend before the start of my college career. We went to Walmart and picked up some supplies for independent living—soap, shampoo, deodorant, and the like, and a Smith Corona typewriter billed as a word processor, with a tiny LCD screen about the size of a medium Band-Aid. This, along with school supplies and a backpack, we stuffed into a few laundry baskets before driving to Blinn midafternoon on Sunday. Robert parked right in front of Regents Hall, and we went inside.

When I got to my dorm room, I found the door unlocked, and there was Justin—sitting in the sparse room, waiting for me or who knows what else.

He popped off his bed and sprang to help. "Hey! You're Chris? Awesome! I'm Justin!" He shook my hand and Robert's. "Let me help you guys out! Is there more in your car?" A few minutes later, everything I owned was in that tiny room. I gave Robert a hug, and he wished me luck. He said he would come back for me Friday evening.

Justin and I hit it off quickly, and it was clear that we had similar interests and amenable personalities. He was tall, blond with geeky glasses, and most important, he had a car—a 280ZX. They had put us together as roommates likely because we had the common bond of New Mexico, even though we were both Texas boys at heart. He would go to Carlsbad to throw the javelin during track season (Texas high schools had outlawed the event many years before), but he was mostly an Austin-area kid who went to Leander High School. Before that, he and his folks hailed from Pittsburgh.

It was then, on that late Sunday afternoon, that I learned Mark Napoli, the coach who had recruited me, was no longer at Blinn. He had suddenly taken a job as a coach at a Big Ten university. As much as I have tried to remember, I do not recall receiving word from Coach Napoli letting me or Rene or my family know that he was departing the program. He was the contact person for us and had spoken to Rene about Blinn being a good place for me, but he did not have the common courtesy to keep us informed. Not that it would have changed anything for me. I was going to Blinn no matter what. But for Justin, the oversight was simply inexcusable. His parents were furious, too, especially since Justin had also been recruited by the University of Texas. I think a part of him regretted not going to UT—though another part of him admits we had such a great time there in Brenham.

We went to grab a bite to eat, courtesy of Justin's car, and we returned to find our new coach moving into the dorm room next to us. Coach Tim Landon had a little mustache and a blond flattop that would have made Major Guile, the *Street Fighter* character, envious. The coach would know nothing of throws and was more of a sprint and relay coach. Justin and I were equally unenthusiastic about the guy.

Classes began and I quickly found my footing. My biology class was fun, and I did well from the jump. English was a breeze because I had been trained by the best (Mrs. Espinoza, my English teacher senior year), and I had an affinity for writing that helped me not be so stressed about it. I couldn't even explain how I wrote an essay; I always went by intuition. I had a kind of ear for it.

My prof, a soft-spoken man with hair and beard like the Nazarene, pulled me aside one day to encourage my writing. He said I had a journalistic, almost op-ed feel to my writing that showcased my voice. Initially, I thought he was criticizing me, but it turned out he was encouraging me. That boosted my confidence and made me feel like I perhaps belonged, but my mathematics skills were sorely lacking.

I took a Texas history class with a prof who, looking back, was almost assuredly gay but had to hide it. On the first day of class, as we went around the room, he asked me, "Are you a football player? You have a thick neck!" I wasn't sure if that was a compliment or what, or even proper. He also was very friendly with many of the international track team members, coming to the dorm to take them who knows where.

All the classes, however, were secondary to why I thought I was there. Today, in my various roles at my university, I remind any student I am connected to that their first priority is to graduate with their degree—to persist and persevere to the diploma. But eighteen-year-old me was there to throw the shot put and the discus and to throw each as far as I was capable. I was there to win championships and take the next step to a four-year program. My thoughts were fixed on Texas A&M University, which had a legendary history with shot-putters. I was supremely confident that I could do it.

But that shit vanished quicker than you could say Jack Robinson.

Chapter Fifty

As the time for the first of many practices neared, Justin and I sauntered over to the field house, where our locker rooms were, and made our way to Head Coach Steve Silver's office. He was a tall, lean guy with dark curly hair and mustache and a look right out of a seventies porn flick. He had the quirk of writing with a ruler so that the bottom of his words and letters were perfectly in a line, and he was doing that when we walked in. He was brash, had won many championship trophies, had coached the Olympic team of an African nation, and had been Samuel Matete's coach—an enormous feather in his cap. Silver was a hell of a recruiter, but along the way, he made numerous enemies who wanted to destroy his career utterly. Like, he made people want to obliterate any chances he might have of holding a full-time job. He was protected by the college president at the time, who purportedly gave Silver a huge budget and inoculated him from people who wanted to see him fail. But we didn't know that until much later.

"Hey, Coach," I asked on behalf of both me and Justin. "We had a question about practice."

"Coach Landon can answer your question," he said after some banter. "You'll be with him."

"What you wanna know, González?" Landon said from his tiny Munchkin desk to the left of Silver's, who never took his eyes off the paper he was writing on, his ruler working precise but oversized lettering with flat bases. When he finished, he carefully folded the sheet of paper like a practiced origamist and stuffed it into a manila envelope. Though he was loud, a real Mr. Type A personality, I liked him much more than I did Landon—whom we quickly took to calling Sarge, on account of his high flattop (again, think Guile or Jean Pierre Polnareff) and his pretend intensity. Like a pro wrestling manager brought to life. A low-rent version of Jimmy "Mouth of the South" Hart or something. Eric Bischoff in Landon's dreams.

"Well," I began, looking quickly to Justin for backup. "Do we need to wear anything special to practice? Do we bring our throwing shoes or what?"

Landon smiled, revealing slightly gapped teeth behind his dark blond pornstache. He had one too. "Don't worry, fellas. We're just gonna do some warm-ups. Calisthenics. Stretching. No big deal."

Justin smelled bullshit, and after Napoli ghosted both of us, Justin didn't trust any of these crummy coaches. He had second thoughts about coming to Blinn at all, as he would tell me later. In terms of his college career as a javelin thrower, it was the worst mistake he could have made. He and I coached ourselves with recordings of slightly better throwers with worse technique than our own because Landon had zero sense of how throwing events worked. But in terms of Justin's social experiences and his friendship with me, he was happy to have stayed. I'm so thankful he did. It wouldn't have been the same without him. But here, now, in front of Sarge, who impressed us not in the least, Justin asked, "Are we going to run?"

"Yeah," I threw in as my small token of solidarity. "We need running shoes or something?" I didn't even know what the fuck running shoes were. Neither did Justin. Turns out, we had never owned a pair of running shoes in our lives. We brought our black Nike basketball sneakers with the white swoosh, and it was the only pair of athletic shoes each of us had.

"There's gonna be some running involved, but you guys will be fine. Hell, I once ran a half-marathon in high-tops." Landon seemed to be mocking us. "I'm telling you, you fellas will be fine."

Justin and I left them to their devices and walked back to our room, knowing the next day was going to sting a little. We comforted ourselves with the knowledge that we were elite athletes in our highly specialized events; therefore, what could be the problem? Throwers didn't run—rarely did they run any long distances. I think we were prepared to lift and throw right out of the gate.

That day was gray and laden with a ponderous humidity. It looked ready to rain at any moment, depressing my spirits. My Nike basketball shoes were already concrete blocks. One quick survey of the other athletes, many of whom were still unknown to me at the time, found them outfitted with the proper gear. I had that persistent feeling that I didn't belong.

Whatever it was that we were about to do, the rain would likely make it worse. And, as I found out not long before, rain in that part of the state and at that time of late summer only managed to make the humidity and heat worse. I was sweating before I'd even done anything, and my sweat failed to have the expected effect of evaporative cooling. I dreaded what was about to come. I kept admonishing myself not to be an embarrassment, but plainly I couldn't guarantee it.

Everyone began to gather near one end of the track, teammates I had never even laid eyes on before. I had met Tim Montgomery on my first look-see of Regents Hall, and he was nice enough and welcoming to me. He was small and lithe, and I would never have believed, if someone had told me, that Tim was probably already one of the fastest human beings on the planet. The body has its illusions and mysteries. Sometimes the biggest guys are not the strongest or most powerful. That was a mantra I had to believe like gospel, as I was routinely one of the smaller throwers at any given track meet.

I stood there like the n00b and rube I was, in glorious black Nike basketball shoes with the white swoosh, and Justin looked like he got the same memo about how to dress inappropriately for our task ahead. Landon and a second coach named Vance suddenly told us to start running in an activity they unimaginatively called "continuous warmup."

Vance seemed little more than a kid himself, but he wasn't. Small with a build that hinted he could traverse about ten miles with Yoda in a backpack at a six-minute-per-mile pace before breaking into a sweat. He would soon be such a purveyor of pain and soreness that Justin and I took to calling him "the Villain."

The continuous warmup was six laps of jogging on the track, so a mile and a half. But every hundred meters, we stopped to perform ten repetitions of some calisthenic exercise. For example, we would jog a hundred meters, stop, do ten jumping jacks, then continue jogging for another hundred meters, where we would stop and do ten burpees, and so on, until six laps had been completed.

It was not long before I could see how relatively out of shape I was. I had done little to nothing all summer after the Keebler Invitational in June, and it showed. Plus, the sprinters and decathletes were setting the pace, and I noticed I was falling farther and farther behind. At one point, I skipped a round of calisthenics because everyone finished right as I got there.

With two laps to go, I wondered if I was going to make it. I wondered if I was about to quit, which, if I did, would prove I didn't belong on this team. But I screamed at myself in my mind to stick with it and finish. If I quit now, I might as well call Robert and tell him to come get me. I refused to quit.

With the continuous warmup completed, it was time for the actual practice to begin. No workout was ever harder than that first one nor more triumphant. I was now on my own, set to pursue hard-won victories and degrees, while all the while I drifted further and further away from the shaping forces of my family. It did not stop me. I pushed, fell, rose up again only to fall once more. College, love, friendship, heartache, loss, depression, all stimulated growth within me—all things to be explored in another memoir. But the rising and falling that I endured for the next several years remade me, often miserably.

Until the day came finally when Rene and Mom decided never to speak to me again. I mourned them both on that day, sure I had seen them for the last time.

Book IV

Chapter Fifty-One

Seventeen years after my first semester at Blinn College, I was in Columbus, Ohio, in the middle of a PhD program.

November in Central Ohio could be irritatingly cold for a *tejano* like me, who had experienced snow as a reality only sporadically in his life before then, like extraordinary celestial alignments that invoked dread in folks who knew no better centuries ago. There in the Buckeye State, they measured snow in feet and had varying levels of "snow emergencies." They spoke of inbound snow like a pesky but beloved relative who was due for an inevitable visit and was most celebrated upon their return to wherever they had come from. (Like Tío Pancho, except he wasn't that beloved.) The iron skies unleashed their payload of frozen flakes, and mostly, Ohioans did not complain too much. But there were other kinds of cold.

Buckeye snow was nothing compared to the reality of an incarcerated mother. Cold-blooded. I was not the reason she was there, for the record, but still pretty goddamn cold-blooded. She was there, the freezing concrete against her decrepit, inflamed skin, which bruised easily and tore open if handled with even the slightest inattention. I imagined how her rheumatoid arthritis and gout tortured her knees, the articulation of the femur, patella, and tibia no longer cushioned with precious, underappreciated cartilage.

Enjoy your knees, youths of the world! Take pleasure in your wondrous movable parts, those marvels of engineering and evolution that have extended your range of motion without the hurts meted out by gravity and friction. Abuse them at your peril, for someday the bill will come due.

Rene's bill came due with a vengeance in the form of an unrelenting prison term. There are no real medications in a state penitentiary to ease the suffering of physical pain. Let's get that out of the way now. They don't give a shit about you once you're behind bars. When I was employed by the Texas

Department of Criminal Justice thirteen years earlier, I specifically remember the day the instructors of our mandatory training emphasized how a person's incarceration was, in fact, the punishment for the crime. We employees, we were told, were not empowered or encouraged to make their lives more hellish by insulting them, mocking them, causing them pain or harm, or denying them services. This, of course, is the difference between theory and practice, between idealism and sadism.

At the end of my tenure as a "recreation coordinator"—a laughable job title but actually an important role within the prison system—we broke records for high temperatures and consecutive days of scorching heat across Texas, and especially at the Goree Unit in Huntsville, where I worked. But rather than mitigate unbearable temperatures in buildings deliberately made without air-conditioning, the prison administration made the people in prison endure a lockdown, where they were not allowed to move about the prison as was typical. My own office, perched in a loft in the gymnasium, was even hotter than other spaces, thanks to a little phenomenon known as conduction—in lay terms, heat rising.

When I complained to the warden and assistant wardens about the unbearable heat, they allowed me to temporarily set up office in a portable building that had the luxury of air-conditioning. I was lucky because I wasn't serving time; I only had to work there. Those poor devils whom the criminal justice system had considered deserving of prison time had also, apparently, given up their right to be treated like human beings, when their time locked up was intended as sufficient punishment to fit their crime.

My own knowledge of the workings of a state penitentiary made even modest shadows into monsters, and I was certain that the prison keeping Rene confined and forgotten at that moment was a drafty box after its own fashion, not unbearably hot but instead cold, perched right at the cusp of high deserts and windswept mountains, not far at all from the tectonic insistence of the Continental Divide. Uranium mines lay depleted of their precious and deadly contents, old ones now boarded up as uncomfortable Cold War reminders, and new pockets of radioactive ingredients remained buried in settled quiescence until the day they were discovered and unleashed upon the world.

There were lovely ski resorts not far from the prison, and canyons and parks and Zuni reservations could be accessed a short drive away from the New Mexico Women's Correctional Facility in Grants, New Mexico. It was a three-hour drive from the fabled Four Corners Monument, where parents on summer road trips showed their kids how to be in four states at once. But these places of recreation and geologic tumult were as far from Rene as they were from me in Columbus, Ohio. Only the biting northern winds visited my mother in that place, never her son. Often, I tried not to think of her. Often enough I was successful.

I sat on a comfortable leather sofa of eggshell white, which I had not purchased, in an expansive, well-heated home that was not mine. I was home-sitting for one of my professors who was on research leave in India, the land of his ancestors—reading in preparation for my doctoral candidacy exam in English at the Ohio State University, in easy repose on a cold gray Sunday morning typical of Novembers in Ohio.

Today I read Borges, specifically, plowing through as many of his short stories as I could manage. When reading Borges, one got the sense of straddling a liminal space of our reality, as if we have taken up residence in the fringes of a kind of multiverse. I feel as if I have found myself moving along a garden of forking paths with a certain past behind me and one of infinite possible futures ahead. I recognized my present, my now, as one among many possible nows, and this included Rene's now and the nows of everyone I knew. Borges made me consider all aspects of my life's timeline as if they were pieces of a dissected frog with pins in all the right parts with labels written in a tidy hand.

That sense of a strange, off-kilter world now only intensified in me when I noticed my cell phone activated by a number whose area code I instantly knew. The caller originated from New Mexico: 505. I normally didn't answer calls from unfamiliar numbers, but I had the sickening feeling the call was one I could not ignore and would likely regret whether I answered or not. I knew it was her, and I'd be compelled to think of her now in my now. Our nows had converged once more to become a now singularity.

I answered by saying, "Hello?" in a way that did not mask the dread surging through me. An operator cut me off with a patent lack of respect, and it turned my dread into resentment. This operator must find little pleasure in her job, and maybe it was pleasurable to snap at unsuspecting people on the phone and give petty satisfaction to her likely shitty life. A grating voice intoned, droned, and I hated this woman with the power of a thousand supernovae. A woman was calling collect from the New Mexico Women's Correctional Facility, she remarked in that way that sounded like she could not possibly give one shit about all of this, and would I accept the charges? Which was what she cared about. Confirming it was Rene waiting at the other end, I let this bitch know I'd accept the fucking charges already. My heart pounded from the conversation I was about to have as well as the annoyance at the disembodied operator who had seemed so callous, so lacking in compassion. My heart tried everything it could do to exit my goddamn chest with each violent contraction it could muster. The pounding expressed what words could not obtain or contain. My heart wanted out.

She hailed me from the other end of the line. Rene's voice sounded far away to me, far from the receiver, as if she were speaking at the phone from across the room rather than into it. Her voice was a high-pitched tremolo, almost a child's voice. Had I gone through one of Borges's forking paths and met my mother as a child?

"I'm here," I said, trying to sound confident and compassionate at the same instance. Attentive but not too panicky. "Are you okay?" It was the sort of ludicrous question one asked when one had nothing else of substance to say. (You see someone fall on unforgiving concrete and break her arm, and you ask, "Oh, honey, are you okay?" knowing full well that shit is decidedly not okay. But you say it anyway out of reflex because you don't know how else to show your concern.) My mother was calling from prison, and here I was asking if she was okay.

It became clear that she was not calling to ask how her son was doing, or how his November was shaping up in Ohio, or how his doctoral program was turning him into a professor, or any other of many generative topics for discussion over the phone that parents had with their children. She would not have called to wish me well anyway. Today she sounded rushed, breathless, as if she had sprinted to the phone before a guard could catch her. (This was impossible because her sprinting days were far in her wake, the creaking of a ratty wheelchair now substituting for her once-powerful cheerleader legs.) I feared she was in danger but feared more that I could do nothing to stop it.

"What is it?" I asked, looking for composure in a steady voice.

"Listen," she began, then switched to Spanish. Now, when she says *listen*, I know shit's about to go down and I'd better pay close fucking attention. I intuited her code-switching to denote that she did not want the guard or someone near her to know what she was saying. Probably a reflex because chances were that the guard spoke Spanish as well, but it must give her a semblance of security and privacy. "I need you to do something for me. I need you to write to Governor Richardson for me and ask him for a Conditional Release due to extreme medical hardship." Her words were precise, even if her voice was flimsy as cheap toilet paper.

By now I was scrambling for something to write with, to write on, looking through kitchen drawers and on countertops, but she didn't wait for me. I did not want to forget any of this, and I wasn't sure if she'd be able to call again anytime soon. I remembered I had a pen near my volume of Borges's *Ficciones*, but I was flustered now. She was on a time limit, and I must now run according to her time on her own forked path. Prison time.

In English, she said, "A Conditional Release due to extreme medical hardship." She returned to Spanish. "Don't use the word *pardon*. Use the phrase I gave you. I am not asking that anything be overturned. I accept my guilt."

I wrote in panicked jerks in a knockoff Moleskine notebook. "Conditional Release. Medical hardship. Okay."

"Extreme medical hardship," she corrected. "Let Giro and Rose know what is going on."

"Okay." I was short with her because time must be about up. I wanted her to have as much time as she could get.

"They're killing me," she said in Spanish. An emotional quaver grew in her voice as she repeated, "*Me están matando.*" The mechanical click of the disconnected line let me know our conversation had ended. I was surprised by the stinging tears in my eyes. Surprised because, though I cried easily, I generally shed few tears for Rene. I wondered if those words would be the last I would ever hear her say to me.

Rene managed to call me a few more times on that gray day with further clarifying information that would aid me in writing a letter to the governor: The prison doctor's name. The medical treatment she had been receiving prior to her incarceration. The prescription meds she had been taking for excruciating pain. The notable fact that she was not contesting or questioning her sentence.

I devoted the rest of my Sunday evening to thinking about how to compose a letter to Governor Bill Richardson of New Mexico, a form of writing I'd never done before—requesting an act of clemency for my mother from an elected official. But as I had already discovered during my journey to a PhD in English, an English grad student must master (or at least become temporarily competent with) a very esoteric and specific form of writing time and time again, only to come to the realization that the genre would never be relevant thereafter.

The next morning, I awoke like a man set aflame. I was on fucking fire. Surely this was why I was here, if you wanted a kind of fatalistic spin to it. If I couldn't write a letter in my mother's behalf, then what the fuck was I doing all of this for anyway?

Chapter Fifty-Two

Governor Bill Richardson
Paroles/Pardons
Office of the Governor
State Capitol Building
Santa Fe, NM 87501

November 15, 2010

Dear Governor Richardson:

I write this letter to you on behalf of my mother, Irene Foster (NMCD #72547), who is currently an inmate at the New Mexico Women's Correctional Facility. Under the State of New Mexico Executive Clemency Guidelines, I request that you grant Ms. Foster a Conditional Release due to an extreme medical hardship of such an extent that the medical staff and facilities at NMWCF are unable to treat her condition. This block on her access to proper medical care is in direct opposition to the civil liberties granted her by the State of New Mexico and the United States of America. In short, Ms. Foster must have access to the same life-sustaining medications she received before she entered the NMWCF. Currently, she is either receiving the wrong doses, wrong medications, or no medications at all. Though I am not a doctor, I recognize that any of these conditions imperil her well-being. The medical personnel who treated my mother before her incarceration will be contacting you and your office soon to verify what I am saying. I respectfully urge you to intervene in this matter in as expedited manner as you are able.

My mother was sentenced to eighteen (18) months at NMWCF for committing fraud. Neither she nor any of her advocates dispute the validity of the sentence. However, her debilitating medical and health issues and her age make for a greater punishment than is warranted in her case. She suffers from Type II diabetes, congestive heart disease, hypertension, crippling arthritis—specifically in her knees, which confines her to a wheelchair—and bipolar disorder. In fact, as noted by Dr. Unlaneta, the staff psychiatrist at NMWCF, my mother's bipolar disorder and insufficient medication may have led her to make the choices that led her to prison time in the first place. In addition, her immobility makes her the target of the corrections officers' ire when she does not move fast enough for them during "count time." Simply put, her debilitating conditions limit her ability to willfully comply with the stringent policies and procedures of NMWCF. The result of this is an unnecessary stress and strain on both my mother and the unit personnel. Ms. Foster's punishment is a loss of her freedom; it should not be a loss of her humanity.

Notwithstanding, my mother was fully prepared to serve her time in the most constructive way possible. However, the lack of proper medical staffing at the NMWCF has not only made this an impossibility, the fact of the matter is that I now fear for her life. I fear that she may have a cardiac event in the facility and she will not get the treatment she or any human being deserves. Someone with such an array of sensitive medical conditions and precise prescription doses cannot be given doses of medicine haphazardly. Doing so either shows indifference, negligence, or liability. I am willing to appeal to the greater sensibilities of NMWCF and readily accept that this is not deliberate. But the fact remains that the medical staff has already proven to be unable to give Ms. Foster the right dosage and type of medicine for her diabetes. I do not understand the reasons for this. At any rate, this signals to me that NMWCF is unable to properly care for my mother's medical needs. Such improper care, in no uncertain terms, endangers her life. As a result of the mixed or missed doses, her blood sugar has dropped dangerously low on several occasions, forcing her to scramble and eat any candy or peanut butter she can find to make it through the night.

Surely you must see this is an untenable situation. I respect you, sir, for your compassion and work for our nation and the State of New Mexico. I respect you and your time, so much so that I am reticent to ask you for anything. Yet I am advocating for my mother. Though she has made mistakes that have cost her dearly, I think you would agree that these mistakes should not lead to an endangerment of her life. I urge you to consider granting Ms. Foster a Conditional Release based on her health. She is willing to serve out the rest of her time under probation. If you deem this not to be the appropriate course of action, then it is your duty as Governor of the State of New Mexico to ensure that one of your citizens under the care of one of your agencies is NOT denied medical attention under your watch. If you do not grant a Conditional Release, then you must ensure that NMWCF cares for Ms. Foster's medical needs in a humane and appropriate way. It is a violation of her human rights to do otherwise. As you are aware, such a violation would have the full force of the law against it, and there is no governor in all of our great nation that I would trust more on issues of human rights than you. You have flown to the other side of the world on behalf of a single person (I'm speaking of Mr. Paul Salopek). By comparison, you would have to do very little to uphold the civil rights of Ms. Foster.

This is an urgent case. I recognize that there is a typical backlog of other requests, but I ask that you expedite your investigation of this situation. In the interim, you can ask the Health Services Director, Dr. Vaughn, to immediately ensure that my mother has the proper medication so that her health is not compromised further. I remind you that, as Governor, it is at your discretion to use your elected office's power to aid one of the least of your citizens. I have always admired your humanity, your God-given talents to see a wrong and to make it right—and then DO something about it. Please intervene on behalf of my mother, Irene Foster, NMWCF #72547.

Sincerely,
Christopher T. González

Chapter Fifty-Three

I wrote that letter because I thought, again, that I could save Rene, and I thought the request did what it needed to do. But in the end, I never did receive acknowledgment of my petition being noted or read or doing anything beyond cluttering some bureaucrat's inbox. I received not a jot from Governor Richardson, who would be governor for only another six weeks after that. It is more than possible that he never even saw my letter. And anyway, it was stupid to think he'd be moved to help Rene's situation, which still grates on me today. As did the whole idea that an elected governor, who is almost always not a judge and has undoubtedly led a less-than-blameless life, was entitled to decide who deserved more time behind bars—or even more breath, if the person happened to be on death row. (The latter didn't apply to Governor Richardson, because New Mexico had abolished its death penalty in 2009. Texas still executes inmates on death row and leads in this category as perennially as the New England Patriots make the Super Bowl.)

For the rest of my time in Ohio, I was certain Rene would die from neglect and mistreatment in that prison. I would never see her again. Anxiety and guilt racked me, and I wasn't even the one in prison. I comforted myself with the knowledge that at least we were on speaking terms again, having settled on the tenuous cease-fire of our relationship when I saw her five months earlier at a hotel in Hobbs, New Mexico. In the end, she would survive her prison time despite pain and abuse, accept the consequences of her crimes with whatever dignity she could muster, and turn to the business of living one day at a time, loaded with prescription pills and high-powered painkillers.

Yet after everything that happened, it had become clear to me that our relationship did not survive the initial shock of my leaving home for college in the summer of 1993. It was like a violent earthquake that devastated initially and then continued to confound and instill fear as time passed and the earth occasionally rocked with menacing aftershocks and tremors. A rite of passage experienced by millions of families as a celebratory event was traumatic for my own.

Every time I speak to Rene, even now, I fear the conversation will be our last. Will I say the wrong thing? Will my tone be inappropriate? Will she hold my education against me yet again? To be sure, I tread as lightly as I can.

Chapter Fifty-Four

On the day before Valentine's Day, in 2015, I was preparing to drive 435 lonely miles from rural Commerce, Texas, to Robert's home in Morton, a tiny place near the western edge of the state. Family emergencies—funerals, potential imprisonments, deathbed congregations—were generally the only things that forced me to leave at a moment's notice, for it was rarely a wholesome occasion that pulled me back to that part of the world and that part of my life. Some earth-shattering shit must occur for my family, including me, to darken a doorstep. Even my family wanted to be left alone from itself.

Heartwarming events, mind you, were not a natural occurrence for us. They hadn't been for decades. Goodness—that is, goodwill—and good things had to be conjured, manufactured like a DIY home improvement project. But today's business was not good. It was Friday the 13th. What better day to set out to destroy your childhood home? Ever done that? Demolish the place you grew up in? Would you if the opportunity presented itself? Well, I had to tear down the old place because the State of New Mexico had presented Rene with an order to clean up the property or else. And no one wanted her to go to prison again.

If Commerce, where I lived at the time, was undersized, then Morton was infinitesimal. It existed comfortably in the quantum realm of Texas hamlets near other towns with striking names like Muleshoe and Levelland, Whiteface and Needmore. I had decided to make this trip alone after teaching my last class for the day at the local university, where I was an assistant professor of English at the time, three years on the job. It was a trip I didn't want to make at all. Alone, because there was no need to bring more people than necessary into the situation, and so, like a fool, I made my decision without consulting my wife.

Ginger hates when I do this, how I leap at every opportunity to intervene in my family's behalf. "When your brother calls," she says, "you drop everything and put your world, our world, on hold and go running off." She is correct, and I have paid the price for my rashness—my obliviousness—many times over.

Also not along for the ride: my two daughters, not yet teens.

I have tried to keep them clear of the toxic nature of my family wherever I could, especially when they were younger. Yet every once in a while, they have the opportunity to be around their Tío Robert—to hear his performative logic of the world for themselves, his NSFW language and politically incorrect musings on what he observes in society and culture, and his downright oddness. I generally would let him carry on, giving a warning to my daughters beforehand that Tío Robert frequently says things that are inappropriate, but that he tends to say these things as a way of creating the context for interesting conversation. He will deliberately take a controversial position he heard somewhere and adopt it as his own—temporarily, of course—to see if any fireworks can result from it. He is a fire starter and a bomb thrower, and I have always made excuses for him.

In 2015, my ancestral home—or what remained of it—was calling, and I knew even before I'd had an opportunity to consult Ginger, aware that it would mean my absence on this Valentine's Day, that I had to go. Not that we were especially devoted to artificial displays of mandatory affection. We'd stopped contributing to Hallmark's and Whitman's coffers even before we were married. But our young daughters might not understand why I would be gone, and long-term resentments can grow even from trifling origins, as my family has proved.

Taking my entire household with me would only exacerbate the circumstances. And anyway, I planned to be back by Sunday night to minimize the disruption in our daily routines. So, I left Commerce on a Friday afternoon. Short trip. I could suffer this alone. Enduring these travails in the history of my family had its own kind of masochistic payoff. The crucible burned hot, but it also purified.

It would not be all gloom, I told myself. I enjoyed extended trips on the road, so long as I was the one doing the driving. I loved the feel of the ground beneath the wheels and the different tones the pavement sang when the tires rolled over at high speed. Durable highways, monotonous stretches of interstates, quirky country roads that were more forgotten than neglected, they all told their stories in this way, in this production of sound and song where rubber met road, if you had the courage enough to turn down the music, or to close your mouth, and listen. And feel. The vast spectra of asphalt and concrete thoroughfares were hospitable proving grounds for ideas and deep thoughts and hypothetical situations. For practicing uncomfortable speeches to come.

With the western sun in my eyes in the waning hours of the day as I started my voyage, the gloaming before nightfall arrived right around the time I passed through the sleepy little community of St. Jo, which lay near the Trinity River. By the time I entered Wichita Falls, not far from Larry McMurtry country, it was full dark, the headlights of my Toyota Tacoma working mightily in their own way to overturn a swatch of twilight for the illumination of my journey. A right turn in Seymour heralded the halfway point of my trip. It, too, stood near the banks of a river—this one the mighty Brazos. If I were coming from Austin, I'd be halfway to Oklahoma City, Oklahoma. Because it was night, I was unable to see the contoured canyonland rise up to become the Staked Plains, the Llano Estacado that I always associate with home no matter where in the world I happened to find myself. But I knew it was out there. I did see off in the distance dozens of aircraft warning lights affixed to enormous wind turbines. The lights glowed crimson and angry-looking against the vast emptiness, like an optic monster opening its hundreds of eyes wide in perfect synchronization, then sleepily closing them, dozing for a few seconds before repeating their hypnotic, choreographed warning. They marked what refused to be seen in the stygian expanse.

As I arrived in Morton, I noted that there were a few hours left before I had to subject myself to the following day's all-out exertions. I'd be able to sleep before then with little actual rest, though. After more than seven hours on the road, my evening had only now begun. Robert would want to catch up over food and coffee long into the night, as he was wont to do whenever we were reunited.

I exited my truck, and Robert embraced me in a massive bear hug—no one I know is large enough to give me such hugs except my older brother.

He is a big man with a big beard and a big heart, though not without his imperfections and foibles.

Robert welcomed me inside, saying *pásale*, then pointed out living room and kitchen renovations, the most recent of many improvements he and his wife, Linda, had slowly made to their humble home. Like me, Robert had to learn how to manage money and keep a place neat and organized, and he has done well with what he has. Our places looked nothing like the homes in which we both grew up. Disarray had been the unifying principle of our childhoods. While I still suffer from a predisposition to messiness and financial impulsivity (Ginger gets all the credit for helping me fight against the rip tide of habit), Robert is obsessively neat and clean in certain aspects. Cleanliness is his fixation and seeming raison d'être, and his hoarding is limited mainly to cleaning products, paper towels, and various sanitizers. He can never have enough of these goods. As if he is forever cleaning his surroundings and himself. On the other hand, this is the guy who would blow his nose in the form of the so-called snot rocket on the walls when we were growing up and take a piss right outside our front door. I guess he is maniacally but selectively clean.

Before I even had a chance to sit, he took me directly to the backyard to show me his vast trove of tools, which he also stockpiled obsessively. I stepped outside and saw high-end, top-quality brands of power tools, like DeWalt and Milwaukee, prepped for loading and arranged neatly: yellow, black, and red machines destined to buzz, screech, and rend. "Everything we need is here," he observed as if I were blind. "Will make the job tomorrow a helluva lot easier." I detected the pride in his voice, an acknowledgment of the investment of time and money in the formidable collection. Though some equipment may have been purchased, I'm sure most was permanently borrowed from his work sites. "If I don't have it, we don't need it." The braggadocio of an older brother in his element.

"Good," I said. "But they won't be worth a shit if there's no place to plug in over there." I allowed that his array of tools was impressive, and I was certain that's all he heard me say. He handled them with care, lifted a reciprocating saw in admiration. The machines seemed to shout, *Power! Masculinity! Get the fuck out of the way and let me fix this bitch! I'm about to tear shit up!* They put my meager tool inventory to shame.

I enjoy power tools, but they're hardly a priority for me to seek out and buy. Sometimes I stop at Lowe's and happen upon a sale, and I imagine how I might need, say, a reciprocating saw someday. But after seeing the price—perhaps in the hundreds of dollars, even after a markdown—I'm unwilling to invest or commit. I am not frugal across the board, though. I waste good money on less useful things, always looking to sink funds into something that promises to make our lives more enjoyable, to Ginger's chagrin.

But tools don't make the cut. Robert knows this. As I prepared to drive back home on one of my prior visits to Morton, he gave me a gallon-sized ziplock bag full of screwdrivers, pliers, Channellock tongue-and-groove pliers, a hammer, various sizes of crescent wrenches. "Take some tools with you when you're on the road, goddammit. Fuck! What if you break down?"

"I'll call someone," I had answered as though it were obvious. "Maybe I'll break down in Clyde and call you right as you're about to have dinner." The face he made was pained, cut to the quick at the memory of David's breakdown in tiny Clyde years before.

* * *

It was one of those rare convergences when Robert, Linda, David, and David's second wife, Sarah, would drive to see me east of Dallas, to visit and hang out. For no other reason than to visit. Well, that's not entirely true. One reason was to come see my firstborn, Olivia, a few months old at the time.

Robert and Linda had arrived first, as the sun set. They'd requested my famous spaghetti and sauce, and it was about ready. I was glad to see them arrive safe and sound after a long drive. They had brought in their bags when Robert's cell phone rang. It was David.

I could see by Robert's face that our plan for the next few days was out the window. First, I thought David had bailed and was still at his house, which wasn't all that bad. We'd carry on without him. Then I realized it was worse than that.

Robert ended his call.

"What is it?"

"David. He's broken down somewhere near Abilene."

"Where?"

"Someplace called Clyde."

Having no knowledge of Clyde, I rummaged for a map of Texas. Clyde straddled I-20, situated nearly equidistant from David's home in Lovington and mine. Clyde—another one of these subatomic towns in the state, this one with the motto "Small City, Big Opportunities." What those opportunities are, only locals can say. "Looks like about three and a half hours from here," I called out, then showed Robert and Linda my fingertip underneath Clyde on the map. "It's the halfway point."

And there we went, to go save David before we even ate. (Ginger makes a good point: There's never discussion. No planning. Just fucking go.)

Turned out it was David's serpentine belt that went bust. But we didn't learn that till after we bought a new battery at an Abilene Walmart, then drove down the road a bit, draining the battery until David pulled over ahead of us. If we went much farther, the car would be stranded in an even more remote place. We decided to get back to the Conoco in Clyde off I-20 before the battery croaked altogether. We left the car there in Clyde and drove back to my house. I slept for about two hours; then we drove back to David's car. As luck would have it, the garage capable of repairing David's Cadillac was across I-20 from the Conoco. The whole thing was epically bad, and became such a traumatic event that even mentioning the town Clyde vexes any good temperament. Thenceforth, if the opportunity naturally arose, we stopped in Clyde to memorialize that shitty bit of happenstance.

"I don't need these tools. Seriously."

"Take 'em, bitch! I'm not fucking coming to get you. I don't give a fuck if it's in Clyde or not."

"Fine."

Chapter Fifty-Five

Now in his backyard, Robert cleared his throat, then his nose, courtesy of the snot rocket he had mastered throughout his life. "Giro is bringing a generator." He pulled a small white bottle of nasal spray from a pocket and gave each nostril several squeezes while alternatively sniffing. Squeeze sniff, squeeze sniff. The man is addicted to nasal spray. My understanding is that when the decongestant wears off, your nasal passage swells and you feel even stuffier, so you use more. But he never stops. Same with David.

I noticed Robert had acknowledged my concern about electricity only after I accepted his badass power tools tit for tat, as we brothers always seemed to do. We were always punching and counterpunching, probing for weakness and landing a not-so-gentle hit if the opportunity presented itself.

I nodded approval at Robert's plans to set up a generator.

We went back inside, and dinner was ready in his inviting home. The aroma of fried corn tortillas reminded me of childhood and Mom in front of the stove. Linda had made *enchiladas montadas* at my request, her mother's recipe. My sister-in-law was short with dark brown skin and thus an incongruous match for Robert—fair, tall, and with greenish eyes. She was eager to roll out the rug of hospitality this evening. I asked her for two fried eggs on top of my enchiladas. The chile—a salsa-like condiment of finely blended fresh jalapeños, tomatoes, onions, and cilantro—was spicier than usual, and soon my mouth was negotiating the exquisite torment of pain and pleasure.

As a child, I often wondered how my elders could consume spicy food with steaming hot coffee. I have now become that person by slow degrees on my own journey to *viejito* status. The inevitability of growing up—of maturing. Becoming the older people from your childhood, who once seemed so weird and boring to you. Hot coffee and spicy food: a good, potent reminder of who I am, of where I come from.

We ate. Before long, Robert was telling me stories from his work as a safety manager for a welding and oil field equipment company. Mostly the stories were about his boss, Matt, who owned the company and who never seemed to get that his employees were human beings with material realities that concerned something other than the company he had founded. Matt couldn't fathom why none of his employees cared about his business the way he did, why no one came in two hours early or stayed an hour late. Why no one was willing to make the sacrifices he made all the time.

I'd heard these stories before, or at least ones like them, but I didn't object. I was bored but enjoying the food. And when the tales about work were exhausted and recycled yet again, Robert transitioned to what was happening in the news and the world of pop culture. I commented in all the right places, and I didn't offer any substantive counters to his opinions. We shared many beliefs, but not all, and I knew our disagreements could wait until later. But he thrived on playing devil's advocate. He reveled in debates, as did my entire family—but Robert especially. My brother luxuriated in contrarianism as if it were the most comfortable chair in the world.

I believe that he took outrageous positions to put my mind to the test, to see how I handled a particular argument so that, if necessary, he, too, would have a model for how to answer if it ever came to that. Yet other times, he was merely looking for entertainment, to troll me, and often I obliged because I knew no other way.

During our conversations, I am often left wondering when I will get to tell Robert about how my job is going. I have tried in the past to explain what I do and share amusing career anecdotes, but nowadays, I usually don't bother. My family seems incurious as to my profession, and I suppose they simply take it on faith that I do some form of notable work as an academic at a university. I have written books and essays on a variety of subjects, most about the Latinx community—our community and culture—and rarely do they ask me to talk more about it.

I sat there at Robert's round glass-topped dining table, listening to my uncle-brother in his domain, waiting for my turn to discuss how things were going in my world. Linda didn't take part, preferring to stay in our periphery while we talked, and she jumped in only to add clarifying details or else to confirm Robert's tale or perhaps to admonish him. My turn did not come round, not for a long while, so I didn't force it. I had to be patient, though I was ready to get to the business the next morning. In reality, Robert didn't want to hear any particulars regarding my work, didn't want to listen to me talk about things he didn't know much about. I was not even sure he knew he did this.

My whole family does it. I recall recent reunions with Robert, David, Diana, Mom, and Rene: When we are all together, the conversation sidesteps direct inquiries about what I do. When I force the issue and hand over a recent book I have published, they request a personally handwritten inscription, so I turn to the endpaper and eagerly pen something heartfelt and unambiguous. There's pride in their eyes when they see my book, when they see my name on it, but I know they will only ever read the first few pages. Such is the doom of the academic, to be unknown to those who once knew you best.

My books are about the literature and narratives produced by members of my ethnic group, of notable Latinx creators of impassioned storyworlds. Not only is my family not interested in my work, but they also are not interested in nuanced understandings of the kinds of literary works Latinxs are doing in the United States. Robert often says our family was and is "too Americanized," and it frustrates me when he says it because I believe he's right. It is a phrase I return to. What does it mean for a Latinx person to be too American? I don't know. Likewise, I'll never be American enough for some people.

Soon Robert started in on our older brother, David, who was absent from our current gathering. He was estranged from us both now, even though he lived a few miles from where we gathered in Morton to dine. My family was excellent at turning its collective back on one of our own when convenient. Robert would prove this to me yet again many years later.

Grudges are tenacious in my family, and not even death can lessen their potency, as when Tom died on the operating table during heart surgery while Rene and I were beefing. She turned her back on me at the wake and refused to look my way, much less deign to speak with me. I mean, she literally spun her wheelchair so that her back was to me when I entered the room. Only the ultrasound pictures I had brought of my first child broke her spirit at last and compelled her to talk to me—for the briefest of comments. Mostly, she wanted me to know that my daughter would most likely be a source of heartbreak for me. No doubt, she rooted for that at the time.

I'm not sure whether she feels that way anymore. I don't believe so. Rene lives with me now, and I care for her to the best of my ability. She calls my daughters *mis reinas*—"my queens." They tolerate her. I think they can sense her intermittent unkindness toward me. At a minimum, my girls hold their grandmother at arm's length.

Chapter Fifty-Six

My grudge with Rene was straightforward enough: She called me one day to tell me her electricity would be cut off if she couldn't come up with $450 by the end of the day. Back in 2002, we didn't have PayPal or Venmo; if you wanted to send money instantly, you had a thing called Western Union (still around but not quite so prominent). And it cost a pretty penny. I wired the money, and Rene was seemingly grateful. I was happy to feel like a grown-up and help my family, even though I didn't have that money to give. But Rene had always made me feel guilty for leaving home and going to college, a move she called selfish. I am perpetually looking for a way to prove that I care about my family and that I'm not selfish.

A month later, she needed another cash injection. This time it was over five hundred dollars of money I didn't have. It put my family in a terrible position, and Ginger and I had a huge fight.

"She's my mother!" I argued. "How can I deny her?"

"Easy! You don't have the money!" I can always count on Ginger to parry my bullshit with facts.

I sent money that I didn't have, betraying my marriage in service to my mother's lies.

Back then I thought I always had to be there for my blood. Once I realized they weren't always there for me, I revised this calculus. So, I sent the money, even though it was again for the electricity bill, which had never been paid with the last round of money.

That wasn't all. Before these cash payouts, I had purchased a PC for Rene to use in her small bookkeeping business. After the two wire transfers, my sister tipped me off as to what was truly happening. Rene, pretending to be Diana and twenty years of age, was having these fake relationships online.

She was sending some lucky bastard my money and the computer I had bought for her. Rene was catfishing before it was even a thing.

When I called to confront her about deceiving me, she claimed her heart was hurting her and she passed the phone to Mom, who proceeded to cuss me out and spit venom at me.

"When you give money," she seethed, "you don't tell the person how to spend it. You give it of your own free will."

"You do when it's for a bill to keep your lights on!" I was irate and had never spoken to Mom in this way. "And I bought that computer for her to use, not to give away. How can y'all take my money under false pretense and then use it for something that doesn't even matter? That's like a sin." Mom considered herself religious, so that last one was for her.

"You're such a horrible person. You're terrible. I'm so sad how you turned out. How could you do this to your own mother? And you know what? She almost lost you before you were born. Now I think she should have gone ahead and miscarried."

I let the moment sink in, let the silence build. "You wish I had never been born? Okay. Then you both are dead to me."

I ended the call, and I didn't have a real conversation with them for over eight years.

Our grudges have a way of lasting, and they linger like a permanent stain, even if reconciliation has somehow been made possible. They are like red hot coals buried by innocuous gray ashes, ready to rekindle at the slightest bit of fuel and breath of wind.

Tom, who was Rene's closest brother in age, was himself transformed into something like Meteor Crater at the moment of his death—a livid symbol of a gargantuan trauma everyone wants to forget but cannot ignore. My unresolved grief over his death has left an immense emotional scar. Tom died during an operation to mend his heart, and thanks to my feud with Rene, I did not get to tell this man that I admired him, that I loved him, that I would pay tribute to his memory by living a full life in his honor. As Tom lived with Mom and Rene, he refused to defy or anger them by talking to me. We had no rancor toward each other. Our relationship was collateral damage that resulted from a separate feud, the stupidity of which had nothing to do with Tom and me.

When Robert called to tell me of Tom's death in the middle of my teaching day, I choked out the first thing that came to mind: "Did you tell him for me? Did he know?" I could barely say the words; I was crying so violently.

"I told him," Robert said. "He knew."

Sometimes a lie lessens the hurt.

Chapter Fifty-Seven

Back in Morton, Robert wanted to talk and tell stories. He was in a good mood that evening. "Giro's a little freaked out," he said as we worked through our *enchiladas montadas*. He ate fast, always had, and I was expected to keep up. "David's been asking him for money. Plus, David's all about ghosts these days—spirits and whatnot. He believes he can manipulate things with his mind. Shit like that."

"Are you kidding me?" I was more troubled than astonished. I knew David was fascinated with the unexplainable, and Sarah seemed to encourage that interest and vice versa. For instance, David believed he could communicate with spirits and capture their presence with the aid of a camera. Orbs, he called them. Harmless pursuits, but a slippery slope toward greater conspiratorial lunacy.

"He says he can put a hex on people. Like, he can see someone walking and think, 'Trip!' and that person will trip and fall."

David had clearly seen the movie *Scanners* once too often. "C'mon, man. Mind powers? Maybe he can use his mind to clean up the old homestead for us tomorrow. That would actually be useful."

"He's finally lost it."

The reason for David's estrangement from us, like the reasons why everyone always gets disowned in my family, was a minor transgression turned mortal sin. He had invested a thousand dollars in a personal training venture I launched and lost it when I shut down the business. That had been fifteen years ago, but he was still resentful. Not until I paid him back in 2018 did he treat me like a brother once more. He was on the outs with others in the family for different reasons. David and Sarah testified against Rene at her tax fraud trial. (Robert and Linda did too.) That's how these beefs happens.

Robert and I needed to discuss the plausibility of David's showing up the next day, north of Lovington, when we would be at full throttle, in demolition mode. Having him there would create an unnecessary complication for us and eat up time we didn't have. I was sure David wouldn't show.

I've always felt for Giro, David's firstborn son, a good guy who deserves better than what his father has turned out to be for him. Giro reminds me of a bear that has been domesticated—huge but gentle. Or, he did at the time. It has been several years since my cousin's gastric bypass surgery, and he has slimmed considerably.

We brothers had always made fun of each other whenever possible, but we couldn't do that with David anymore. Not with Giro around. We might tease our brother without mercy, but David was Giro's dad.

"You think David will show up tomorrow?" I challenged. I doubted it. He had always had a reputation as being slow-moving, somewhat lazy, and lacking initiative, yet wildly exacting and detail oriented. Truthfully, he was severely meticulous, almost to the point of debilitation, like most perfectionists. Tom had nicknamed David *el viejito*, and it had stuck. David was always old before his time.

Robert had the opposite problem. He worked so fast that he often screwed up whatever he was doing. *Bull in a china shop* was apt if you had the bull move out all the china while it was breaking everything in sight. Kind of defeated the point.

Robert sat, taking a long sip of his coffee through a straw. Thus he avoided soaking his long whiskers in a coffee mug. It looked idiotic but was well within his eccentric character. He smoothed out his salt-and-pepper mustache from habit because it gave him a moment longer to think before he spoke; then he rubbed his clean-shaven head. "I hope he does. If he does show up, I'm gonna say, 'Listen, bitch. You ain't real. I'm real.'" He pointed at me to emphasize his words. But it was comical, which was his aim because he wanted me to laugh.

I did laugh, not even sure what he had meant. I guess that the paranormal shit David was into wasn't as real as Robert's words and actions? Robert always had a style of telling stories, or posing hypotheticals, in ways that had me roaring with laughter. Something in the tone of his voice or an expression on his face cracked me up. He had the timing of a comedian and a knack for vocal impersonation.

"He and Giro were over there the other day. I think they had a backhoe and tore down most of what was there. Both trailers, for sure."

"It's already demoed?" Another surprise. "Where are we going to put it all?"

"There's a huge dumpster already there."

"The backhoe still there?"

"Doubt it."

"The dumpster can't be big enough. Two fucking trailers? Whole mobile homes? Bullshit. We'll need to have it emptied and brought back." I reflected for a moment, calling up a memory Robert and I shared. "Maybe we can burn it in a bonfire," I said, thinking back to the burlap onion sacks in Tulia all those years ago. "Burn it all."

Chapter Fifty-Eight

During summers, we worked helping Mom and Dad in the onion harvest in the greater Lubbock area. For years, Mom and Dad were the supervisors for the hired workers who would do the actual work of harvesting the onions. Robert and I (and sometimes David and Tom) had the job of tallying the bags of clipped onions so the workers could get paid, moving the port-a-potties from job site to job site, and always ensuring there were enough empty burlap sacks for the workers to fill. It meant going to previously worked fields, where another group of workers, unconnected to us, loaded the filled sacks onto a portable conveyor and dumped the onions into a large truck. The crew would leave the empty sacks in mounds for us to gather later. The members of this other crew surely were bastards, especially in the last years we did it.

The process for supplying workers with sacks was this: go to where the mounds of empty sacks were, load them onto our trailer, then unload them where the workers would be working. It was a dirty job, literally. Mike Rowe should try it. You'd be covered in dust and papery onion skin, no matter how careful you were. You'd blow mud out your nose for days afterward. But the worst was when the mounds got wet after a storm. By the time you'd get to load them, they'd still be heavy from being waterlogged. Your fingers and nails would be sore beyond belief. But the second worst was when the other crew would create oversized mounds out of the sacks—mounds over ten feet high. Such mounds were impossible to load into the trailer with any sort of speed or efficiency, and good luck if they got rained on. And that's why the other crew was made up of bastards of the worst kind. I think they knew how hard they were making it for us, but that didn't stop them.

In Tulia, we found the last sacks of the season, which we needed to return to the co-op warehouse in Petersburg, where they would be stored or recycled. Tulia was about an hour's drive north of Petersburg, making it a two-hour round trip to return these sacks. Not only were the mounds produced by these bastards of the jumbo variety, but the field itself must have been over twenty acres.

We pulled up to the acreage, and the mounds were as high as I had ever seen. They had done a number on us this time. "You fucking believe this shit?" I groaned as I turned down "Plush" by Stone Temple Pilots, which we had on repeat. I quickly surveyed the mounds, calculated how many loads would be involved, and estimated it would take days to finally complete the job.

"This ain't gonna work," Robert answered. He knew what I knew, but he was prepared to go where my imagination hadn't dared. "So, we're gonna fucking burn them."

"What?"

"Burn these motherfuckers," he repeated. "We'll take a couple of loads, then burn the rest."

We took several loads back to Petersburg, which took most of the day. On the last trip, Robert set fire to the remaining enormous mounds of burlap sacks. We watched them go up in flames from a safe distance in this field outside of Tulia. They probably could have seen that fire from space. I expected to get caught, or at least to have the bosses in Petersburg chew us out mightily for this reckless dumbfuckery. But so far as we knew, nothing ever came of it. Nothing that ever came back on us. And it was the last time we worked there—the last time the co-op worked in onions. Turned out to be a grand farewell, like Luke Skywalker setting his father's funeral pyre ablaze.

Back in Morton, Robert shook his head like he was trying to wake up. It was getting late, but neither of us wanted to be the first to admit it. "Too dry to start a fire. And too windy. We'll set fire to half of New Mexico and part of Texas." Now, he was mindful of fire and wind and getting caught, but I'm sure he was looking for an angle like that.

He was still thinking of David, though, and he wanted to keep roasting him. "Yeah, that's what I'm gonna tell him. 'Listen here, bitch. You ain't real. I'm real." He knew he had found a line that would keep me laughing, and so he was going to wear it out for the whole time I was there—because I'd do the same. And I was going to keep prompting him to say it because I knew it couldn't be worn out, no matter how hard we tried. We were brothers even if we weren't.

"Yeah. He's finally lost it," he repeated, as if he could scarcely believe it himself.

"We'll take a couple of loads, then burn the rest."

Chapter Fifty-Nine

The next day, Robert and I left for Lovington as the sky had begun to lighten to a beautiful, cloudless cerulean. The sky was always the most impressive thing about the Llano Estacado because of its flatness, and this day did not disappoint. I was always at ease in flat prairielands, where I could see from horizon to horizon, and I gazed deeply along the division of earth and sky as Robert drove his Ram truck toward Lovington. He played the SiriusXM loud, as he always did, turning it down only when he wanted to discuss something, which was hardly ever. I saw the deep red earth, dirt that looked like it should be on Mars, to either side of the highway, where cotton and other crops would soon be planted. I recalled all the times I had toiled in farm fields before I earned a diploma—a diploma, I would soon discover, that would be cast away as easily as spent toilet paper. Those days of grueling work were behind me; indeed, they had helped mold me, but I reminded myself how fortunate it was that my daughters would not have to endure such hardship. That did not stop me from constantly reminding them how easy they had it, however.

We pursued a southerly direction then turned west as we talked about how the events of the day would unfold. Robert perseverated on whether David would show, and I told him the chance of Julia Roberts pulling up to the old homestead was better than the likelihood of our estranged brother rolling up. I asked questions to help wrap my mind around what needed doing. How much demo had David and Giro done already? Actually done, not imagined done. What would be the best way to attack this? I mean, what's the strategy here? Were we going to get a hotel at the end of the day, or were we driving one hour back to Morton?

Robert's answers were uncertain and cautious. He hadn't thought any of this through. I wondered how much it would cost to have someone with heavy equipment handle all of this for us and whether it would be worth it. I threw money at problems wherever and whenever I could, even if I didn't have it.

Robert changed the subject abruptly, like always. "Giro needs to lose weight," he says.

Here we go again. "Don't we all? And by 'we,' I mean us. Which is to say, you."

"Yeah, but Giro's supersized." I was not surprised by this observation; Giro had always been a large guy in a family of large guys. Six feet six inches when he decided to stand fully upright and not slouch, and easily 450 pounds. Thank goodness he was sweet, cerebral, and dedicated. An angry and violent man of his size could do real damage to himself and others.

"He's fallen through the floors at Mom's house," Robert voiced as if trying to convince me. "I mean, he's literally fallen through the fucking floor. Plus, it's not healthy for him. We need to tell him to lose weight."

"Those floors are rotted, though. Anyone would fall through eventually." It was true even the last time I had been over there, years before. "That's another house that has problems we're gonna have to contend with at some future point."

He ignored me and continued his fixation with his nephew and my counterpart. "He's too big."

"Right," I said, then took a sip of coffee. "But we don't want to embarrass him. Like, how would you like it if someone came up suddenly and said to you, 'Listen, you fat bastard. You need to lose some goddam weight.' I mean, how would that actually make you feel?"

"Fuck you."

"I'm just saying, you know? You wouldn't like it if someone said, 'Look here, you sloppy fuck. You're gonna die if you don't—'"

"I ain't saying that, bitch. Listen to what I'm fucking trying to tell you, goddammit." Robert was working to convince himself as much as anyone. "We'll tell him we love him and that we want to see him well. Tell him maybe he should get that stomach surgery to help him lose weight quicker. But he has to lose weight."

"Okay," I said. "Let me know when you want to tell him, and we'll do it. You can start by saying, 'Look, I know I'm one to talk. But you look like you're gonna keel over any moment.' Then I'll follow up with, 'Yeah, you know I heard about this stomach surgery a woman got. She lost a lot of weight, and it nearly killed her, but—'"

"Hey, man. What the fuck? No scary shit."

"But it's fucking risky, okay? People honestly do have complications. Plus, I think it's pretty expensive." I sipped more coffee, delighted to be in the passenger seat, indulging in the quiet few minutes before shit hit the fan.

I didn't care, to be honest. Not now. It seemed out of the blue. I hadn't come here to get Giro on a diet. Yet a part of me always enjoyed giving Robert the business, and things were going my way this morning.

As he grew older, Robert steadily became more and more the family ascetic—the one who reminded everyone that we were killing ourselves by what we were eating and drinking. His diabetes was an omnipresent foe in his life, and he took turns battling it with berserker obstinacy and ignoring it with general lassitude. Someone had a little anemia? Robert would go on about how the best thing you needed to do was eat liver and onions, or maybe even raw liver if possible. Or eat red meat four times a day. That would surely get your anemia corrected. Were you taking enough garlic pills? How about vitamin E? Don't drink straight Cokes (that's what we called the regular ones with all the sugar and corn syrup). He was addicted to Diet Cokes, though; don't remind him of that. And so on.

Right now, Robert had set his sights on Giro's health, but I knew the concern was rooted in Robert's fear of his own sliding health. He and I had seen so many in our family take that familiar retrograde about-face: Dad, Tom, David, Rene. It felt like predestination. Destiny by DNA. Robert called diabetes the perfect disease. You literally killed yourself with indulgent food, and you did so gladly. It was insidious. But I always felt that not only did he protest too much, but what he needed to do was worry about his own health. Get that under control first, then try to help others. Otherwise, it was hypocritical to tell people to eat salads with lemon juice instead of ranch dressing while you devoured two jumbo double meat chili cheeseburgers from Pete's Drive-In No. 1 in Lubbock (529 Thirty-fourth Street), one of our all-time favorite places to clog arteries. Don't worry about somebody else's sugar intake when you gorged on two large meat lover's pizzas in a sitting, all right? That's what he could never understand, and he'd get pissed if I pointed this out.

In truth, like so many folks on the lower socioeconomic ends of this astral plane, we never did anything in a healthy fashion. Oh, we loved going to the doctor. But we could not even contemplate preventive health. Everything we ate was full bodied and of high caloric value. We would buy many cases of Cokes (twenty-four cans) at a time, and these cases would last a few days, tops. Enriched white bread with all meals (Mrs. Baird's, naturally; Farm Pac, if Mrs. Baird's wasn't available). And when we weren't making our own rich food, we were getting fast food like we owned stock in it. A few buckets of KFC tonight, maybe some Long John Silver's tomorrow, and Sonic burgers later in the week, would be a typical stretch for us. Even when we didn't seem to have much money, we still managed to have enough for fast food and junk calories. That patrimony of unhealthy eating was a legacy that was difficult to shake; it was so deeply ingrained in our sense of identity.

To this day, Robert would rather eat at a tried-and-true fast-food chain like McDonald's or Burger King than a taco truck or locally owned restaurant. It's his curse, you see, his own personal Green Mile—one that my entire family seems foreordained to walk.

As we neared our destination, he thought to call Rene to let her know we were almost there. She answered in a pert voice, high pitched, seeming excited and eager to see us. Sounded fake to me. She asked what kind of breakfast burritos we wanted, and she would bring them to us at what I was already thinking of as the demolition site. But I wasn't much interested in breakfast now. I had an itch to get there already and start tearing things up.

When the call ended, I looked at Robert. "I didn't know she was coming. To help?"

He shrugged. "She won't be out there for long. Be nice to her and don't start shit."

"I'm not." I frowned. "She's going to be in the way. She can barely stand." This wasn't exaggeration. I didn't think having her out at such a dangerous site was going to do anybody any good, but perhaps she wanted to bear witness to this destruction like the rest of us. Or perhaps it was that because this was a burden that fell to her, she owed a debt of responsibility to see this through to the end.

We exited 82 and merged onto 206, heading north, with the pavement looking like it always had to me—a way out rather than a way in.

Chapter Sixty

"Wanna see Dad and Tom?" Robert asked. It had been years since I'd seen Dad or Tom, and to say no to Robert's query would be utterly disrespectful. It would piss him off, and he was clearly going to go anyway, so why say no? And I wasn't there to start a fight. Sitting there, I had no real feelings either way, so I said, "Sure. Let's go."

The cemetery was past the electric plant, along the west side of 206. Almost as soon as Robert asked and I answered, we were turning into the cemetery, an unimpressive patch of land that, despite the best efforts of the groundskeepers, was dirt and yellow grass lined with puny trees. The sun was out in full now, and we cast long pointy shadows that looked flattened by an eastern wind. I stood before Dad's grave, and Tom's was to the right, with enough space between to accommodate another future permanent resident. Father and firstborn son, Tomás and Tomás Jr., with that middle spot already reserved for Mom when her time came to leave this world. Over five years hence, she would join them in eternal rest.

On this morning, Robert talked to Dad and Tom as if they were with us, as if they were sitting there waiting for updates and conversation, but I couldn't bring myself to do likewise. Perhaps it was because Robert was a real son, a real brother, and I was a fake. I missed them both beyond measure, and I was far away when each of them died. I felt the loss of time, the loss of opportunity, and it was part of the price I paid to pursue an education and leave home. Had I not done so, I would most likely have been with them in their final hours. Despite this, I was asked to eulogize them both, doing my absolute best, given the circumstances. As any good son or brother would do, fake or otherwise.

These two men haunted my dreams weekly, if not nightly, since their deaths—Dad in 2001, Tom in 2004. I suppose that was at least one measure of what they meant to me, and another measure of the guilt I felt in not having been with them at the end of their lives. They were always so alive in my dreams, and I consistently (and conveniently) did not recognize that they were dead.

Tom, with his ever-present black cowboy hat on his head and a huge bushy black beard, usually did not have much to say. His eyes were still hidden behind darkened glasses, but I imagined them lively and expressive nonetheless. Neither Tom nor Dad had aged in these dreamscapes, of course, and they went about doing the kinds of things they always did. They were alive and well in the mysterious neuronal apparatus of slumberland, still the Big Scary Brown Guys they had been in life—a clear signal that my mind continued to turn this unresolved issue over and over as if it were some puzzle to be solved. This was the kind of haunting I believed in—because it was real, and generally of our own making.

After a few minutes more, Robert said his goodbyes, and we continued toward our destination. We had been on the road for only a little more than an hour since we left Morton, though it felt as if we'd been on a quest for days.

But something bothered me, a mental itch I'd had since we stood near the graves of these beloved men. Finally, I thought I had it.

"Hey," I said, "wasn't Tom's gravestone supposed to be an actual, upright stone? Not a flat one?"

A few beats passed, and Robert turned to me but didn't say anything. He was staring at me, as if trying to process what I'd said. It might be that he also felt something was amiss with Tom's grave. Robert and I had footed a large portion of the tab for Tom's funeral, and Robert, especially, was key in selecting the headstone. My observation had stunned him, and for the rest of the day, he'd ruminate about what this all meant, trying and not finding some sort of mystery or conspiracy in this observation. At random intervals throughout the day, he'd stop and say, "That fucking headstone was supposed to be standing up, man. Not one of those flat ones. Right?"

"Shit, I don't know," I confessed. "I mean, I think all the ones in that cemetery are flat. Maybe they have a rule or something," I tried, not sure what else to say.

When we turned right onto Crockett Road about five minutes later—what used to be called County Road 114 when we lived there—and at last onto our property, I had that queasy feeling of vertigo. Time and nature had begun to reclaim this place, and everything seemed closer and smaller than what I remembered. Years of neglect had encouraged the weeds and grass to grow tall and dominant, and some of the structures—glorified chicken coops and DIY barns—lay on their sides or leaned like a drunk with all his weight on one foot. Old trucks had been sitting there for years without being moved. Once we were out and surveying the scope of things, Robert walked over to one of the trucks, a defunct '68 Chevy.

"This one is my year," he said. Robert always looked for the opportunity to remind anyone who would listen about the historical significance of his birth year. I always conceded to him that 1968 was monumental but would have been so regardless of Robert's birth.

"It would be great to restore, but who's got the time?" I thought that was a kind thing to say. This was the same truck I had raced after as Mom drove away in search of her missing lamb, whom she was so certain had been kidnapped.

Farther into the property sat a two-tone brown Ford dually. Its short bed made it a hot commodity for restorers, and for years, people had tried to buy it from Mom, who held the title. The truck once belonged to her brother Juan, whom we called Tío Johnny when we were kids. I remembered the time years before when they'd hauled the truck over. The thing came here to die, having never been moved in over twenty years except to make way for another piece of junk. Our family tended to hoard things as hoarders did, with no real plan to ever put the stuff to good use. The desire to keep and hold on to objects that should be let go of was another of our defining traits, and our inability to release things was like a curse upon our house.

I took a few pictures before the demolition began for the sake of posterity. With so much work ahead of us, I already felt overwhelmed.

There were, or had been, two trailer houses on the property perpendicular to one another in the shape of an L. There is the one I think of as the main trailer—the trailer that was the first one there on the property. The one in which Rene had slung me across the kitchen. The front door faces north and the front entrance to the property. The other trailer, the second trailer, arrived years after, say, the late 1980s. It was another Rose hand-me-down and was parked not far from Levelland and Morton when she lived in it. I remembered when both trailer houses were new. Seeing them wrecked and disintegrated was almost like seeing dying family members. Decades of memories right before us, and we were now creating one last memory with them for all time. The ultimate memory.

David and Giro had indeed knocked down the outer shells of the trailers sometime before, and now the trailers lay with their inner guts exposed to the elements. Those inner guts were the things of our past selves.

I got to work with a sledgehammer, as I methodically knocked away the floor of the westernmost room of the main trailer, one tantalizing blow at a time, with my thoughts wheeling into the past.

Chapter Sixty-One

Several miles north of Lovington, New Mexico, stood two mobile homes where I lived from the ages of eight to eighteen. For a whole decade, I got to know every inch of the ten-acre plot of land that hugged the east side of NM 206. That I spent several of my formative years on that bit of rural land surprises and shocks me now (it feels like the middle of nowhere and, well, it is), and I wonder what the odds were that I would have started there and ended up where I am today. When I lived there, our nearest neighbor was at least a quarter of a mile away to the east, a deputy sheriff, and other neighbors even farther away.

Today my dreams often find me in one of these mobile homes, and they form one of the two childhood homes of my youth, both ultimately razed. I could not have fathomed it when I lived there, but it only makes sense that these flimsy structures would meet their end sooner rather than later. They were like tin cans on plywood, after all.

What I didn't realize back then was that I would have a hand in taking them apart. How many people have a chance to demolish the place where they grew up? It is traumatic and cathartic at the same instant. For me, there was little choice. The State of New Mexico had given Rene a citation for keeping the property in such disrepair, and the state now compelled her to do something about it or face some serious consequences. After her incarceration, she no longer took things such as citations lightly. Someone had the idea to demolish everything and have it hauled away to a landfill. That somehow felt right. If I could only click my heels three times and make this wreckage vanish. Nothing was ever that painless, though.

I struggled with the fairness and legitimacy of this state mandate. If we owned the property, then who cared if no one was living there or if the grind of time was proving unstoppable? Was New Mexico basically a supercharged HOA? I drove by old barns that must have been decrepit when Tom Joad and his ma made their way west and no one appeared to give a rat's ass about them. Deteriorating metal buildings, rusted through and undoubtedly hazards, stood as monuments to glory days of old. But today they looked terrible. I'd seen acres upon acres brimming with defunct automobiles, and these weren't junk dealers with an actual business. It was just a big-ass yard with tons of salvage cars.

It must have been that our prominent little plot right next to the highway was too much for the Land of Enchantment, and the forty-seventh state demanded that we clean up our act. How can a land enchant with our two trailer houses mucking things up? And let's face it, the southeast corner of the state was not what you'd find pictured on touristy postcards. (That would be Santa Fe and parts west and north.) Tough for me, as I had not lived there as a resident since before my eighteenth birthday, and yet here I was. Not wanting more havoc to rain down on Rene and Mom, I was obliged to act. Even if they were upset with me at the time, they had had enough punishment as I saw it.

Truthfully, I wanted this chance to tear the place apart. Remember when Jenny visits her childhood home as an adult in *Forrest Gump*? When she starts throwing rock after rock at the palsied structure because it symbolized the source of so much of her trauma? Jenny, filled with rage and anguish, walks right up to those decrepit buildings and Forrest stayed the fuck back. He knew what was about to happen. Those buildings couldn't hurt Jenny, but the trauma was alive and well in the memories that kept her up at night and motivated much of her self-destructive behavior. "Sometimes, I guess there just aren't enough rocks," Forrest muses. Goddamn right, Forrest.

My return was a little like that. I was not abused as Jenny had been. That is, sexually, even if it was mistreatment nonetheless. I associated so much pain and injury with this place, even if it had shaped me in substantial ways and not all negative. Part of me wanted to help put the place in some order, even if it meant scrapping it all and starting over. I wanted to destroy it. To literally take hammer and saw to it all.

Since no one had lived there since Tom died, nearly eleven years before, the place had become an enticing location for vandals and local kids who wanted to do some *Breaking Bad*–type activities while hiding from prying eyes. I envisioned a site free of the flimsy trailer houses and junk cars and dilapidated barns. I wondered if something new might be placed on this land to resurrect some of the good times that were a part of my life. Destroy to create—the death and rebirth of the phoenix, that sort of thing. Or, hell, give someone else a chance to do something with it. I was certain that I did not want the land. I saw it as anathema.

The reality proved way more difficult, as ever. Physically, there were too many things to accomplish in such a short time. A couple of days was not enough to finish demolition without earthmoving equipment. I stupidly had faith that we could bring order to the place with our bare hands and a few tools. Emotionally, I was unprepared for the treasure hunt that resulted. I would find a box in what was once one of the bedrooms, and within it, I would find artifacts that cast me into reverie. There went ten minutes. The plurality of it held no interest for me, but it nonetheless hurt to trash so much of what I found. A notebook that had Mom's handwriting throughout it: five minutes. A school project Diana had made during her elementary school years: another five minutes. A blanket someone, most likely, Mom, had crocheted: yet another five minutes. The whole day was like a perverse version of that show *This Is Your Life*. But the greatest wound came in the midafternoon, when I found a white plastic bag holding my high school diploma.

The bag, lying in the bed of the derelict '68 Chevy, had been exposed to the elements for what must have been years, and now the blue diploma cover was warped and weathered. Mold and water damage had added new designs of their own. I opened the cover as Robert, who could only bear witness to this depressing little scene, watched over my shoulder. He didn't say a word, but I knew what he must have been thinking. He was like Forrest watching Jenny about to explode. It couldn't be my diploma, could it? Sure enough, my name was on the certificate. It was nothing more than sad proof that, though I had graduated from high school, no one bothered to care for my diploma. It meant nothing to anyone but me.

It made me wonder why my diploma, which I had left at home for safekeeping when I went to college, had been junked as though it were yet another piece of garbage. It suggested to me that my family's views on education were empty words.

In reality, this is what I imagine happened: All "important" keepsakes were hauled over to the house down the road, which my family later moved into once I was in college. That was the house with the floors Giro was in danger of crashing through. My diploma remained at the property north of Lovington. I cannot say if resentment—of me and my absence—separated my diploma from the lot that moved with everyone else, but it is more than likely.

One may reasonably ask why my high school diploma was not with me. Certain things always seemed to be in Mom's custody. She had boxes and suitcases filled with important documents, a haphazard system at best. My diploma stayed with Mom in a secure location of her choosing, and I figured I didn't need it where I was going when I left for college. By contrast, Rene's and Tom's diplomas were prominently mounted on the wall next to the TV for as long as I could remember. I didn't care either way, but leaving it with Mom gave me confidence because she was notoriously careful with such things. I knew whom to ask the day I needed access to the diploma.

Yet here it was, carelessly tossed aside. I smiled as I held my diploma in my hands on that Valentine's Day, not from mirth or enjoyment but as perturbing confirmation of what I had known since the day I left for college, nearly twenty-two years before. Finding that diploma was like finding a Valentine's Day card two decades after the fact:

You remember the sweetness of the idea, laden with possibility and promise. Soon cynicism follows, and you want to move on because you recognize you have done even greater things than what was intimated in a trite Valentine's card. True, the diploma was only a piece of paper. I was sure I could pay for another one if I wanted it that badly. But the desecrated diploma, which felt like an assault on my own educational success and worth, was too much to take seriously in that surreal venue.

Chapter Sixty-Two

That I discovered my high school diploma in such a sorry, ruined state in Lovington did not surprise me. Seeing the familiar royal blue cover, one I had not laid eyes on in many years, only corroborated what I felt about Rene and how she most likely felt about me. The diploma was like a miniature portrait of Crisito—cruel synecdoche. I could not see how it might have symbolized anything other than that, as brutal and neglectful as it appeared to someone outside my family.

But for us, it was merely how we went about the business of being us, and I had long come to this understanding. In a display of sheer irony, Rene and Mom, ever since Dad and Tom died, had found beatific significance in even the most ordinary pieces of refuse so long as it had a connection to these two men.

That empty Coke can? It was the last one Tom had. We can't throw it away. That candy wrapper? Can't toss it. Dad had eaten that piece of candy. But Chris's high school diploma? Who even knows where it is? And stop whining, Chris. Your high school diploma wasn't that big a deal if we're truthful. Eye roll. It was expected.

I opened the stiff cover. Its spine cracked in protest, but I was impervious to any sentimental care for the disregarded thing now that my sadness had turned to anger. Nothing could have seemed sorrier than that little blue cover, the urge to be rightly offended held at bay only by the spite that surged through me. If no one had thought to care for it, why should I give a damn about it? And yet, I did give a damn that it had been so disrespected.

The situation was made even more absurd because Mom had insisted on keeping it with her so that she could keep it safe. Once, after my sophomore year in college, I asked her where it was. "Somewhere safe," she quipped. She could not, or would not, produce it. "Why do you need it?" she asked. The truth was that I didn't need it, but I wanted to see it. As it turned out, leaving it with Mom was the worst thing I could have done with my high school diploma. I'm not saying she deliberately tossed it. But somehow it had gone from her care to the bed of a used-up '68 Chevy truck.

Remember, when I was growing up, other high school diplomas were prominently displayed in conspicuous locations in the house for all to see. Rene's diploma was next to Tom's. I was raised to believe that these symbols of academic, educational achievement mattered. That they were worthy of admiration and respect. I believe I recalled those beautifully framed diplomas when I saw the wreckage of my diploma that day. Why was mine here, forgotten to the elements and time? Why mine? (Existentially: Why me?)

I snapped it open and was surprised to see the actual diploma in relatively good physical shape, though the pungent smell of mildew had worked its way into the tiniest paper fibers. It was ruined in a way that I would never allow myself to be. That was perhaps the greatest lesson I took from seeing a symbol of one of my significant accomplishments at the time—the paper is not the man, and the man is not the paper.

I stared at my full name printed in an elegant font on that piece of paper. Such a pompous, ridiculous name. One that strikes a wrong note for me whenever I write it out:

Christopher Thomas González III

At some point in every person's life, the time must surely arrive when they ask for the origin story of their name. This is especially true if the name is not altogether obvious, such as Gabriel García Márquez's Buendía family. Throughout my life, I have asked Rene about the source of my name. I have done this so often because, the first few times I inquired, I thought she was laughing at my expense. I did not think she was being forthright with me.

"The Third?" I said suspiciously.

"You were the third Tomás in the family." Rene had a way of making even the most outlandish things seem perfectly acceptable.

"But you named me Thomas. It's Anglicized. It's not the same thing."

"It goes with Christopher, which I always thought sounded British. Christopher Tomás doesn't have the same ring to it."

"What about Cristóbal Tomás?"

She made a face like something stank. "Nope."

Here I would generally try to use some logic, which Rene always touted as a virtue and signifier of her interest in the *Star Trek* universe. Thank goodness for the Vulcans! I said: "Using suffix numbers is often indicative of fathers and sons. Right? So, my father would have to be Tomás. Plus, the name is typically an exact match. Like Dad and Tom. Tomás González and Tomás González Jr."

"That's just how I wanted it," she remarked, closing the conversation for the time being. She was more interested in some other whimsy, but she had one more point to make. "But Christopher wasn't my first choice."

I remember the first time she told me. She had revealed this on several occasions because, I think, she had forgotten that she had already told me. So, I get to hear this on repeat, and I also hear it when she tells this story to Ginger or my girls.

I humored her. "What did you want to call me before you decided on Christopher?"

She didn't hesitate. "D'Artagnan."

"D'Artagnan? Like from *The Three Musketeers*?"

"Exactly. I had read *The Three Musketeers* in high school, and I thought it would be a perfect name for a son if I had one. When I was expecting you, I told Mom that I was going to name you D'Artagnan. She said, *'tas loca!* and told me to pick another name. I decided on Christopher. She didn't like that either. But it was better than D'Artagnan, in her mind."

Yeah, I thought. In my mind, Christopher was better too.

I kept staring at my diploma, thinking how close I had been to the pressure of rising to the expectation of so weighty a name as D'Artagnan. And D'Artagnan was a surname, but that wouldn't have stopped Rene, the illogical person of logic. Only Mom or Dad could have stopped her. And no one would have called me by D'Artagnan, I am certain of it. I would have been some unholy diminutive that I fear to imagine. I'm thankful that I'm a III, I suppose. *C* is the third letter too. But D'Artagnan was the fourth Musketeer, so it doesn't work. Often, I ignore the suffix or drop it altogether because, like so much of my family history, it is too complicated and awkward to explain in brief conversation. So, unless I am dealing with legal documents, I omit the III.

Chapter Sixty-Three

My diploma also reminded me of a long-standing tradition Rene and I shared. In May of 1993, I prepared to graduate from high school. As all high schools did around that time of year, Lovington High School made ready for its ceremony. We secured our robes and invitations, walked through our rehearsals with giddy exuberance, and generally looked with anticipation at this august milestone.

Since then, I have seen many graduations at all levels of education, and I am always gratified in the joy that is expressed by graduates and family alike. But I also feel a bit melancholy at missing out on all the fun. When it came time for me to graduate from high school, I was in for a shock. It did not dawn on me until nearly the day of the event that Rene had not mentioned the graduation or her planned attendance. I had simply assumed that she would attend. She had generally attended way more trivial stuff.

Like the times I was in elementary choir. There I was in the fourth grade, singing *Dem bones, dem bones, dem . . . dryyyyyyy bones* and other amateurish fare typical for school programs. The next year, I was recruited to be a narrator for a Christmas choir performance, and I think the expectation was that I was going to memorize an entire script that was like twenty pages long. I memorized somewhere around the first two pages, and then I had to rely on the script printout. My choir teacher was unhappy with me, but what did she expect?

Rene had come to these sorts of programs. But with the most significant ceremony now a few days away, she let me know that she had no intention of going to my high school graduation.

"You're not going?" I asked. "To my graduation?" as if I needed to clarify and emphasize the importance of this day to me. I was old enough to remember David's and then Robert's graduations. We had actually decorated the trailer with signs that said CONGRATULATIONS! and I helped do it!

We never went that far in birthdays or other such anniversaries as to fucking decorate the place. We were lucky to get some cake and a few bucks to spend at the store, but there were rarely birthday cakes, to be honest.

Rene was utterly dismissive of my achievement. It was like I had been given a participation trophy. "High school is expected," she said with an ease that I disliked immediately. "High school is not a big deal for you. College is the thing! That's the graduation I'm going to go to!"

The problem was that high school had been a big deal for me. Though I had inherent talent as a student, my early high school years were plagued with slouching grades and a who-gives-a-shit attitude. Rene had been there to remind me to get my act together, but mostly I slept through many of my classes—figuratively if not literally. Even as a student athlete, I would rally at the end of a grading period only enough so that I could continue to be eligible to compete. Luckily, I turned it around my senior year.

But usually, I would be sick for many days at an alarming rate. I would be unwell for a week or two at a time, and then I would be substantially behind in my schoolwork. Thus, I was always playing catch-up. This happened so often that people at school didn't know what to make of it. But we would dutifully go to the doctor, where I was diagnosed with some respiratory infection or flu or whatever, and I'd get a doctor's note to be out of school for however many days. It was a minor miracle that I graduated at all. Not through lack of ability or talent, but because I had missed so many days in a school year.

As I write this, there would be no way I could miss that much school in this day and age. And from where I sit, I wonder if all or most of it wasn't somehow psychosomatic. At times I ponder if this wasn't a kind of Munchausen syndrome by proxy thing where Rene would, if not convince me that I was sick, at least encourage me to believe that I was not well. It seems we spent a lot of time in the doctor's office. Sometimes several doctors' offices over a short stretch of time, if our access to health insurance changed for whatever reason. For her part, Rene had always grappled with some malady or injury.

In the end, Rene had said her final word about my high school graduation. That was it, and there was no use in trying to argue the point with her. Thus, Rene did not attend my graduation, and, as it turned out, she would later refuse to attend my graduation from Sam Houston State University when I received my bachelor's degree, or from Texas A&M University–Commerce for my master's, or from the Ohio State University with my doctorate (granted, she was in prison for that last one).

I would have taken all of this in stride but for one damning point. Rene went out of her way to attend Giro's high school graduation. Giro, David's son and Rene's nephew, was the one who got Rene to go to a graduation. Does that make any sense? Giro had a father, a mother, stepparents (because his birth parents had divorced when he was around ten). He had Tom as a surrogate father, and Rene, Mom, and Dad. So, she went to Giro's graduation but never went to any of mine. She didn't go to Diana's graduation either. Rene's refusal to go to my graduation, even her dismissal of it, was ultimately a presentiment of this pathetic piece of mildewed paper I now held with disgust. That paper was worthless, and Rene had already predicted as much.

Days later, when I was back home in Commerce, I told Ginger about my diploma. She was at once incensed and unsurprised. It upset her that anything I had achieved should be so carelessly discarded, and it angered her more that I stubbornly refused to salvage it from amid the refuse of my wrecked childhood. "That belongs to your children!" she groused. "They would want that . . . someday."

"Nah. It's only a piece of paper." I sounded like Rene. "Besides, the girls wouldn't want that. I can probably get a new one . . . but why?"

It was too late for all of that, and the ravages of such dismissive attitudes towards my achievements had already done their worst. For all I know, my high school diploma continues to molder where I last saw it over six years ago. Or maybe someone has finally cleared the land of the proof that I was ever there that day or any day. I have not been back to those geocoordinates since Valentine's Day 2015. And as for her skipping my graduation, Rene explained to Ginger in 2021 that she didn't go because she didn't want to embarrass me. After a whole lifetime with her to that point, why would she think that would embarrass me and not the countless other *chingaderas* she did at my school along the way? Instead, Mom and Dad came to my graduation, and perhaps that was all I needed.

Chapter Sixty-Four

It took me a long time to realize this, but I am a kind of rara avis in the United States. Being rare is different from being elite, a term that gets hurled as if it were a curse at people who, typically because of intellectual prowess and educational achievement, have notable ability in a given area of specialization. To be elite means understanding one's rank within a given category, as if one were nestled snugly in a top-ten list. The proof of being elite is nearly self-evident: You win a national championship. You accept the Academy Award for Best Actress in a Supporting Role. You are awarded a MacArthur Fellowship, or "Genius Grant." Elite status is readily confirmed by external acclamation. You don't need to go around claiming you're elite. (If you do, you're probably not that elite.)

A rarity is something else entirely. Being one requires a kind of awareness that isn't so readily clear. It may require that people repeatedly tell you that you are someone seldom seen. (Bragging about being exceptional doesn't make it so.) Rare bird status also doesn't automatically denote greatness. Rareness may simply mean that, somehow, the unseen forces of extinction have not gotten around to you yet. Or you're that scarlet ibis, like in the story. In more recent times, we refer to a singular individual as a unicorn—all too often, a designation resulting from serendipity, fortune, or plain happenstance. Luck.

I hated being lucky. Standing amid junk and garbage where I grew up, in the middle of nowhere on the Llano Estacado, and knowing I came from that, I couldn't help but feel extraordinarily lucky. Again, this notion of serendipity worked in concert with a phenomenon known as impostor syndrome, which manifested as a voice insisting that you weren't good enough, that you didn't belong, that you were here as a matter of happenstance. People of all stripes were afflicted by the condition, but belonging to an underrepresented community tended to exacerbate its effects, in my opinion. The kid who grew up on ten acres north of Lovington would never have believed he could be a professor or work at a university. I had to leave home and forget where I came from to succeed in my way.

My reflections might sound antithetical to what you often hear from others who have come from impoverished circumstances, and thus extremely ungrateful. The exhortation "never forget where you came from" is generally understood to mean that you must stay humble, or hew to the values you were raised with. But my family was toxic in so many ways, something I didn't realize until very recently. I was always told that I had turned my back on my family simply because I was selfish and an asshole. But if I had stayed close to them during the critical period between college and where I find myself today, I likely would have struggled like the rest of my family.

Oh, I absolutely appreciate being lucky when it turns out that way. But I detest the notion that something over which I had little control had happened to me, inuring to my benefit. Like many of us, I want to believe that I am the driver of my life rather than a passenger. I enjoy successes when I feel I have consciously earned them. I generally believe that you must still climb steep trails when they are revealed to you. Or as my mentor and friend Hunter Hayes (the professor, not the singer) told me after something he had helped me with, "You did all the heavy lifting." I'm not so certain that I did all the heavy lifting, but I'll allow that I did a lot of it.

As I drew closer to the age of emancipation and my departure for college, Rene became another person. No longer close to me, she stopped confiding in me about serious matters, stopped initiating deep conversations. I could feel her resentment growing the older I got and the more education I attained. I am also certain that my philosophy of doing things on my own and not relying on anyone else further estranged us.

I've learned not to accept too much help from my family, because they are always quick to rub it in when it suits them. I try to keep that kind of ammo away from family and friends. By the same token, I don't ask for help from people who have my best interests in mind, unfortunately. I want desperately to accept a friend's offer of aid, but even if it involves something minor, I can already imagine a future version of them reminding me how I would not have amounted to anything if not for that time they gave me a ride home from work. I would never do that to anyone, but I default to thinking others will readily do it to me.

I work hard to accept help from others. And every time I do, I am beside myself with discomfort as I force a smile and say, "Thanks!" My upbringing keeps my friends at arm's length, and I am saddened and disappointed every time I have to confront this in myself.

Today, Rene tells me she is proud of my accomplishments, and I try to take her at her word. But when I am in her company, she rarely asks me about my job or my personal life. Instead, she stays within her sphere of experience: sometimes in the immediate present, mostly in her past. She will go on for hours about the television shows she watches or how tough it was for her as the head cheerleader at a Black high school. She spares only a few minutes for understanding me or what I do. Rene is more absorbed with my daughters, her "*reinas*," but these days they are too old to be cute or enchanting.

And still, Rene will continue to tell me that I've done a good job about this and that. But then she will stop herself and say, "Well, that was expected." When every accomplishment you've worked hard at is taken for granted, you start to wonder what the hell those expectations are.

"Hey, Rene! I became mayor of Fantastic City!"

"Oh, wow! But then, it was expected."

"Hey, Rene! I've been elected Wizard of Oz on my first try!"

"Really? Well, that's expected."

"OMG! Rene! My start-up became a multibillion-dollar company!"

"Well, how about that! But, after all, it was expected."

Complete hogwash. As this memoir shows, nothing I've done could have been predicted when you consider where I came from and the maladroit people with whom I share genetic material. I had to break from my family for many years, piss them off, offend them, disappoint them, so that I could reach some of the life goals I've thus far attained. Such as breaking the poverty cycle. Or breaking the cycle of children sacrificing everything for their parents. Or the cycle of going into debt to cover the funeral expenses of those deceased who left behind nothing but regrets and lost opportunities.

Chapter Sixty-Five

Back in Lovington, I stood surveying this place where I had spent so many youthful hours dreaming of other locales. I faced a sort of reckoning with the memorabilia, proof that I had lived there with a clan of fellow miscreants. Too quickly, I had whipped myself into a frenzy, and if I didn't watch out, I would not be able to continue this pace long.

I set aside the twelve-pound hammer I had been using to demo the trailer and strolled over to Robert, who gazed at the wrecked buildings, arms akimbo. That he wasn't actively laboring at the moment made me think something was fermenting in his brainpan.

"What do you think?" I asked, trying to recover from swinging the sledge. I was in no shape to do that, but I didn't want to admit it. I'd pay later, in the form of soreness and perhaps injury, but right now I wanted action. I was Jenny, slinging goddamned shoes and rocks.

The wind was building. I could tell it was shaping up to be one of those breezy days that whipped dirt high into the sky. Robert cleared his throat. Took a deep breath. Exhaled loudly.

Robert always cleared his throat before launching into a point of discussion. It was his tell, part of his ritualized style of speech. He had always struggled with a mighty stammer, though when we were kids, he claimed it was a stutter. (Stammer? Stutter? Is there a difference?) Either way, it made him anxious to speak to a group, let alone in a public setting, as our little excursion in Albuquerque at the state track meet proved. Certain words triggered his stammer, and they proved to be significant impediments to his expression. He had developed workarounds for those quagmires of language and irksome phonemes.

I have a touch of this stammer as well, though it is not so vexatious as in Robert's speech. My language nemeses tend to be words that begin with *cl* or *gl*: *clear, class, glue.* If I start a sentence with such a word, there may be a problem. When my stammer engages, I feel as if I have a mouthful of peanut butter, but I am reminded of its existence only a few times a week. Like Robert, I have workarounds. That's why I know his utterances involve a degree of forethought. We are both cautious speakers by nature, a trait often interpreted as introversion or reticence. But given the right circumstances, we are also known to say stupid shit, just like everyone else.

"You see what David and Giro already managed to do," he said, waving a hand over the wreckage as though blessing it.

Both trailers' foundations were still intact, but with the metal outer shells and inner wood paneling yanked clear of the floors. But we saw no debris piles or signs of organization. It looked like they'd simply used the backhoe to rip the trailers' walls from their foundations.

"It's a goddamn mess," he observed in a way that didn't come across as stating the obvious. "They used a backhoe, the kind I wish we had right now."

"Yeah, and they made a shit job of it, it seems. What the fuck were they thinking?"

"Maybe if they had a bulldozer. Could have pushed this shit into a big-ass mound."

"Well, let's get going already. This shit isn't going anywhere on its own." To be honest, I didn't want to talk. I was ready to make progress on the jumble of trailer guts, yet angry about being there.

Though I struggled daily to remain organized and neat, when it came to doing a complete reorganization or a deep cleanse, I generally began in one section and worked my way through it until whatever I was working on was overhauled, cleaned, reorganized, and so on. If I could only begin, it would only be a matter of time before all this was set aright through sheer determination and brute force.

But time was a luxury we couldn't afford—the typical result of Rene's procrastinating nature and her dogged desire never to ask for help until the situation was so far gone only superhuman effort could make a difference. It was as if she always waged unwinnable battles because they somehow highlighted her toughness and spirit. I was that way once, less so of late.

I wanted to start trashing whatever I could fit in the dumpster. To break things down into more manageable bits. I wanted to make progress. *Now.*

"Let's see what else we got besides the trailers." Robert could sense me itching to start, but he was forcing me to slow my efforts without telling me in so many words.

We walked around and through the remains of what was once our home, and I was shaken by overwhelming fumes of nostalgia. On my drive to Robert's house the night before, I had remembered the trailers as I last saw them in 1998: humble but functional, livable. Then after Robert mentioned their disrepair and half-assed dismemberment at the hands of David and Giro, I had imagined the trailers as undifferentiated stuff, akin to detritus in the aftermath of an Oklahoma EF5 tornado. I was surprised to find the contents of the trailers lying there, discrete objects waiting for us to deal with them.

I had come home after being so long gone, and a part of me desperately wanted to sift through every last item I saw. An archaeologist from the future would have wondered what this wreckage indicated in its perverse mystery. That's overselling it. Still, to me, every little thing, from weathered notebooks and magazines to curtains and broken furniture to dishes and tattered clothing, all of it had a story to retell me.

I wanted to stop, pick up an item, talk with Robert about its consequence, and wallow in the flood of memories. What did it say about who we were? I wanted to find meaning amid the refuse of our lives. It would take weeks to do that, and we had mere hours. But if I could, I would catalog everything in sight, for I too was a hoarder at heart. And this was the ultimate hoarder situation. Everything I saw was at once both garbage and of value to me. I wanted to trash it, then sift through it, then trash it again in a Sisyphean cycle, struggling perpetually with the ponderous weight of memory.

What was trash and what was a keepsake? Was a piece of paper a keepsake? Maybe, but it must be especially important to the possessor. Was my diploma any more valuable to me than a candy wrapper that Dad had handled on his last day on earth? This convergence of relativism and materialism was a question for philosophers. Here and now, I could only sense that all of what I saw before me needed to be disposed of. It didn't matter if any or all of it had been meaningful in some recent past.

I followed as Robert retraced the steps we had made thousands of times before. With every footfall, I was at a different point in my past, but it was all jumbled together as glimpses of moments once lived. Unlike me, Robert was generally not a sentimental sop, so I doubt that he was fighting the urge to give in to rumination. That was why I wanted only to work myself into exhaustion today. Through physical exertion, I wouldn't have time to think about the day's emotional cost. But moments like this, walking across the property with my uncle-brother, made me wonder if I had agreed to a kind of psychological masochism.

The complex of *jaulas*—the original set of rooster coops located at the northwest corner of the ten acres—appeared to have caved in upon itself. It had been erected almost as soon as the main trailer was sited, and I'd spent so much time there learning from Dad and Tom about the secret knowledge of cockfighting and life in general. The coops connected in a roughly rectangular shape, leaving ample open space in the middle that we used for sparring the roosters. It once had the feeling of an open-roofed barn. Now it was a heap of grayed, faded lumber, rusted nails, mangled chicken wire, and corrugated galvanized steel with sharp corners and oxidized skin.

I could see the large green tank that held the well water we used to drink. It was exposed on its side and waited patiently for someone to do something with it. Nearly everything that once stood there now seemed to have collapsed from fatigue. There were only a few exceptions, both smallish structures Tom had built when I was in high school. One was a tiny, one-room shack—a homespun version of the kind of prefab sheds you find at Lowe's—made of plywood. It would not last much longer.

The other edifice was a sort of barn to the southeast of the trailers, and we headed straight for it as if we had an appointment to keep. Robert and I hadn't exchanged many words as we toured the property, but we were sympatico. A lot of family history scattered out before us, and soon, no one would know who had lived here and what they might have done in life. I was confident the neighbors saw this place as a junkyard, or perhaps as a bit of land that provided a space for spirits to knock about, far from judgmental eyes.

Unlike most of the others on this property, this barn was still well preserved. Today we would say that the materials used to construct it were repurposed, but for us at the time, it was a matter of using what we had and what we could get our hands on. Tom had built it as a place to hold roosters who were on a keep—a training regimen of sorts—and it consisted of a long aisle with large rooster pens to either side, with an area near the front door to train the roosters, or to sit with a beer in hand and have a chat with someone. Tom always had apprentices to the cockfighting trade, and this was a spot where the young men would often wind up to take in lessons from the master. I was once a *gallero* in training, but one who knew a full conversion would lead to a dead end. I always fell far short of true devotion.

The sun cast long morning shadows that shrank by the minute, and amid the wrack and ruin, the interplay of light and shadow made the setting untenable for me. I was in what to an outsider would look like a dump—a landfill that stood as a tribute to transient and perishable human life. Tall prairie grass covered the ground; I could no longer detect the caliche driveways that would crunch under our car tires when we came home. Well water and boiler tanks, toilet bowls, barbed wire and steel fenceposts taunted and teased. The large rented dumpster appeared undersized for our needs, as I'd feared. Still farther beyond where the remnants of the main trailer were, a third truck, a Chevy Silverado, sunblasted and forlorn, pointed eastward in permanent repose. Even these three trucks on the property were disorderly, at odds, each one facing a separate cardinal direction, ready to get the hell out of there and away from each other.

Robert and I entered the metal barn to have a look inside. It was not a dank place but, rather, cool and dry, with good natural light at the far end but dark near the entrance. There were ten large *jaulas* with nothing in them, yet I could easily imagine the sounds of roosters clucking and crowing and screeching every time something flew overhead, a particular quirk of these animals that only people who had lived with them would know. They made a high-pitched whine whenever something flew overhead. It sounded like a warning, which was probably spot-on.

I went inside one of the pens to take a piss, as there were no public restrooms for miles. As my urine started to flow, I was unnerved that the barn looked exactly as I had remembered it while the trailers, where we actually lived, lay in utter ruin. How did this place go so untouched by time? I wondered. It was one of the last additions to the property, as if Tom had finally happened upon a design that worked for him. It was a sturdy structure, and I recognized it might be the last place that felt like a part of my childhood home that was still standing. A three-hundred-square-foot hut meant for jungle fowl—animals currently illegal in most of the United States. For a moment, I felt at home, but the moment burned off in the morning sun like fog.

I didn't want to linger in here, so I finished up and prepared to exit the barn. Though I did not want to say it aloud, I felt as if Tom might suddenly burst through the door, wisecracking and laughing as he so often did, perhaps with a rooster in the crook of his arm. I cast my eyes to an area of the barn I had not noticed upon entering, and I checked my breath at what I saw.

Anger surged through me like an electric current, and before I knew what I was saying, I blurted out, "What the fuck is that?"

But I knew what it was. Anyone would. The perfectly formed slip noose was made of thick nylon cord. Smallish, but sturdy enough to get the job done for someone determined and desperate. It hung from a beam in one corner, yet another reminder of death on this property. Not thirty minutes ago, I had literally been in a cemetery, and now I saw a crude hangman's gallows. It made me queasy, and my first thought was that someone had played an awful trick on us. Trespassers up to no good. Or perhaps it was a warning. A threat.

But Robert merely thumped the noose with his finger and chuckled. "Fucking Tom." Years before, in one of his moments of morbid humor and before he truly became sick, Tom must have fashioned this small noose out of boredom. I still didn't like the look of it, and I exited the barn, leaving it behind me for the final time.

Yet the noose haunted me for another reason. I was already in college, or perhaps I had already graduated, when Tom decided to fashion that noose. He flashed in my mind, sitting there, alone, perhaps hurting from his diabetes and failing kidneys, his scarred hands pulling the rope taut until an iconic noose took shape. Had he wanted to die?

Chapter Sixty-Six

I was glad to be once more in the full morning sunshine when Robert disrupted my thoughts. "So, the way I understand it, we need to focus on the things that are considered eyesores." At long last, Robert sketched out his plan for me. "This barn is fine. If we could move these trucks out of sight, that would help. Or we could put up a fence and hide it all. That was one choice they gave Rene."

"Why don't we put FOR SALE signs on the trucks? They'll be sold before the end of the day." Because our property hugs a relatively well-trafficked highway, people often would stop to look at one of these old trucks and maybe buy it. It was precisely that sort of visibility that gave us cause to be here at all.

Robert shook his head. "They'll never let us do that. Rene already told me."

We weren't allowed to get rid of anything connected to the men in our family who had died, making this an all but impossible task.

"Plus," Robert added, "who the hell knows where the titles are? How could we sell them without those?"

"There's a process. Pain in the ass, but a process that won't help today," I said. It's always something, I thought. "It would be easier to make up a story. Tell Rene and Mom that we decided we wanted to restore these vehicles. If we ask for the titles and say we're going to take them back to our homes, they'd never know. Right?" A correct statement because Rene and Mom would never think to visit us of their own accord, and Robert knew this.

He considered my ploy for a moment. "That could work."

I smiled because it was something he hadn't thought of before, had not predicted, which surely annoyed him.

"We could mention it to Rene when she gets here. Go from there."

I thought it was worth a shot, and I could tell Robert liked the idea. We were desperate already, and any amount of lying that would result in commonsense actions was considered within bounds. In this case, the ends justified the means.

We worked our way back to the ruined trailers. I saw an oxidized old camper shell, weakening before the ravages of time. I remembered when it had stood in our yard in Lubbock, and here it still was now. If there had ever been a time when the truck cap was put to the purpose for which it had been designed, I couldn't recall it.

My family never could leave the past where it belonged. The past was always with us, bound up with renewed vitality in the things that were left behind. Breaking free of the past required a painful event, such as a familial falling-out. The trauma of what Rene called a knock-down, drag-out was preferable to letting go of the past. Everywhere I looked: reminders of who we once were. And though it all lay neglected, trashed, and nearly forgotten, it all still existed within Mom's mind as it had many years ago. Like me, she had not been to this spot in over fifteen years. Rene hadn't come by recently either. And yet, we couldn't rid ourselves of the junk. It oppressed us even when it was out of sight.

Robert and I walked by a sizeable hole in the ground behind the second trailer. It dated back to when I was in junior high, and we were going to install a septic tank to replace the system we had. For much of my childhood, about twenty-five yards from the back door of the main trailer, not far from this large hole, there had been a literal open sewer that we called "the cesspool" without irony. It was situated to the south of the trailer, and the northerly or westerly winds that often predominated would carry the smell away from us. The stench was a miasma that stayed at our periphery, and when it did intrude, olfactory fatigue would set in. Such is the phenomenon of going nose-blind and becoming desensitized to whatever reeks. The in-ground reservoir was covered with steel grates and sheet metal, scraps from construction jobs; occasionally, the cesspool had to be "pumped" by means of a small motor with a hose on each end. One thick rubber hose plunged into the gurgling recesses of the cesspool, and the other emptied onto the ground on the other side of the contraption. When our toilets stopped working, someone would have to go out and turn on the motor to let it run until the cesspool was sufficiently drained. For days, you would have to avoid the drainage area, but I was a kid, and sometimes I'd forget until it was too late and I was taking squishy steps in it.

At some point, it became clear that we could not continue in this fashion—perhaps some government agency found us out, perhaps a neighbor reported us—and we had to have an actual septic tank installed. Tom got a construction buddy to bring over a backhoe, and they dug a great hole in the earth, breaking through layers of caliche all the way down. But the cavity I was peering into was evidence that we must never have installed the septic tank, which meant we didn't have enough money to finish the job.

It was yet another emblem of growing up here, next to our own jury-rigged cesspool and leach field. The symbolism was too potent and too perfect to be fiction: Imagine these rubes who lived near their in-ground cesspool and kept a menagerie that comprised hogs, goats, roosters, peacocks, geese, turkeys, dogs, cats, emus (for a mercifully short time, thanks to David's failed scheme to sell emu meat), and other improbable denizens. Who knows how much we were poisoning ourselves all those years. How often did we fall sick because we were in close proximity to raw sewage? How did it not seep into our groundwater source and contaminate our tap? I guess the well was too deep for that, but still. And in pure ignorance, I would play around that cesspool as a child, thinking the most dangerous risk was that I might fall in and drown. I never learned how deep the reservoir was.

Robert pointed to the empty hole. "See," he said. "That's what we should do. Dig a bigger hole and have all this shit pushed into it. That's the kind of easy solution we need."

"Yeah, that will go over well with the state," I replied. "It's not like they would look or anything."

I gazed at the dumpster. It appeared as big as a semitrailer, but basic logic told me it would not accommodate the debris from two mobile homes plus the flotsam of our possessions. I scratched my head, and Robert knew what was running through it.

"I don't think this is going to work," he said as we watched Giro and Rene pull up to the property. They had brought breakfast.

Chapter Sixty-Seven

She did not so much exit the vehicle as wriggle out of it, working her way slowly, like a plump caterpillar on a precarious tomato vine. Rene's weight made her unsteady and as likely to topple over as an inverted Weeble.

Prison had not diminished her physically, contrary to what I'd imagined, or perhaps her body was already wrecked before she served her time. She was fifty-six years old when she entered the penitentiary, and when she'd called to tell me she was going to prison, I had been certain that I would never see her again. Or rather, I was convinced that she would never be the same Rene as before her incarceration—whatever that meant. Prison changed people. It altered them, for good or ill. I had expected to encounter a shadow of my mother, a husk like the empty cicada exoskeletons that clung to the house in Lubbock. Like Miss Sophia from *The Color Purple* after she got out of jail for sticking it to a white lady. To my surprise, Rene looked unaffected and undaunted by her time behind bars.

Later she would say that prison toughened her up. Yeah, sort of. Whenever she had to eat something not to her liking, say, an Indian recipe we decided to try when she lived with us during the outset of the COVID-19 pandemic, she would remind us that she was given food labeled NOT FOR HUMAN CONSUMPTION in the chow hall, so she guessed she'd eat this Indian food. That felt nice and was in line with her personality and character.

And let's not even talk about her run-ins with prison gangs and how they came to respect her for being such an insufferable bitch, with her big mouth and her fearlessness. She had always staked her reputation on being the one you didn't want to cross, which surely didn't hurt in the penitentiary. How she managed to do that against much younger gang-affiliated women in prison was easy for me to understand. Not much made Rene flinch, she had abundant intelligence, and at the time, she was old enough to be a kind of mentor to the younger women in that prison. They eventually regarded her as a maternal figure. Those poor girls were desperate to be loved by a mother. I could relate.

Her knees, a source of constant and considerable pain and the living reminder of athletic successes of yore, were blasted and barely supported her weight either while standing or walking. Remember, she was the head cheerleader at a Black high school, as she often told us multiple times in a week.

While I often rolled my eyes or left the room when she cued up her own rendition of "Glory Days," I knew all too well how the injuries of youth had a way of coming back to haunt a person in later years. Unlike Rene, it's not my knees that cause me so much agony but, rather, my back. I had suffered several serious lower back injuries in high school and college because of my weight lifting and shot-putting, and I pay those debts in full at every sunrise. Years from this day in Lovington, doctors will confirm that Rene has zero cartilage left in her knees, which is what caused her to become severely bowlegged, diminishing her already short frame.

On this particular Valentine's morning, she leaned on a cane—Dad's cane—and she smiled when she set her eyes on me. The cane was special only in its sentimental value, and it looked like a beaten-down version of every adjustable cane you can find at any pharmacy. Shaped like a curvy number 7 with a foam handle and a rubber foot, the cane had a scratched-up copper-toned finish. Dad, who often butchered English for fun, called it his "walking chain," rather than walking cane.

Though I wanted to believe Rene was genuinely happy to see me, I had come to learn the hard way that I must make no assumptions. Everything she did and said was "under review." Rene always had a way with the truth and, especially, how she expressed what she was feeling. She, like her mother before her, has a semipermeable memory, which often got intermingled with her own version of events that were verifiably false. Like, she would make up whole sequences of events that never happened. For instance, when she lived with me during the pandemic, she reminded me of that time when my good friend confessed his undying love to me as we romantically found ourselves on some Texas lake, alone in a boat.

"Remember when you told me that?"

"What? I literally have no idea what you're talking about."

She smiled and said, "Yes. You said you and your friend, who was a guy, said he loved you and confessed all this to you in a boat out on the lake." Rene said it with such conviction, I started to wonder when the fuck it was that I had my own *Brokeback Mountain* moment.

Ginger laughed at the absurdity. I turned to Rene. "Nothing like that ever happened. I think I'd remember. Either you dreamed this or it's a movie that you're confusing with my life."

This sort of thing happened often enough to be annoying but not so often as to make me worry. But she has such certitude in her memories, along with her penchant for telling you what she's thinking or feeling. Rene is nothing if not willfully transparent. But often what she expresses is not what she's feeling or thinking, which is unsettling.

For my part, I was happy to see her alive. Not long before, I thought she would die in a New Mexico State prison. That seemed to me excruciating, tragic, and harsh. But the tax collectors have such inflexible reputations for a reason, and when they have the might of state and federal governments, they will not be cheated or denied, your poor health be damned.

"Hey!" she shouted with glee. "What are y'all doing?"

It wasn't an actual question; she knew what we were doing. But it was an expression of hers, like the way people say "What's up?" or "How's it going?" A bit of throat clearing to get ready for deeper subjects of conversation.

"Oh, I don't know," I said as if I were truly pondering the situation. "Thought it might be a good idea to show up randomly to this disaster area on a Valentine's Day. Guess I got nothing better to do."

Rene's fake happy-go-lucky façade vanished like mist on a hot day, and the real Rene appeared before me. "You asshole," she muttered, and meant it. Her insult did not bother me; she called me that all the time.

Besides, I guess I am an asshole, which in my family simply means not sugarcoating or pretending everything is fine. Or it means to be uncompromisingly, sarcastically truthful when you should probably keep your trap closed. In a family often allergic to truth, a truth teller can seem like someone who is out to wreck things and mess up a good vibe. I'm the truth teller in the family, and so I am often at odds with Rene, most especially because she is the most accomplished and skilled liar of us all.

Not that I tell truths out of some moral superiority or unshakable integrity. And I lie out of convenience if the lies are of the small and inconsequential variety, so I'm no saint. As Ricky Roma says in *Glengarry Glen Ross*, "Always tell the truth, George. It's the easiest thing to remember." Then again, Ricky Roma is consistently on top of the monthly sales board, selling swampland to deadbeats precisely because he is a magnificent liar.

Chapter Sixty-Eight

I smiled and gave her a hug because I wasn't a total monster. "It's good to see you," I said, and I meant it as much as her quip about my being an asshole. It was hard for me to believe this fragile woman went to the state penitentiary and came out hardly changed at all, at least from a physical perspective. Later she'll claim prison was like a country club for her, which I thought was total nonsense.

She smiled. "I brought breakfast."

"Okay."

I had to eat or else it would have caused more strife and angst. Giro was there, too, and he looked happy, as he always did. He had lugged a generator as Robert said he would, positioning it for later use. As soon as he could, he dived into his breakfast burritos. Robert was right: Giro was huge and probably needed help. Yet I always balked at telling people how to live their lives, just as I didn't want to hear from well-wishers how I needed to stop eating so many sweets or cut back on my coffee intake or go for more walks. Interventions were not my thing. I didn't want them, and I didn't want to prompt or orchestrate them, either.

I gobbled up the egg, potato, and chorizo burrito because I felt like I'd been up for hours and hadn't done a damned thing, so I might as well eat. I knew the goal was to clear this plot of land—to make it less of an eyesore (good luck!)—but things kept getting in the way. Basically, a metaphor for life. The best of intentions didn't amount to much, and in the end, we were left with what-might-have-beens and what-I-should've-dones.

After we ate, Rene piped up. "How can I help?"

No one said anything for a moment until I answered, "You can go home. I know you want to help, but there's not much you can do. Hell, I'm not sure how much we can get done." Home for her now was the little house south of town where she, Mom, and Giro lived, where Dad and Tom had lived their last days. It, too, was falling apart. With Tom and Dad no longer around to maintain them, these homes had deteriorated or were on the road to ruin. It also didn't help that Mom and Rene had allowed pet dogs to run amok inside the houses.

If my remark wounded her, she didn't show it. "I can do something."

"Have a seat and keep us company," Robert suggested. "You might get hurt if you try getting into this stuff, and that way you can direct traffic from where you are. Sit there and hang out with us." He was being helpful, and he could be caring and loving often enough to counter the times when he was a blunt instrument. Like I was right now.

I thought of who we were in that moment, taking stock of our corporeal selves locked inside imperfect bodies that we treated with such indifference. In my family, we tended to care about our bodies and our health once it was basically too late. But our bodies were terrific accountants and miserly bookkeepers that missed nothing we had borrowed (or taken) from them. Their invoices would come due in full course if we lived long enough. My family's financial cluelessness mirrored our ignorance of health, and I couldn't help but see the parallels between money, health, and the place we all once called home for many years.

Even when we didn't have much money, which was most of the time I was growing up, we seemed always to eat in excess. A strange outcome, counterintuitive perhaps, when one brings to mind stereotypes about poverty. Remember poor Oliver Twist: "Please, sir. I want some more." Or the Cratchits, and how Bob's meager wages essentially would have malnourished Tiny Tim to his death if the monstrous Ebenezer Scrooge hadn't changed his ways in a single night. Or maybe it's John Steinbeck's Tom Joad and his family, staying ahead of starvation by migrating to California, and the dying stranger suckling at Rosasharn's teat by novel's end. We think iconically of poverty as having nothing to eat; it's a hallmark of not earning enough to make ends meet. Maslow's hierarchy of needs lists food among the most fundamental needs that must be met, which later experiments have cast doubt on. It's a psychological theory, after all.

I recall seeing an experiment which featured two surrogate mothers that a baby monkey could alternate between. It's known as the Wire Monkey Mother experiment conducted by Harry Harlow. One cage had a wire frame vaguely reminiscent of a momma monkey shape holding a bottle of milk, while the other had a warm surrogate mother but no caloric supply or nourishment. In time, the baby monkey spent far more time with the warm surrogate mother that had no nourishment to offer. Ostensibly, it preferred love and tenderness to food. To me, poverty is not simply about possessing enough food. A person (or monkey) can be impoverished in many ways, sadly.

But often, at least as it applied to my family, it's not that you have nothing to eat, it's that you make unhealthy choices in your food intake, and you tend to eat a lot of it because you inhabit a psychological reality that constantly reminds you that you don't have enough as a rule. You may not know when or from where your next meal is coming (or your next paycheck, for that matter), and so you'd better fill up while you can. "Eat, drink, and be merry, for tomorrow we die," is an easily remembered scripture because it's true, especially for people like us. Live now. Carpe diem. Die another day but not today. All that.

Chapter Sixty-Nine

We made merry through food whenever we could throughout my life. We ate a combination of fast food and home cooking, with the latter supplying the greater part of our nutrition. By eating so much, we fooled ourselves into thinking we weren't so far below the poverty line as we were. We had commodity foodstuffs from the US government with the USDA shield emblazoned on the containers. (That logo reminded me of railroads for some reason.) Butter, cheese, peanut butter in the largest packages you'd see until Sam's Club and Costco came along. I didn't even know this was the "welfare" that Republicans on television were always grousing about, all red-faced. They made it sound like such a scourge, but it couldn't have been that expensive in relative terms. They'd rather give illegal moneys to Contras in Nicaragua, I guess, than give butter and cheese to poor Black and Brown people in their own nation.

The cheapest cuts of meat can make the best-tasting dishes. Ask any food historian. Pork chops, pork butts, ground beef, and chicken quarters were the basis for so many terrific meals of which Mom was the chief architect. Thank goodness she was a great cook with an intuitive sense for what makes a succulent dish, even if she herself couldn't articulate it or bother to record it in a recipe. Hers are still the best flour tortillas I've ever eaten, yet no recipe for them exists. I watched her make them countless times when I was a child—the familiar large Tupperware bowl of a hue of yellow that made it stand out easily, her kettle of hot water at the ready, all-purpose flour, shortening, the little can of Clabber Girl and container of Morton Salt imprinting on me that this was surely woman's work (thanks to the brand mascots). There were no measuring cups or spoons in sight. She would pour salt into her cupped palm or pour out steaming water from the kettle directly into the bowl, her eye the only measuring implement she required. And yet, Mom's tortillas were consistently wonderful every time she made them. I'd take a tortilla right off the comal, slather one side of it with that government butter, roll it like a cigar, and eat it as if it were the very ambrosia of the Olympian gods that fueled the ichor in their veins.

Whether it was *caldo de res* or *arroz y frijoles*, *tamales* or *barbacoa*, Mom churned out miracles in her kitchen, feeding such large appetites with the metaphorical five loaves and two fishes on the daily. Growing up, I rarely felt that we didn't have enough. Sure, we didn't eat out often enough for my liking, but there was always good food at home. Our utilities were regularly cut off due to lack of payment, but I never equated that with being poor. Rather, it was suggested to me that the utility companies were unreasonable and that we were unfairly treated. I also thought of poverty (what I expressed as "being poor") as homelessness. Well, we had a roof over our heads and food, so I never thought we were living in poverty. Plus, my family members were grandmasters at hiding shit, and they understandably hid from me that we lacked many of even the most basic resources.

My family coped by overcompensating with food. We were stress eaters before it was labeled as such. We devoured pots of beans, rice, *fideo*, *menudo*, and never complained. Meanwhile, our indulgences in food coincided with a precipitous drop in all the adults' health. I'm certain this never hit home until Dad had his first heart attack in the early 1990s.

Chapter Seventy

I suppose everyone has a wake-up call in their family—the moment when everyone realizes they've been living dangerously, and they need to rein it in a bit. Maybe it's gambling for some people, or crime, or any other risky behavior we might conjure. For our household, the patriarch's heart attack woke up many of us, but only temporarily.

When Dad returned home from his hospital stay due to said heart attack, we all marveled at what he was given to eat while he was there. It was like a child's plate! Airline food! Not that we knew what that meant beyond small portions. Cruel and unusual punishment! No human could live on such little food (except white people, probably). No more Cokes and sweets. Forget ice cream, milkshakes, and hamburgers. KFC and LJS? *Olvidate, 'mano.*

Now Dad had to eat salads and much smaller portions of things we didn't normally eat. Vegetables (not from a can, if possible) steamed and not fried. It depressed him severely to eat that way while we all continued devouring calories like never before—Gargantua on a strict diet while all around him a horde of Pantagruels consumed with gusto, oblivious as to the implications and the psychological hurt we perpetrated on him. Wouldn't you then feel sorry for poor old Gargantua with his little portion of "ants on a log" (a celery stick with a smidge of peanut butter and a few raisins)? Mom gathered us outside of Dad's presence to admonish us to stop eating around Dad. But the solution was simple enough, and I'm sure I'm not the only one who thought it: *Why don't we just eat what Dad eats? Won't that make it easier on him and everyone else?*

Well, there were many problems with that line of questioning, even if I can't recall anyone making that suggestion. Thinking on it now, we ate the way we did precisely because Mom and, later, Rene, could make large meals on string budgets. And the way you feed large groups of large human beings is to use small amounts of meat with copious gravy, rice, noodles, tortillas, bread, and other "fillers." It's all refined, simple carbohydrates and sugars.

Drinking Cokes was such a natural pursuit in my family that my elders once worried about me—about my health—because I was a kid who seemed to, shockingly, prefer water to a Coke or Kool-Aid. Why wasn't I eating three or four slices of Mrs. Baird's enriched white bread or a stack of tortillas with everything I ate? Why was I using a goddamn fork and not tortillas? In fact, my family drank Cokes as if they were water.

I have never felt the pull of cigarettes, alcohol, recreational drugs, sex, or anything else like I do a Coca-Cola with lots of ice. I've even quit coffee for long stretches with only a few minor headaches. No problem at all. I gave up all animal products for nearly half a year. Easier than I thought, though not easy enough for me to sustain in perpetuity. But leaving Cokes is a herculean effort for me. Like Pookie in *New Jack City*: "That shit just be callin' me, man! It be callin' me, man!" Clearly, I outgrew my preference for plain old water.

Because making heart-healthy meals for Dad was so foreign to us, to say nothing of expensive, we would cut corners with microwavable meals by such brands as Healthy Choice. (Now, I guess they were a healthy choice compared to sugary or fatty crap, but I'm not sure anything microwavable in five minutes is exactly healthy.) It was a convenient and simple alternative. But soon those little frozen containers were almost like snacks between the real meals, and we went back to our ways because we had known nothing else. Comfort is convenient because it is a well-worn groove, and similarly convenience is comforting. This new healthy way seemed suspicious and contrived, and we despised it.

Here in Lovington, I saw myself with members of my family who were all deeply unhealthy, each in individual ways, in a place that was beyond salvation. My own journey through wellness was fraught with ignorance, misunderstandings, poor hygiene, and a noisome affinity for doctor visits. Rene would often take me to the doctor throughout my childhood, at times without my being certain that I was sick at all.

I abused this health anxiety at some point, once I became conscious that Rene would take me to the doctor even if I feigned a sore throat or stuffy nose. The ruse got me out of a lot of school. My absences would be many days in a row, and frequent. Once I think I was absent a full two weeks and maybe even a few days beyond that in a single stretch in junior high. That was over half a month! I was ridiculed and mocked, naturally, for being gone so long.

"You got cancer or what?"

"Why the fuck are you absent so much anyway, dude?"

"Um, because I was sick! I even have the doctor's notes to prove it." (I did have doctor's notes!)

"Yeah, sure, fucker."

While I most assuredly abused that arrangement because I often did not enjoy the education system once I hit middle school, I did have enough maladies to be semi-truthful in my absenteeism, making it all plausible. The great problem I had early on concerned my teeth, which were riddled with cavities and sore spots almost for as long as I can recall.

Lubbock's water is notoriously fluoridated, and *Men's Health* magazine ranked Lubbock as having the worst teeth in the nation in 2008. Too much fluoride can cause brown or even white stains on teeth, and one of my incisors had a few small but prominent white blemishes that always made me want to hide my teeth whenever I smiled. Over time I have seen these small white stains, which began at the center, now hover near the end of my tooth. It makes the saying about being *long in the tooth* a reality. Also, I don't remember being instructed to brush my teeth as a kid, and I rarely saw the adults brush their teeth, as if they saved it for special occasions. They tended to chew mint gum as a means of tamping bad breath.

I may have consumed more water than Cokes, but I took all the sugar I wanted from bubble gum and candies of all sorts. My sweet tooth was so unchecked that I didn't get the kind of demineralization and tiny cavities that are the early warning signs of dental peril. Instead, whole chunks of my teeth crumbled away, leaving behind what looked like craters to me. These would in turn fill with food particles. I remember standing in front of the large mirror near the living room in Lubbock, clearing out packed food from molars with a toothpick. It smelled awful, and on occasion I would touch a sensitive spot where an angry nerve lay exposed. I was between five and seven years old, and so many of these deteriorating teeth were of the permanent variety. My teeth never had a chance.

Chapter Seventy-One

At some point, likely because I was in such constant dental pain, I began regular visits to the dentist. See, my family doesn't put one bit of stock in prevention, but it assuredly moves heaven and earth to fix the problem when it's too late. Maybe that is much more common in people than I imagine, but it is undoubtedly a defining characteristic of what I saw growing up. I'm convinced that much of this is cultural, a function of ignorance of a purposefully obtuse and byzantine health care system, to say nothing of the perverse economics of health. My contributions to all of this were my wretched tooth issues, and it set me on a journey of pain, shame, and self-discovery that would follow me like some bosom companion for much of my life.

Fillings, root canals, crowns, bridges, caps—all new words to my expanding vocabulary! Also, I think I had the misfortune of always going to dentists who, philosophically, didn't believe in administering relief from pain. Maybe it was because they worked with lower socioeconomic folk, and they didn't give a shit about a poor person's pain. Probably deserved it, they likely thought. *Well, little fucker, you should brush and floss way more than you do and quit eating so much goddamn sugar. Serves you right.*

It was always, "You might (*might!*) feel . . . a little sting" or "You're probably (*probably!*) going to feel . . . a little pressure." This shit was always so far from reality that I began to think these motherfuckers were deliberately getting off on my pain. (I wouldn't have thought it in that way. I likely would have thought, *These dentists either don't care that I hurt or they like to see me hurting.*) Unfortunately, the agony never seemed to stop, even into adulthood. One bastard both removed a temporary crown and then replaced it with a permanent crown *without a painkiller.* I imagine it's comparable to placing a live electrical wire directly on a tooth. I have never been so close to wanting to commit actual homicide. I would gladly have shown what a little pressure felt like coming from my fists of fury.

It turns out that I'm also one of the smallish percentage (about a tenth) of folks who are allergic to penicillin. This miracle of the modern age, to my young mind, was like a poison that could not only hurt me but actually kill me. Unlike chemicals that had huge warnings on them or were locked away in places that were inaccessible, doctors were dishing out penicillin in megadoses to help their patients. At an early age, I distrusted doctors and, as a result, felt I always had to double- and triple-check that I wouldn't be given the antibiotic by accident. Physicians are supposed to do no harm, but they make mistakes too.

I remember one time in particular, a confluence of these two early childhood horrors: demented dentists and poison penicillin. Mom took me to the dentist in Lubbock, and it's likely that my teeth were an absolute disaster by then. I probably set fucking records for that dentist—a case study of the worst tooth decay he'd ever seen in a child so young. The waiting room had the typical children's amusements, and at the time I was fascinated by the simple water toys known as Waterfuls that had little pieces of plastic that would move about in a water current produced by the simple push of a button. On this day, I was toying with one that had little rings that moved about and landed on the snout of a toy dolphin that rocked in the water. Before long, my name was called, and I went behind the door to meet my destiny.

Ordinarily, Mom or Rene would never have let me go alone with a doctor. But this was a children's dentist, and they reassured Mom that I was in good hands. I was led to the chair, and they said all the usual things dentists say to give kids a false sense of security. I was scared to be there, and the reassuring water toys were no longer within reach.

The dentist, an older white man, talked to me but I heard nothing he said. My mind's eye was fixed on the sore spots in my mouth—spots he probed with what felt like a sharp and angry hook. I could feel the scrape of it, and I would involuntarily jump when the hook contacted my teeth. That was a moment I knew I had to be brave; Mom would not have taken it lightly if I ran out of there scared shitless, as I had almost done at Anthony's when Darth Vader wanted to turn my hair into socks. Mom probably would have told me to get my little ass back in there and get this taken care of. I had to gut this out, hoping it would be over soon. And that's basically my attitude toward dental visits even today. Like forcing your tongue into an electrical socket, it will all be over soon enough.

I didn't know what the guy was doing. I knew shots were involved, which are always painful. But soon something else happened. I felt like I was having trouble breathing. I could not seem to catch my breath, and it got worse from one moment to the next. I didn't know what anaphylaxis was, but on that day, I was getting to know it intimately.

Mom burst into where the dentists practiced their sadism. I could hear her voice, and she was livid. She roared, "I *told* you he was allergic to penicillin!" She had recognized an emergency right under her nose because she saw hygienists and other employees running around frantically. They must have thought, *This little Brown boy is gonna crash and go code blue right here in the fucking dental chair!* I'm sure they were prepared for this contingency, but they sure acted like they didn't know what to do. They panicked, and Mom bursting in there like a crazed Latina mother likely made them panic even more.

I used to think maybe I had made this up, but it was a story Mom herself told every so often. I often wondered why a dentist would be giving antibiotic shots. But then again, if my teeth were so bad that there was infection, no wonder they did that.

Today I take no chances. Going to get takeout? I let them know I'm allergic to penicillin. Buying a car? Okay, but remember, motherfuckers: I'm allergic to penicillin. Once a nurse, of all people, asked me what would happen if I had penicillin. "I'd drop right here on this very spot, lady, and you're gonna have a hell of a time getting my big ass the fuck back up, so fair warning." As a kid, I feared it, but then it made sense because even Kal-El had one *huge* weakness. Penicillin was and is my kryptonite.

Chapter Seventy-Two

It was not until my young adulthood, when I discovered athletics and sports, that I tried to get healthier, but old habits died hard. And I could see proof positive in the three people I was with on that Valentine's Day. Robert talked a good game, but he had such difficulty in keeping healthy habits. Rene always claimed she was a hypochondriac—she often said this aloud when I was growing up. Something was always wrong with her: Ulcers. Migraines. Respiratory infections. Nervous breakdown. Hernia.

Once she had a gross cyst at the base of her neck, where it met her upper back. It caused her immense pain, but in this instance, she did not want to see a doctor. Her brothers had convinced her that they could remove it. That. They. Could. Remove. It. Such a dangerous and ridiculous idea! Right here, feet from where I now stood, was where they prepared for this unsophisticated butchery under the New Mexico stars and bright moon.

Drinks were flowing for everyone as light morphed to dark, but mostly it was Rene and a bottle of vodka. Smirnoff. Like in some Western films when the protagonist drains a bottle of whiskey, then has a partner yank a bullet from his shoulder, Rene was convinced that if she was drunk enough, she would not feel this literal operation. Worse, they performed the surgery outside, in front of the mobile home—at night! I have no idea why, but I suspect no one wanted to clean up blood and gore off the kitchen floor. The mise-en-scène recalled the hundreds of dubbings Tom and I had completed. Maybe Tom had determined that the blood was in Rene's feet and that she would not bleed much.

Rene was sitting on a stool, understandably agitated, with a faded pink towel around her shoulders. The cyst made her look like she had a small hump on her back, like she was Quasimodo's little sister. Someone was holding a goddamn flashlight to see better. Maybe it was me—I don't rightly remember. But I do remember watching with an equal measure of horror and fascination. I was around ten years old.

David was the one with nerves of steel, and he wielded the scalpel. This dude was unshakable and not affected by things that made normal people queasy. He was the guy in the family who would eat the eyes of a beef's head when we made *barbacoa*. The one never fazed by creepy-crawlies and disgusting, slimy things. (I'm not sure if he has ever vomited in his whole life.)

When David made his first incision, a top-to-bottom cut about an inch and a half long, Rene let out such a wail of pain and agony that it shriveled some part of me deep inside, some tender realm where the shit of the world doesn't generally penetrate. Well, I felt her scream but did nothing more than bravely bear witness to what was happening. She was in such torment, and it had barely begun. But we could not go back now. He had cut her open.

"Ohhh! Ayyyy! Owww!" Her articulations of distress rang out across the property. If neighbors had been closer, they would have called the cops because surely they were witnessing a gang initiation, torture, or perhaps a murder.

David made another quick incision, this one left-to-right, so that the wound looked like a large plus sign. More anguished screaming. Then David quickly took up some tweezers, gave a mighty squeeze, and pulled out the cyst with the assistance of the pressure that had built up. Even more bellowing from Rene. I jumped back when I saw the splatter go everywhere. The cyst looked yellow and hard, like one of those super high-bounce balls you could buy at a convenience store for a quarter.

Then it was out. It was over. I don't remember if there were stitches. There should have been because the size of the wound was outrageous. And for the rest of her life, Rene would have this gruesome scar at the base of her neck. I would stare at it when I took her to her doctor appointments during the COVID-19 pandemic, appalled at the butchery of years past.

Now, why the fuck would everyone agree to do what they did to Rene? She could have died if she'd bled out! Or she might have survived the DIY surgery only to die from an infection. What made a person think, *Oh, you have a cyst? I'm happy to cut it out for you, if you want. Drink half a bottle of Smirnoff, and we're good.*

Chapter Seventy-Three

With her neck scar now long since healed, Rene sat not far from me as I tried to break apart more of the trailer. That sledge exhausted me, but wielding it was preferable to having to talk to Rene. I suppose I resented her. We had to do this because of her, I felt. Perhaps that was unfair, but I had been wanting to help her for as long as I could remember, and she continually did things that made it so difficult. More than once I had said to her, "You and your siblings make things so much harder than you have to."

She wanted to ask me about the family. How is Ginger? How are her *reinas*? How was the drive over?

"Everyone's fine. The drive was fine."

Rene must have sensed that I didn't want to talk, and she grew quiet after a few more attempts at generic, safe questions. Morning was turning into noon in these flatlands, the wind scudding dust over everything as if it meant to sandblast all this wreckage in my behalf. The wind wasn't that strong, though, and I didn't have that much time. After maybe thirty minutes of trying and failing to engage me, she asked Giro, without rancor or upset, to take her back home.

I kept working as if I did not notice. Then I said "later" to her over my shoulder. Exeunt Rene and Giro.

A large measure of my silence, I would realize later that day, was that I did not know how to speak to her after her incarceration. Rene would always make me feel like I had committed a huge transgression against the family in my decision to leave for college, and she reminded me of it at every turn. These reminders—insults, to be sure—always made me overcompensate when I had an opportunity to help. Case in point, my foolish notion that I could sweep in and load two demolished mobile homes into a dumpster and call it a day.

If my sheer determination could have spared the family any hurt or stress, then there was nothing I wouldn't have done for them—even at my own financial and emotional expense. But Rene regularly robbed me of that sort of agency. It was as if she blocked chances for me to help her because she knew it hurt me more to have my efforts rejected.

And she and Mom, in their incendiary, legendary spite, would deliberately endure humiliation, degradation, and embarrassment because the hardship was bound to rend your flesh and discomfit you without offering them the slightest comfort or relief. Their pain was my pain, and they knew it. But the helpless anguish of having the ability to help yet being forbidden from doing so was a type of pain that was mine alone. And that, to them, was enough retribution for my insolence and temerity, my ambition.

Rene's incarceration was the pinnacle of this sort of injury by proxy. She would write me letters from prison, and they would arrive to my address in Columbus, Ohio. I would read of her ordeal and wonder about her true condition, chastising myself for being a poor excuse for a son.

I would ultimately find the time to write back to her in the midst of my doctoral studies, and I would often fall asleep perturbed as I imagined her in a state penitentiary. *Is there anything I can do?* I would write. *Could I send you money for commissary at least?* Always, she would refuse these requests, and I often wondered if she did that as a kind of punishment to me. Was she playing a kind of martyr because she knew her deprivation would make me hurt? But she would write back about how Mom, Giro, and Rose would visit her all the time and how she was so thankful that they helped her when no one else would. So again, I would ask, *What can I do?* And she would reply, as ever: *Nothing.*

In my work as a professor, I confer with Latinx students and families who might be considering a college degree. And I often speak to my non-Latinx colleagues about the intricacies and difficulties that a path through the university presents to students who come from my culture. For many first-generation students whose parents are newly arrived to the United States, surpassing their parents is a true hope shared by the whole family. Often they are landless farmers or laborers who took a risk in coming to the US, so they will encourage their children to pursue opportunities even if those breaks take them away from the family.

And I have found that many students whose families have been in this country for more than two generations have the opposite burden. Their parents want them to defer college or not to go at all, especially if it means leaving home. If they do leave, their selfish act disrespects the family and all it has sacrificed for them. At times it feels like a type of indentured servitude, where you stay at home and work for seven years before you are given permission to move (not too far down the road, *por favor*) and start a family of your own. They don't want to disrupt or break up the family unit.

Chapter Seventy-Four

To leave home and go out on your own was not only frowned upon in my family, it would get you cast out. Like, they would tell you to leave and never come back and literally turn their backs on you! Now, I had seen this happen often in my childhood, but never for reasons that had to do with education. Generally, someone wanted to get married or, you know, do the typical kind of shit people did once they hit their early twenties, such as get an apartment, maybe move a few towns away, and so forth.

One day I came home from school to learn that Rose had been excommunicated in this manner for something like wanting to leave her husband (who was a good man and well liked by our family) and be with some other Latino who floated her boat. I didn't see the showdown, but I heard about it secondhand from Robert and Tom. It was epic. She was banished, and I did not see her again until Dad lay in his casket at his wake—a span of nearly a decade.

It happened to David at least two times because of whom he married—an older white woman named Penny who, understandably, didn't want to live with us—despite inhabiting the more recently added trailer house that we were also set to trash on this Valentine's Day. They lived there for at least a year before she said *fuck this* to our weird bullshit and told David to get ready to be a man and move out. Rene and Mom hated her guts for this. Ironically, Rene was the reason Penny met David in the first place; Rene and Penny were coworkers at a place called Caprock Communications in Hobbs, New Mexico.

After a couple of years, they all reconciled tenuously and definitely not permanently. David was welcomed back (he had a son, Giro, now—and so naturally he was invited home), and I rejoiced to see my older uncle-brother once more. But he teased me, unkindly, I thought, and we somehow got into a weird macho thing where we were punching each other on the upper arm and deltoid area. My punches had no effect on him, and he kept hitting me harder and harder, until I finally collapsed on the floor in tears.

He sat next to me and laughed. "What's wrong?" I could tell he didn't like that he'd perhaps inadvertently caused me real pain.

"I missed you," I said through tears. Yes, his punches motivated some of my tears. But what had hurt me more was his absence in my life. "I'm happy you're back."

"I missed you, too, *cabrón*." He took me by the back of my neck and gripped it with a tenderness his punches had not shown. "C'mon. Let's go see what everyone's doing." He hugged me, and I rejoiced at having my brother return to me once more.

There and then did I understand a little bit of why the father rejoices to see his prodigal son return. The joy in once more having what you'd thought lost is so rapturous, so exhilarating, that you're willing to forget all the stupid shit that made you separate to begin with. For this my brother was dead, and is alive; he was lost, but now is found.

When both Rose and David were banished, it was like these slightly elder figures were suddenly wrenched from my life, and I hated it. Yes, Rose was and is quirky, but she also loved me, serving as another stand-in for my life. Another terry cloth mother surrogate without food but who cared? And she would at times bring me presents as a way of showing this little Brown boy that he fucking mattered. Or she'd take me with her for weeks at a time, and I loved it.

Like when I wanted nothing more than a football to throw around with Robert. Some boys play catch with a baseball and glove, but we would throw around a football for hours at a stretch on our big patch of dirt, until the daylight had drained from the sky. Robert had managed to bring one home from football practice—his sticky fingers were always a great asset—but with all the thorns and burrs on our land, the football was abruptly punctured flat. We did triage and stuffed that bastard with rags so it might hold its shape, though now it was way heavier, but it was hopeless. I tried to devise anything that might approximate a football; we threw around a rolled-up towel, a two-liter bottle, and lesser imitations.

And then one Sunday afternoon, like a traveler who has been to fantastical lands and returns to their tiny, disbelieving hamlet, like Melquíades who brought the miracle of ice to Macondo, Rose showed up bearing wondrous gifts. I was napping in a room I would later demolish in 2015, and Robert ran in to wake me up from my nap.

"Chris! Look!"

I roused myself, disoriented in that way when you don't know what time of day it is, wiped drool from the corner of my mouth, and stared at him in wonder.

"Look!" he exclaimed again. "Rose bought you this. Let's go!"

In his hands he held a brand-new Wilson football, still in its carton. Robert passed it to me as he ran out of the room.

She must have caught on to my situation. Rose must have known that I was agonizing, trying to get my hands on a real football. And she must have resolved that she would not let Crisito go without something so basic as a football. This time, and at a few other instances along the way, Rose came through in glorious fashion. And I loved her for it.

I think of these memories and many more—memories of me trying to fit into a family that paradoxically loved me, was proud of me, but begrudged me the very gifts and talents that had allowed them to so love me in the first place. And Rene was the end and the beginning of that contradiction.

Chapter Seventy-Five

In the summer of my senior year, a few weeks after I received the diploma I would find in such a dilapidated state decades later, I had become aware of Rene's consistent animus toward me. She was clearly and visibly angry whenever we interacted. Though at first I laughed it off, before long I was stinging from her verbal taunts and abuse. Like her mother, she could always wound with words and her tone of voice.

In those weeks after graduation, everyone had gone to Lubbock for the onion harvest while Tom and I stayed behind. I didn't mind it. Anything to do with onion crops was a much harder job than whatever Tom was going to have me do with roosters. I had to go to Lubbock only once that summer, and it was to take some state-level joke of a standardized test called the TASP (Texas Academic Skills Program) exam. My testing site was on the Texas Tech University campus, but no one would be around to drive me because they would all leave at four in the morning to go to the Field of Onions, as Bugs Bunny famously said. I suggested that I could take a taxi, which seemed outrageous. But it was my only way to take this test I needed if I was to go to college.

And so, for the first time in my life, I took a taxi from my house in Lubbock, Texas, to Texas Tech University. I luckily found the correct building and passed the TASP.

But other than that, I was with Tom all summer in Lovington without a car. Because we're misanthrope pains in the ass, we had no one who could bail us out in a pinch. Or maybe we did, but we weren't going to ask. Rene would drive from Lubbock to Lovington with food supplies and more for us. It was as if Tom and I were on some remote outpost in the Antarctica, and we were restocked and resupplied occasionally.

Without fail, Rene was an utter bitch to me whenever she would show up. She was annoyed by my presence, and I became acutely aware of it.

I finally turned to Tom one evening when we were alone and Rene was back in Lubbock. I had worked up the courage to ask, and this was my shot.

"Do you notice it?"

"Notice what?" he replied. He was sitting on the floor of the living room with the ugly baby blue carpet, reclined on one elbow, in the direct airflow of the swamp cooler. I sat across from him in our knockoff La-Z-Boy recliner. It was night with no more rooster work that needed doing. We were both drinking cheap MD 20/20. David Lynch's *Dune* was on TV, the version where William Phipps narrates the clarifying expositional knowledge at the beginning. "How Rene talks to me now," I answered. "Do you notice it? Or am I seeing shit that isn't there?"

He took a moment to himself, then nodded.

I took a swig of the cheap wine. It was light green and probably had fake kiwi as a flavor. "Why does she do that? Did I do something wrong? Am I not a good son? I don't make her proud?"

He hesitated. I'm certain he was careful because, after all, it was his big sister we were about to potentially criticize, and Tom was always loyal as fuck to his elders. "She's jealous of you."

Tom's words crushed me like an imploding building, and a metal shard penetrated my heart, a sharp sliver of steel that continued to work its way deeper with each passing year, like the kind Tony Stark was worried about.

"Jealous? Seriously?"

He sipped from his own bottle of Mad Dog. I think his was strawberry banana or some weird shit. "Yeah. I mean, look at you. You're getting to do the kinds of things she could have done but never had the chance to. You're going to college. You're gonna get a degree. You're gonna have a life." I could tell that he was defending her and that he cared for her deeply. His last sentence was a real kick in the nuts for me. But as my own daughters remind me when I criticize them for something they're not doing, they didn't ask to be born. Neither did I.

I took a breath, absorbing what Tom had said. And I sensed that that was as far as he was willing to go. I turned to the TV again. "That fucking Baron Harkonnen," I said. "What a disgusting bastard."

Tom laughed. "Yeah."

A few weeks later, as Robert and I prepared to make the drive that would ultimately end at Blinn College in Brenham, Texas, everyone gathered in front of the main trailer house to send me off. I remember everyone who was there—Tom, Diana, Mom, Dad—but I cannot remember Rene. I cannot remember what she may have said. I can remember no farewell or hug from her. No words of wisdom to take comfort in. In my memory, once more, she is absent from this red-letter moment in my life. And that is why I always tell anyone who will listen, when they ask about how it was that I went to college and got an education, that my relationship with my mother was forever altered the day I left home. That was the price I paid.

It was never the same between us.

Chapter Seventy-Six

For the rest of demolition day in Lovington, we managed to break shit into smaller pieces and move it around from one pile to another. Like a kid pushing their food around on a plate at dinnertime because it's unappetizing, we managed to rearrange the debris into a slightly more organized state. It had all been a mockery, and we finally realized it was pointless to be out here at all.

Giro, who had returned after taking Rene back home in the morning and listened to us mildly suggest that he lose some weight, went back home at last. He and Rene were going to drive to Robert's house in Morton later. He had invited them to come over so we could all visit once more.

When Robert and I drove back to his house, I couldn't think. I was exhausted and wanted to shower desperately. Giro and Rene arrived later, and I could not help but ridicule, mock, tease, and disregard everything Rene said. After one particular exchange, where I essentially said she didn't know what the fuck she was talking about, Robert came over to me where I had isolated myself on a couch away from everyone else.

"Hey. Cool your shit, man. No fucking fights."

"Whatever," I returned. "She says wrongheaded shit and no one ever calls her on it."

The next morning, I was up before everyone else. Rene had fallen asleep on one of the couches with the TV on, which she had done for years. Old reruns of *Saturday Night Live* were on VH1. She awakened and we watched the TV in silence, in the dim morning light that refused to penetrate the dark living room, as we had done so many times when I was a child.

Later in the day, we watched the movie *Magnolia*, a Paul Thomas Anderson joint that is a masterpiece that thwarts the average filmgoer. Rene, who had started watching late, began asking questions. Robert and I answered. Then she began to dismiss it.

"This movie is fucking weird. I don't understand it," she complained.

"Of course you don't understand it," I snapped.

The room got fucking quiet.

I pushed further. "You're not smart enough to understand it."

That was too far and obviously untrue. But in the moment, I wanted to hurt her, and calling out her intelligence was the most powerful weapon in my arsenal because I was the only one in the family who could say it with any sort of credibility.

Without another word, Rene retreated to the dining room and ignored the rest of the film and me along with it.

After some time, when I finally managed to sidle over to the table where she sat, she talked tentatively to me about prison. I listened and nodded in all the right places. I was the good son again, the one I would be during the pandemic, and the angry, disrespectful son was sealed into a box in the attic of my mind. For now, I listened.

Rene never developed that sense of checking the potentially hurtful quality of her words. That is, she knows her words can hurt; she doesn't worry about the consequences until months, or even years, have passed.

Any woman in a Latinx family has her work cut out for her. Rene was her parents' firstborn, and she admittedly never had what most would call a traditional childhood. Before she was even a teenager, she was like a mother to her younger siblings, and so in her formative childhood years, she was cast into the role of the disciplinarian, with the tone and mindset to match.

On this day as I listened to her tell me stories of prison, it seemed to me that she was like a child, perhaps for the first time. Not that she was childlike in her intellect. No, she was like a child in the jokes she told, the things she found entertaining, the issues that triggered her to upset and anger. Age has worsened this childlike quality in my mother. That quirk was on display when I sat with her at Robert's table.

Suddenly, she stopped talking about her prison experience and shifted to tell me this story of her childhood:

When she was a little girl, she had woken up one morning. Mom commanded her to prepare breakfast for Mom and her *comadre*. Rene was probably around ten years old, if not younger, and she still had much to learn about cooking because who the fuck knows how to cook anything worth eating at ten years old? Some kids are still making goddamn mud pies at that age.

She had to make a full breakfast with, like, potatoes, eggs, bacon—all of it. She fucked up the eggs because eggs can be tricky even for adults. Mom wanted over-hard eggs, and after some failed attempts, Rene plated up what she thought were acceptable eggs. Only they weren't. She had plated several runny, undercooked eggs. They weren't even close.

Mom raged, and I could only imagine how it must have been when she was young herself, full of piss and vinegar. Mom was outraged at her little girl. In response to fuckups and mistakes, Mom got vindictive because, deep down, she truly believed you fucked her over deliberately, to disrespect her authority. So, naturally, she made Rene eat the runny, raw eggs as punishment. All of them.

When Dad got home from work, he was beside himself at what his wife had done to their daughter. He tried to console his firstborn, his baby girl, but the damage was done.

Those raw eggs have haunted, imprisoned my mother her entire life. I like eggs over-medium, and Rene will still comment on those runny eggs she was made to eat as a child if she sees me eat eggs that have runny yolks. When she brings it up today, she is again reduced to tears. This childhood event is but one of the many things that happened to her that shaped her as an adult and as my mother. She was abused, psychologically tormented by her own mother, and she never had a real chance at agency in her life. I remember all these ignominies she carries around with her (those that I am aware of), and I try very hard to consider these things when I feel that she is less than kind to me. But in the end, she chose her parents over me, and I cannot ignore that.

In that moment, as I sat there next to her at Robert's round table with the glass top, I reflected on Rene as a total, imperfect human being and tried with great effort to keep one thing in mind above all else. The cycle of abuse and neglect and disregard could be broken, and I would have to be the first one to do it, even if it had cost me my own position in my family.

With the day now growing old, the time for me to return home had come. I had traveled to correct mistakes and clean up disasters not necessarily of my own making. Futile endeavors. Instead, I viewed my past, my family's past, and my complicated relationship with Rene with a clarity I'd never had. This was not the end, and there would be much more to come. But I no longer wanted to fight and settle old scores. Understanding and grace were still feasible. And I wanted desperately to give Rene some of the life Tom had spoken of and a taste of the happiness that had eluded her. I had always wanted that for her.

"You got any tools if you break down?" Robert asked as I loaded up my Tacoma.

"Nah. I'll be fine."

"Goddammit." He went over to his truck and took out a few things like pliers and screwdrivers and put them in a plastic grocery bag. Handed it to me and said, "Just in case." He hugged me. Linda gave me her patented side hug. "Be careful on the road," she said. I nodded.

I hugged Rene last.

"I love you, *mijo*," she said. "*Cuídate bien.*"

"I will. Love you too."

I gave them a wave from my silver Tacoma, rattled off a few pert honks from the horn, and then I let out a deep breath to hold back the tears. I left Morton for Commerce once more, driving with the afternoon sun of late winter gleaming at my back like a spotlight over my shoulder and the flat land of my youth all around me. I wondered again, as ever, how my family had gotten to where we were now and imagined where we would find ourselves in a future that was nothing but uncertain.

I was now coming into my super Saiyan form as a Big Scary Brown Guy, like some *Dragon Ball Z* character. My path had consistently taken me away from my family—a price I had once thought I would never be able to afford. The truth was that I could pay it and survive, but the cost could often feel like far too much to give up.

Sometimes I think of the little Brown boy I was, and I remember those times when we were all in the house together, laughing and joking, eating good food and telling stories. We were so focused on our present then that we never gave thought to a future time when our family would recede like a vanishing point—when even such simple pleasures that filled our darkness would fade like cherished photos left out in the elements too long, sun bleached and inexorably weatherworn.

Epilogue

As I was finishing up the final portions of this memoir, Rene died of what the medical examiners called a cardiac event. She had been with Diana in Ruston, Louisiana, when, on MLK Day, January 17, 2022, one day before she was scheduled to return to live with me in Logan, Utah, she died in her bed.

After Mom's death in September 2020, I invited Rene to live with me for a while. I knew she had been Mom's caretaker for decades, stubbornly sacrificing her own well-being in service of her mother's. I asked her constantly why she did this, and her answer was always the same: "I made a promise to my dad."

To my surprise, she accepted my invitation. After Mom's funeral was over, Rene was to return home with me. Over a fifteen-hour drive from Robert's house, she talked about many things, including the abusive treatment she'd endured at her mother's hands for much of her life. "Mom never loved me. Never wanted me," she said.

It sounded like words I'd often thought of with respect to Rene. I felt like she had never loved me, even though she often said things to the contrary. Her actions showed me that she didn't want me. As I drove, she told stories of her own childhood and long-forgotten family lore, some of which I had not heard before. She spoke for most of the fifteen hours. I focused on the road and mostly listened. It was as if she finally had the chance to let it all out. I hoped that it was cathartic for her.

We drew closer to the significant land changes as we entered Utah—the red rocks of the Canyonlands and the Arches areas, some of which you can see right from the road as you approach Moab. I wanted Rene to see this beautiful landscape. To notice it. She scarcely mentioned it. When I deliberately pointed it out, she discussed her fear of such places. They seemed high to her, and she wanted nothing to do with them.

Before she had agreed to come, she asked about my house. We knew her mobility was next to nothing. I told her there were a few steps to get into the house, and there were a few steps to get to the bottom level of the house. If it was a problem, I told her she could do everything from the top floor.

When we arrived and she considered the seven steps to get into the house, she balked. "I can't do that," she said flatly.

"You have to," I returned. "Or I can carry you in."

"You have a bad back."

"It's not bad enough that I can't carry you inside."

"Why did you buy this house?"

"Nearly all houses here in Utah have this split level. Plus, I didn't know you'd be living with me when we bought it."

She decided to climb the stairs after all. She wrapped her upper body around the rail and went up the steps with excruciating slowness, panting and cussing the whole time. Once she was inside, she sat on her walker and rolled about to explore.

Ginger welcomed her and did all she could to make Rene feel at home. She was so gracious and loving the whole time Rene lived with us, I heard Rene tell Ginger once, "You're so kind to me. You treat me better than my own daughter." I'm sure Diana, who allowed Mom and Rene to live with her for years, would've loved to hear that.

Rene finally caught her breath. "If I had known you had that many steps, I wouldn't have come." She was angry, but I ignored it. She was much better off with me.

Despite her initial annoyance with me and my house, we soon resolved to prioritize her health. I took her to countless doctor appointments, at times going to work, then coming back home to get her, then taking her to the doctor, back home, and then me back to work. It was ceaseless, but I couldn't complain. Our roles were reversed, and now I was the one taking her to doctor visits and interceding on her behalf. Me the adult and Rene the child.

I complained to Ginger over and over when I was exhausted or frustrated. "I asked for this, didn't I?" I had only myself to blame. Ginger had asked me initially if this was such a good idea. I felt I had no choice. Rene was my mother, and this was my one chance to take care of her.

Over several months, we managed to improve her health—at least in terms of mobility—by managing her pain and exploring the possibility of a knee replacement. During the tests before her surgery, we both realized how unwell she was. Her cardiologist asked her with Eastern European bluntness, "You've had heart attacks, yes?"

"I don't know," Rene mused. "Maybe."

"Think hard."

She obeyed. "There have been a few times when I thought I might be having a heart attack."

"They probably were. I can tell." The doctor with the stern face observed her as he roved about her torso with a stethoscope. His straightforward manner was refreshing. No bullshit as far as the eye could see. "Deep breath," he commanded.

I listened and watched from the other side of the examination room.

"You've had COVID?"

"No," Rene replied truthfully.

"Ever smoked?"

"No," Rene lied.

The doctor harrumphed like he could tell she was full of shit. She had smoked cigarettes and weed regularly, though she never did when she lived with me.

The cardiologist sat on his stool and made his face grimmer. "You are not well, but you probably will be okay for the surgery. We will see what the stress test says."

She was cleared for the surgery, in fact, and had been working hard during physical therapy to improve her strength and mobility. She hated PT, but I made her do it anyway. I'd leave her with her tormentors and go to Starbucks to work on this memoir. I told her I was writing it.

"Ooh! I'd like to read it!"

"You can read it when it's done. But I'll be honest with you. I call out a lot of shit as I saw it. You might not like what I have to say." I was sure she wouldn't like it, and I looked forward mostly to her objections. I had no doubt she'd see certain things differently than I did.

She made a face like she had considered it and thought it fine. "I can't wait to read it."

"Okay."

She never got the chance.

Her knee surgery was dicey. She had fallen getting out of the shower early that morning, and Ginger and I had to help her get back up. "No, I can do it! Don't come in!" she hollered from the floor. We ignored her, ignored that she was nude, and got her into a seated position on her walker. She was already exhausted.

Once we arrived at the hospital and they began to prepare her for surgery, I could tell the nurses were abuzz. They were concerned about Rene's O2 levels.

"Are you on oxygen at home, dear?" the nurse in charge asked.

"No," Rene said dismissively. "My oxygen gets low when I sit because I have a giant hiatal hernia." The hernia was a fact, but I had seen this song and dance at other doctors' offices. To me she always seemed to be out of breath, but she accounted it as no big deal.

I could see what the oximeter read: 52.

"Dear, I don't know how you're still conscious," the nurse said in a way that was not a joke.

Minutes later, once Rene was in the preop bay, the nurse sought me out. She called me over from Rene's bed, out of her earshot. "Who are you again?"

"I'm her son."

She whispered to me. "What's going on? Why is her oxygen so low?" She was damned near accusatory.

I knew what I wanted to tell her, but this was a long story. So, I abbreviated where I could. "She lives with me. She gets exhausted easily under even her normal circumstances. This morning, she was disoriented upon waking, fell getting out of the shower, and getting to this spot was like her running a marathon. She's winded even for her."

"She needs to be on oxygen."

"No argument from me," I agreed.

When the anesthesiologist, a youngish man with dark hair and blue eyes, came in to give his opinion preop, I thought he was nervous and uncomfortable. I could see he was worried, but he also gave us clear reassurance. The surgeon, though, was unflappable, the badass that he was. He looked like a guy who spent his days off climbing mountains and bouldering because he could.

And then they took her away, and I waited until it was over.

Turns out she didn't die on the operating table as I feared, but they did put her in an ICU room because of her low oxygen. From then on, she was never without oxygen for as long as she lived with me. She began to get better sleep, which helped her apnea, which she refused to believe she had. When it came time for her second knee surgery, a surge in COVID-19 took up all the ICU rooms, and on the day of her surgery, we had to postpone indefinitely.

The holidays were nearing, and Rene had mentioned she would like to spend them with Diana, who has two little ones of her own. After a year with Rene in the house, I was ready for the break.

I never saw her again. She had always requested no funeral or ceremony, preferring to be cremated rather than buried. Though I honored her request, I find it so hard to think of her as gone without that final goodbye. I catch myself still thinking of her as alive but elsewhere, the way she had been for most of my life. Alive, but elsewhere.

In my career, I often have the opportunity to talk to other Latinos who carved out successful vocations as professionals—having taken a path that led them away from home and into unexpected or even unsanctioned areas of training and study. When I ask them how it was for them and how their family handled their leaving, it is as if they are telling a similar story to mine. They talk about rebelling against their parents or somehow imperiling the relationship they had with parents by seeking knowledge outside the home. We who do this are almost instantly albeit unwittingly cast into a heroic role because the hero's journey necessitates leaving home, by force or otherwise, with the understanding that if you are able to return home, both yourself and your home will not be the same. And you never feel like a hero, of course. On the contrary, you feel like a failure to your family. As if you betrayed them at some level.

But my family was even more extreme than any stories from other Latinos that I've heard. At times, members of my family actively seemed to work against me, as if hoping for my demise was the right thing to do. If I fell in love, there would be a serious problem with her. If I made a friend, he was insincere or would soon betray me. If I got a decent job, I would be a dupe or a fool.

In the last few years, I have found myself at times with the invitation to talk about how I got here—how it was that I became a teacher, a writer, an educator, and a Big Scary Brown Guy. People ask about my parents and, especially, about my mother. I must disappoint them when I say my mother was either not there or took a laissez-faire attitude with me. I wish I could say that she was there for me every step of the way, or even some of the way. But I always felt her unwillingness to claim me. Saying love and showing love are not the same thing, after all. It was as if she had cut her losses with me and turned instead to other children caught in the immense gravity of her orbit like temporary satellites, children who she thought would appreciate her, need her, and love her as she presumed I did not.

But we always try hardest with parents who we feel love us the least. We think if we can come through this one time. If we can save the day for them this one day. If we can sacrifice enough blood and treasure for their benefit just once for all time, we will finally earn the love they have denied us our whole lives. We will at last prove our worthiness. Yet love cannot be earned through sacrifice alone, nor can it be won by conforming to someone else's mold. It requires a transcendent choreography between two souls. And the love in a family can be as complex as an algorithm.

The day before Rene died, we exchanged a few text messages. As usual, Rene, Rose, Robert, David, Diana, and myself were irritated at one another. Some of us refused to talk to the others. Only one of Rene's texts was substantive on that day. It may be the truest thing she ever wrote to me:

"Yes, it's shitty not to be able to talk to your family. No matter how crazy they are."

Acknowledgments

FlowerSong Press and their imprint Brown Ink Press gave this book new life when the unimaginable happened. Once again, Frederick Luis Aldama, you were the right person at the right time in my life as you have been countless times before. Edward Vidaurre, may you be blessed a thousand times over for your guidance and generosity. You came through like the utter professional that you are.

Thank you to Rochon Perry and everyone affiliated with Cedar Grove Publishing who initially believed in my memoir and my voice even when I had begun to doubt. You took a chance to publish this book and helped give birth to it. I will be forever grateful. Rest in peace, Rochon.

Robert Mixner conjured miracles at Cedar Grove, picked up the pieces, and actually made it possible for me to move to Flowersong and Brown Ink. No one will ever know just how hard you worked for me when the world was falling down all around us. You're the best, and I mean it.

My thanks to Eliani Torres, the editor I've been looking for all my life. Your precision and patience inspired me, and the steady drip of your encouragements sustained me more than you know.

Thank you also to J. Gonzo for the spectacular cover art. You are a phenomenal talent and a champion for Latinx arts and design. Bravo!

Olivia González, my daughter, supplied the interior illustrations that were not drawn by J. Gonzo. I cannot thank you enough. I'm excited to see where else your extraordinary artistic talent takes you.

Marc DiPaolo, Keri Holt, and Jennifer Sinor graciously took the time to read and comment on very early drafts of this book. Your encouragements gave me the first indications that I should see this through to the end. Thank you all.

Thank you to the SMU Department of English for its support, and specifically to Richard Bozorth, David Caplan, Tim Cassedy,

Katie Condon, Darryl Dickson-Carr, Rhonda Garelick, Jayson Gonzales Sae-Saue, Richard Hermes, Dan Moss, and Beth Newman for the goodwill and splendid conversation. I so enjoy working with you all!

I would also like to thank the following friends, mentors, and camaradas for more than I can express here: Jason Allcott, Pamela Arias Allcott, Frederick Luis Aldama, Janet Anderson, Teresa Batts Peña, Noelle Cockett, Waqa Damuni, Mauricio Espinoza, Tracy Floreani, Evelyn Funda, Christy Glass, Amy Gore, Justin Gurney, M. Hunter Hayes, Mary J. Henderson, Lalita Pandit Hogan, Patrick Colm Hogan, Joe Kraus, Wenxin Li, Kim Martin-Long, Suhaan Mehta, William Nericcio, Hyesu Park, Domino Renee Perez, Theresa Rojas, Samuel Saldivar III, Parama Sarkar, Mehmet Soyer, Cristina Stanciu, Ilan Stavans, Gary Totten, Robert Wagner, Rebecca Walton, Michelle Wang, Joseph Ward, Charles Waugh, Sean Yeager, and Wenyin Xu.

In memoriam: Tomás González, Tomás González Jr., Elva González, and Irene González Foster. QEPD.

My deepest gratitude to David González, Linda González, Robert González, Chencia Bryan, David Eric González, and Rosemary De Los Santos.

Finally, I am indebted to my family for all they mean to me and more: Ginger, Olivia, and Emilia. You are my treasure beyond measure.

About the Author

Author Illustration by J. Gonzo

Christopher González was born and raised on the flatlands of the Llano Estacado, straddling the border of Texas and New Mexico. He received his PhD in English from the Ohio State University and is the author, co-author, and editor of many books including the International Latino Book Award-winning *Reel Latinxs: Representation in U.S. Film & TV*. He is a professor and holds the Jacob and Frances Sanger Mossiker Endowed Chair in the Department of English at Southern Methodist University in Dallas, Texas.